Fundamentals of
Service-Learning
Course Construction

Fundamentals of Service-Learning Course Construction

Campus Compact

Kerrissa Heffernan, Ed.D.

Special thanks to Dr. Richard Cone of the University of Southern California for his generous assistance with this project. Dick is the originator and co-author of the six models of service-learning and the section, "Describing the Service Assignment." His contributions to the publication and to the service-learning field have been invaluable.

We would also like to thank Amy Sellin, research associate at Campus Compact, for her assistance in assembling this material and the faculty who have so generously allowed us to print their service-learning syllabi in this publication.

Campus Compact

Funding for this publication is provided by The Ford Foundation.

Campus Compact
Brown University
Box 1975
Providence, RI 02912
PHONE: (401) 863-1119
EMAIL: campus@compact.org
WEBSITE: www.compact.org

ISBN: 0-9667371-6-4

Table of Contents

Preface

While there is an expanding body of literature that offers a powerful rationale for service-learning, there are few publications designed to specifically assist faculty in course design, development, and construction. One of the most frequent requests Campus Compact receives from faculty is for assistance in course construction—designing effective courses with guidance from sample syllabi. We generally direct faculty to web-based resources that house diverse service-learning syllabi. Yet these resources often do not offer guidelines for determining what constitutes a good syllabus.

Concerned about the uneven quality of service-learning syllabi, Campus Compact recently examined over 900 service-learning syllabi. This review confirmed that although there are vast numbers of service-learning syllabi available, there are few standards to help distinguish those worth recommending from those which are less exemplary, and few resources to assist faculty in constructing a service-learning syllabus.

One good resource is Janet Eyler and Dwight Giles' 1999 book, *Where's the Learning in Service-Learning?* In their book, Eyler and Giles assert that "many of the intellectual goals of higher education, including learning and application of material, critical thinking and problem solving, and perspective transformation, depend not on service experience alone but on how well integrated theory and practice are through application and reflection." (Eyler and Giles, 1999, p.166) To assist faculty in planning how to integrate theory and practice in their respective courses, the authors offer characteristics of effective service-learning and link these characteristics with intended learning outcomes. These characteristics—placement quality, application, reflection and community voice—are defined and then linked through research to specific student outcomes. Eyler and Giles ground these characteristics in research and offer them as markers for constructing effective service-learning courses. This information is enormously important, not only to faculty, but to the field of service-learning as it establishes benchmarks for quality.

In an effort to improve the quality of service-learning syllabi, Campus Compact has revised its web-based syllabus collection and created this volume, *The Fundamentals of Course Construction,* a revised edition of the 1994 Campus Compact publication *Redesigning Curricula: Models of Service-Learning Syllabi.* *The Fundamentals of Course Construction* is the third in a Campus Compact series on integrating service with academic study. The first volume, *Rethinking Tradition: Integrating Service with Academic Study on College Campuses* (1993) was a collection of essays and best practices that served as an overview of the service-learning field prior to 1993. In 1994, Campus Compact published a companion volume, *Redesigning Curricula: Models of Service Learning Syllabi,* a collection of syllabi and discussions by select faculty on teaching, learning, and course development. Based on the recent syllabi project, this new volume, *The Fundamentals of Course Construction,* is designed to assist faculty in constructing a good service-learning syllabus. The volume offers six models for service-learning courses, a cataloged sample of service-learning assignments, sample service-learning syllabi, and sample syllabi from service-learning courses that serve as civic bridges.

Introduction

The syllabus is the presentation of the structure of a course and, as such, is critical in shaping educational outcomes. Designing an effective syllabus is an art, as the syllabus must clearly convey to students what they will be expected to master in the course and how that mastery will be evaluated.

Service-learning introduces students to a particular pedagogy or teaching strategy that faculty hope will facilitate the acquisition of particular competencies, skills, attitudes, and appreciations. The degree to which faculty utilize service-learning should be directly related to course goals and objectives. Thus, the syllabus must clearly explain the role of service in the course, how service connects to content, why service is the pedagogy of choice, and what the service component will entail.

At Campus Compact, I am in the unique position of having access to hundreds of service-learning syllabi in a wide range of disciplines (and, perhaps more importantly, I have access to a wide range of faculty). After years of teaching, it was enlightening to examine syllabi from another perspective and in most cases as a disciplinary novice.

The majority of the service-learning syllabi I examined while researching this project were overwhelming and confusing documents. After reading stacks of diverse service-learning syllabi, I pulled out my own syllabi, sure that these would offer clarity. My syllabi were terrible. They were confusing—full of gaps, leaps, and assumptions. Like many faculty, I conflated course goals and objectives, presented the syllabus in a format that was misleading (relegating the service experience to page three), and chose assignments that were incongruent with course goals. After revisiting my syllabi I was unsure how the readings, assignments, and service placements I had selected served the learning goals for my course in Women's History. Having assumed that the service project could "stand alone" as an assignment, I had not allowed the service to inform my course organization.

I have since learned that to be truly effective and to minimize the potential for harm, service-learning must be well planned and integrated into the course with a clear sense of **how to structure** the service component and **why this service** activity is being utilized in this course.

- **How to structure the service component:** Define the nature of the service and introduce a service model for the course. For example, will students perform community-based action research, problem-based service-learning, or "pure service?" (see section 2)

- **Why this service activity in this course:** Define the service placement or project in the context of the course and the discipline.

Organizing a service-learning syllabus within the framework of a particular service model and its academic purpose can also assist faculty in addressing the question: "How will service assist students in the acquisition of particular foundational knowledge?" Initially, faculty may see this as a "zero sum" argument: "If I add service to my course, what content must I remove?" Service-learning is not about what stays and what goes. Rather, it is about identifying a pedagogy that best facilitates the acquisition of foundational knowledge that consists of specific competencies, skills, attitudes, and appreciations. A growing body of research suggests that service-learning is such pedagogy.

(Astin & Sax, 1998; Balazadeh, 1996; Bacon, 1998 (dissertation); Balazadeh, 1996; Batchelder & Root, 1994; Boss, 1994; Cohen & Kinsey, 1994; Driscoll, Holland, Gelmon, & Kerrigan, 1996; Eyler & Giles, 1999; Eyler, Root, & Giles, 1998; Fenzel & Leary, 1997; Foreman-Wood, 1996; Gray, et. al., 1998; Greene, 1996 (dissertation); Hall, 1996 (dissertation); Jordan, 1996 (dissertation); Kendrick, 1996; Osborne, Hammerich, Hensley, 1998; Oliver, 1997; Markus, Howard, & King, 1993; McElhaney, 1998 (dissertation); Miller, 1994; Nigro & Wortham, 1998; Rhoads, 1997; Smedick, 1996 (dissertation); Schmiede, 1995; Sledge, Shelburne, & Jones, 1993; Western Washington University, 1994). (I)

(I) Please see *Introduction to Service-Learning Toolkit: Readings and Resources for Faculty* available through National Campus Compact, Brown University, Providence RI, 2000.

1 Course Organization

"How one understands service has direct implications for how one teaches. Whether one envisions service as a continuum, as a set of paradigms, or in another coherent, consistent way, coming to grips with one's understanding of service is an important step in selecting the type of service that will match the purpose of a given course, defining the impacts one expects service to have, and determining the criteria by which success or failure will be measured."

KEITH MORTON,
ISSUES RELATED TO INTEGRATING SERVICE-LEARNING INTO THE CURRICULUM.
(IN JACOBY AND ASSOCIATES, 1996. P. 282)

There are four basic principles that should guide faculty in organizing and constructing a service-learning course:

1) **Engagement**—Does the service component meet a public good? How do you know this? Has the community been consulted? How? How have campus-community boundaries been negotiated and how will they be crossed?

2) **Reflection**—Is there a mechanism that encourages students to link their service experience to course content and to reflect upon why the service is important?

3) **Reciprocity**—Is reciprocity evident in the service component? How? "Reciprocity suggests that every individual, organization, and entity involved in the service-learning functions as both a teacher and a learner. Participants are perceived as colleagues, not as servers and clients." (Jacoby, 1996 p. 36)

4) **Public Dissemination**—Is service work presented to the public or made an opportunity for the community to enter into a public dialogue? For example: Do oral histories that students collect return to the community in some public form? Is the data students collect on the saturation of toxins in the local river made public? How? To whose advantage?

Once faculty have addressed these four principles, they should begin to plan the manner in which the service component will be presented in the syllabus. The presentation of service in the syllabus can be critical in shaping the educational outcomes for the course. Service cannot be presented as a mere sidebar to the course; rather, the syllabus should explain why this kind of service is a part of the course. This requires instructors to think about the explicit connections between their course and departmental objectives; between the university's mission and the community's expectations; and, perhaps most importantly, between their goals and their students' expectations (Woolcock, 1997 p. 10). These connections are further clarified for students in how faculty structure the service component in the syllabus. This is most often evident in how faculty conceptualize the course within a specific service-learning model.

SIX MODELS FOR SERVICE-LEARNING

Whether creating a new course or reconstructing an existing course using service-learning, faculty should explore the appropriate model of service-learning. While one could argue that there are many models of service-learning, we feel that service-learning courses can basically be described in six categories:

1) "Pure" Service-Learning—These are courses that send students out into the community to serve. These courses have as their intellectual core the idea of service to communities by students, volunteers, or engaged citizens. They are not typically lodged in any one discipline.

EXAMPLE: CALIFORNIA STATE UNIVERSITY AT MONTEREY BAY
Service Learning 200: Introduction to Service in Multicultural Communities:
Course Focus: Youth and Elderly

Purpose: To prepare students for active and responsible community participation. To learn the skills, knowledge and competencies necessary for this type of participation, students will engage in an on-going process of service and reflection throughout the semester.

Community-Based Assignment: With faculty guidance, students will choose a service site that will allow them to learn about themselves and their community. For a minimum of three hours a week, for 10 weeks, students will be engaged in the work of a local community agency, school, or other organization. In addition to hands on work, time at the agency site will be spent observing, listening, and engaging in dialogue with community members.

One of the purposes of the community placement is to afford students direct experience in a community or sector of a community with which they do not have previous experience, and which they may have initially perceived as "other." The topics this section will focus on are infants, children, young people and people who are elderly. Some course readings, class discussions and activities and all placements for this section will focus on these topics. Several community agencies have agreed to serve as site placements for this section. Students will have the opportunity to learn more about them from class discussions and from the Service Learning Placement catalog distributed the third week of September. Students will be able to meet with agency staff at the Placement Fair held September 20.

Time spent in the classroom and in the community is of equal importance.

Related Assignment: Weekly journal, three service learning projects (one per month) with related essays. Final group service presentation (to be designed by students in conjunction with faculty).

Because service is the course content of pure service-learning, it is easier to build an intellectual connection between the course and the community experience. But pure service poses a danger in that the "content" of the course is service-learning, volunteerism, or civic engagement. It is not that these topics can't be taught in intellectually defensive ways. Many of these courses use a multi-disciplinary approach to examine the philosophical, social, and intellectual underpinnings that support a movement or a historical/philosophical approach to a phenomenon like volunteerism. But all too frequently, detractors accuse these courses of being lightweight excuses to give students credit for service with a reflective component that is more conversational than analytical, (all in the guise of an intellectual frame). As a result, faculty often view these courses with a great deal of skepticism. There is also a danger that such courses may serve to marginalize service-learning because faculty may be reluctant to envision a more rigorous or content-specific model.

2) Discipline-Based Service-Learning—In this model, students are expected to have a presence in the community throughout the semester and reflect on their experiences on a regular basis throughout the semester using course content as a basis for their analysis and understanding.

EXAMPLE: SACRED HEART COLLEGE
History 252: Medieval Europe

Purpose: This course aims to study the development of a distinctly European Western civilization that emerged from the Mediterranean and Classical world as well as other northern "barbarian" tribes. We will seek to understand the development of a distinctly "western civilization" in Europe by (1) focusing on political, economic and religious institutions, (2) by looking at the ideological and cultural system and the collective mentality, and (3) by looking at a variety of people who inhabited these worlds. In the Medieval world each person had a fixed place in society, and entered their role through birth and "calling": they had a duty to live in society in a certain way.

Community-Based Component: (A course option in place of a paper.) You may do a student-teaching internship with sixth-graders at Winthrop School, Reed School or Moran School. Students will present units on the medieval world, work with reading skills, and design and run projects with the sixth graders.

Related Assignments: A written report of your experience (15 pages) is due at the end of the semester.

CHALLENGES

Discipline-based courses are generally easier to defend intellectually. But the link between course content and community experience must be made very explicit to students. And the more explicit the link, the more one limits the types of appropriate community experiences. This can make placement logistics and monitoring difficult and frustrating. Perhaps because of this constraint, discipline-based courses are more apt to use service in lieu of another assignment, as extra credit, or as a fourth credit. This can present additional challenges to the reflective component as not all students in the course are engaged in service.

3) Problem-Based Service-Learning (PBSL)—According to this model, students (or teams of students) relate to the community much as "consultants" working for a "client." Students work with community members to understand a particular community problem or need. This model presumes that the students will have some knowledge they can draw upon to make recommendations to the community or develop a solution to the problem; architecture students might design a park; business students might develop a web site; or botany students might identify non-native plants and suggest eradication methods.

EXAMPLE: UNIVERSITY OF UTAH
                     Civil Engineering 571: Traffic Flow Theory

Purpose: Transportation studies encompass a wide range of disciplines. The Traffic Engineering Course has been designed to provide you with an insight into traffic control and management techniques.

Community-Based Component: Students in this class provide a needed service: The Millcreek Lion's Club and the county of Salt Lake have approached me requesting that I work with them to address traffic control problems in the Millcreek neighborhood. Traffic routed improperly has become a safety issue and has greatly contributed to the deterioration in the neighborhood especially for seniors and children. Too much traffic on neighborhood streets has cut off access by foot and isolated parts of the neighborhood from what used to be a more cohesive unit. Students will work with the community residents to understand the problems, then to design traffic solutions. Students will present their findings and solutions to the community and the county in public meetings and will get feedback from both as to how to continuously improve the project.

Related Assignments: In addition to collecting research and designing solutions (presented in a series of reports), students will write about how their designs have been influenced by community concerns.

CHALLENGES

Problem-based service-learning attempts to circumvent many of the logistical problems faculty encounter by limiting the number of times that students go out into the community (students go into the community long enough to identify a problem and/gather data). The rationale is that students are responsible for surveying communities and identifying specific needs. Students are then responsible for coordinating their own schedules to develop a product in response to these identified needs. There are two difficulties associated with this approach:

1) The limited exposure of the students to the community minimizes the likelihood that their solution will address the full magnitude of the problem.

2) There is a danger in promoting the idea that students are "experts" and communities are "clients." This heightens the perception of many communities that universities are pejorative entities that promote insular ways of knowing and understanding the world.

4) Capstone Courses—These courses are generally designed for majors and minors in a given discipline and are offered almost exclusively to students in their final year. Capstone courses ask students to draw upon the knowledge they have obtained throughout their course work and combine it with relevant service work in the community. The goal of capstone courses is usually either exploring a new topic or synthesizing students understanding of their discipline. These courses offer an excellent way to help students transition from the world of theory to the world of practice by helping them make professional contacts and gather personal experience. (See Appendix)

EXAMPLE: PORTLAND STATE UNIVERSITY
In Other Words: The Women's Community Education Project

Purpose: To design an outreach program to raise local teen girls' awareness of resources and activities at In Other Words and the Women's Community Education Project. To provide a space for teen girls to think, talk, and write about current issues in their lives.

Community-Based Component: Your primary task for this course is to make contacts with teen advocates in the Portland area and to conduct several rap sessions with teen girls, encourage them to participate in our project, solicit submissions, and design our 'zine. You will negotiate a secondary task applicable to our project. This task is an opportunity to use skills specific to your major and should reflect a personal interest in an issue related to teen girls or the bookstore.

Related Assignment: Portfolio, Capstone Plan, and proposal for group facilitation research reflective journal.

CHALLENGES

Capstone courses place much of the responsibility for placement on the student. It is assumed that the senior year is an appropriate time for students to bring their skills and knowledge to bear on a community problem, developing new knowledge in the process. Capstone courses generally offer communities students with specific skills who can invest a significant amount of time in research and practice. The danger is that when students graduate and leave the community, they take with them valuable knowledge and insights that cannot be easily replaced.

5) Service Internships—Like traditional internships, these experiences are more intense than typical service-learning courses, with students working as many as 10 to 20 hours a week in a community setting. As in traditional internships, students are generally charged with producing a body of work that is of value to the community or site. However, unlike traditional internships, service internship have regular and ongoing reflective opportunities that help students analyze their new experiences using discipline-based theories. These reflective opportunities can be done with small groups of peers, with one-on-one meetings with faculty advisors, or even electronically with a faculty member providing feedback. Service internships are further distinguished from traditional internships by their focus on reciprocity: the idea that the community and the student benefit equally from the experience.

Purpose: The Practicum is designed to prepare you to work as a Community Assistant for the Feinstein Institute for Public Service. The Practicum is also designed to develop and improve the practical skills that will help you to work effectively as liaisons between service-learning courses and the community-based organizations that operate as service sites in these courses.

Community-Based Component: The Practicum is a yearlong required course for the Public and Community Service Studies major. While the two semesters differ significantly in terms of course content and objectives, they complement each other. During the first semester your focus will be on developing a comprehensive knowledge of your site, the population it serves, and the neighborhood where it is located. You will be responsible for "managing" the service for the group of students assigned to your site. You will be asked to reflect upon your motivations, your intentions, and your impact in light of the relationships you develop over the course of the semester. During the second semester your focus will be on analyzing the relationship between the Feinstein Institute and your site and you will be asked to reflect upon and write about responsibility and impact at the institutional level. You will consider the history of the relationship between the Institute and the organization and be asked to make concrete recommendations regarding the advancement of the relationship in the future.

Related Assignments: Organizational action research, critical incident journal, grant application.

CHALLENGES

Service Internships require students to produce a body of work that is of value to the community or to a specific community site. However, they generally require a level of oversight from the community partner that can be taxing. And, as with capstone courses, students graduate and leave the community site, taking with them valuable knowledge and insight that cannot be easily replaced.

6) Undergraduate Community-Based Action Research—A relatively new approach that is gaining popularity, community-based action research is similar to an independent study option for the rare student who is highly experienced in community work. Community-based action research can also be effective with small classes or groups of students. In this model, students work closely with faculty members to learn research methodology while serving as advocates for communities.

Purpose: This course will involve teams of students in community-oriented research projects. Students will participate in the design and execution of a specific research project identified by a

Lehigh Valley development agency. The results of this research will be communicated both orally and in a written report to the agency.

Community-Based Component: Students may choose one of seven research projects identified by development agencies. For example:
  • Transportation Barriers to Successful Welfare to Work Transitions
  • Community partner: Council of Hispanic Organizations
Students will assist the council by researching and documenting the extent to which women living in the inner city of Allentown are limited in their search for employment by the current configuration of bus routes. Student teams will meet with LANTA planners to identify ways in which routes could be changed or new services developed to enhance the possibility of successful transitions from welfare to work
Related assignments: Large research paper and presentation.

CHALLENGES

Undergraduate community-based research shares many of the same pros and cons as traditional research-focused courses. This model assumes that students are competent in time management, are self-directed learners, and can negotiate diverse communities. These assumptions can become problematic and the ramifications of students' failures can impact the community.

These service models can assist faculty in conceptualizing service-learning within a specific disciplinary framework. For example, mathematicians and faculty in the hard sciences often react favorably to problem-based service-learning since it reflects their disciplinary training, which is primarily problem-based. Faculty in the humanities often respond favorably to disciplinary-based service-learning since it values the analysis and synthesis of information, which is reflective of disciplinary training in the liberal arts. But creating a service-learning course raises larger questions for faculty about the construction of knowledge.

SOME REFLECTIONS ON THE CONSTRUCTION OF KNOWLEDGE

Introducing faculty to service-learning within the rubric of the six service-learning models may allow them to entertain larger questions about the construction of knowledge and the teaching-learning process.

Reflecting upon my own experiences creating and revising service-learning courses, I suspect that a significant challenge to my students' use of the syllabus was not just a lack of clarity but also the gulf between our (my students' and my) respective conceptions of knowledge. Many of the students I encountered in my courses seemed to conceive of thinking in an academic setting as linear and concrete. Lofty and abstract discussion of the emotional quality of working class women's lives during the progressive era were met with questions such as, "Will this be on the test?" or, my favorite question, "Do we need to know this?" While my students did enthusiastically engage in class discussions and grasp abstractions, these were not familiar classroom behaviors. Though I assumed that students were thinking about the possibilities information held, they generally preferred to remain in the now—to dwell on the immediate regurgitation of the information. Discussions with colleagues revealed that this gulf between my conception of knowledge (abstract) and my students' (concrete) was a common and taxing problem for faculty.

Moreover, the various developmental levels (affective, emotional, and moral) of students further exacerbated this gulf.

As faculty, we are often drawn to teaching because it is about possibilities—about abstractions, ideas, and the possibilities inherent in our disciplinary interest. We construct our work environments so that they are highly autonomous and we assume that students prefer to think and work as we do. Our course syllabi often reflect our assumptions and our preferences about the acquisition and use of knowledge. But research suggests that many of our students are not of a like mind. When designing syllabi, instructors cannot dismiss the gap between how students have been taught to conceive of knowledge (concrete) and how faculty tend to perceive knowledge (abstract). Research confirms that many undergraduates perform best in learning situations characterized by "direct, concrete experience, moderate to high degrees of structure, and a linear approach to learning" (Schroeder, 1993 p. 22).

A well constructed service-learning course may assist students in several ways. As faculty, we might think of our syllabi as maps that guide students as they develop cognitively, affectively, emotionally, and morally over the course of the semester. But even when syllabi are linear and concrete, well-considered, and structured in a manner that is coherent and appealing to students, many students will simply ignore the information at hand. "The vast majority of difficulties in reasoning demonstrated across a diverse population were not logical fallacies or other problems of a formal nature, but rather problems resulting from the subjects underutilization of available information" (Perkins, 1982 p. 32).

When we design a syllabus, we hope that it accurately reflects the intent of our courses. We hope our syllabi speak to students about the value of mastering the content or the discipline we love. We hope that the experience of being in our courses will challenge students intellectual and moral timidity; will serve as a measure to students of what they can aspire to be and understand. It is painful to realize that our discipline—our course—holds little more than a vague attraction for students; that the service placement we have so carefully cultivated is but one more responsibility a student must attend to each Thursday afternoon; that we have very little control over how our students prioritize and utilize information. I am not suggesting that the duty of faculty is one of leading the distracted, concrete learner through an "enjoyable" process. I am suggesting that we cannot diminish the importance of our (students' and faculty's) respective conceptions of the use of information and the construction of knowledge. As faculty, we should think of our syllabi as maps that guide students as they developmentally move over the course of the semester. Developing the map requires faculty to attend to a course sequence and an order, to create a syllabus that can bridge the gulf between faculty and students' conceptions of knowledge, and to assist students in learning how to utilize that information.

2 Implementation

"…the goal is to blend service and learning goals and activities in such a way that the two reinforce each other and produce a greater impact than either could produce alone."

BARRY FENSTERMACHER, COMBINING SERVICE AND LEARNING: VOL. II, 1990, P.195

Exemplary service-learning syllabi:

- Include service as an expressed goal

- Clearly describe how the service experience will be measured and what will be measured

- Describe the nature of the service placement and/or project

- Specify the roles and responsibilities of students in the placement and/or service project, (e.g., transportation, time requirements, community contacts, etc.)

- Define the need(s) the service placement meets

- Specify how students will be expected to demonstrate what they have learned in the placement/project (journal, papers, presentations)

- Present course assignments that link the service placement and the course content

- Include a description of the reflective process

- Include a description of the expectations for the public dissemination of students' work.

THE COMPONENTS OF AN EFFECTIVE SERVICE-LEARNING SYLLABUS

Regardless of how dynamic the instructor or the service project, the addition of service to a course requires that faculty reevaluate each category in their syllabus and, if necessary, broaden categories to reflect the integration of content with service. The syllabi examined tended to be organized using all or a combination of the following categories:

- Heading that includes the university name, department, course title, catalog number, semester/year, and faculty contact information (including rank, office hours, email, office and/or home phone, and office address)

- Course description

- Introduction, overview, purpose, or rationale

- Course goals and course objectives

- Required texts/readings

- Weekly semester schedule

- Overview of course assignments (or the primary assignment)

- Explanation of the grading policy

- Supplemental or recommended reading list

A course outline/syllabus that is coherent and offers a clear connection between each of the above categories enhances teaching and learning and facilitates a confident transition for students from the campus to the community. In the following pages we will examine each of these categories and discuss how service might impact the presentation of that category.

The Heading

Course title, catalog number, semester/year, university, department faculty and co-instructor* contact information (including rank, office hours, email, office and/or home phone and office address

These basic administrative components are fairly self-explanatory. However, the majority of syllabi I reviewed omitted one or more of these items (frequently the university or the department). Faculty tend to reference their courses in acronyms and catalog numbers, indicating that they tend to perceive syllabi as strictly internal documents—not meant to be read by those outside the course or department. But syllabi should be considered public in nature. They are kept and passed along to other students. Libraries, computer centers, and campus writing and learning centers keep syllabi on file. Websites and organizations like Campus Compact and the National Service Learning Clearinghouse collect syllabi and post them on their websites. Each of the items in the syllabus heading is important and faculty should make them as clear as possible.

FABER COLLEGE
School of Education; Fall, 2001
SED 320: Sociology of Education
Associate Professor John Blutowski*
Clara Barton, Director of the Faberville Literacy Collaborative

* Some syllabi list the community partner as the co-instructor. This inevitably raises questions about rank and distinctions of power. Many faculty leave their rank off the heading as they feel it inappropriate to create distinctions in power between themselves and the community partner.

Course Description

The course description is the first opportunity to truly describe the course. While brevity is often prudent, the instructor should introduce the non-traditional nature of the course—the service component—and clearly articulate the relevance of the service to the course.

UNIVERSITY OF RICHMOND
LDSP 305 – Leadership in Community Organizations

The focus of this course is on leadership within community and voluntary organizations and how this context affects and shapes leadership. Organizations in this context run from permeable boundaries of social movement to those of formal, for-profit and government organizations. Leadership in this context, thus combines elements of leadership of social movements with leadership in formal organizations of the corporate and political contexts. Students will find lessons derived from other contexts, social movements, formal organizations, and politics, especially social policy, applicable here.

This course will focus on an array of community and voluntary organizations. We will spend a great deal of time examining the differences among organizations within this context that impact on their leadership. We will focus on concepts of participation, representation and empowerment to distinguish this organizational context from others and to distinguish organizations within it. Much of the new emphasis in formal organizations, including corporate structures, incorporate these concepts. Thus, an emphasis on the distinct factors of leadership in community organizations does not suggest these factors are unique in this context. We will spend considerable time examining leadership as organizing and as administration. We will also examine and discuss specific leadership tasks that are common in this context: fund raising, conducting meetings and working with boards.

CONNECTICUT COLLEGE
ES 410 – Environmental Studies/Geophysics:
River Hydrology and Hydraulics

The development and evolution of natural channel systems will be investigated with a special emphasis on environmental river restoration and aquatic habitat. Topics include the physics of flowing water, sediment transport by rivers, flow and substrate characterization techniques and flood hydrology. Laboratory requires the students to jointly design a river restoration project for an environmentally degraded channel.

Introduction, Overview, Purpose, or Rationale

While many faculty choose to fold the course description and the course introduction together, the two serve different functions. The course description briefly describes the course. The Introduction is an expanded version of the description in which faculty can elaborate on the course, discuss prerequisites, and more fully introduce the service-learning component of the course.

University of Richmond
LDSP 305 – Leadership in Community Organizations

Perhaps nothing distinguishes America from other nations more than the reliance on the non-profit sector to address public problems. Ranging from large formal voluntary organizations, like the United Way and the American Cancer Society, to small informal groups, like support groups and neighborhood associations, Americans join together to provide services to those in need and to advocate for political and social changes. The non-profit sector beckons many Americans, in diverse roles and varying degrees of commitment, to combine their potential and responsibility for leadership. This area of study is central to the University's goals for the Jepson School to "challenge students by broadening their perspective on themselves and deepening their understanding of controversial contemporary issues and values conflicts [and] motivate students to seek positions of leadership as a vehicle for service…"

Connecticut College
ES 410 – Environmental Studies/Geophysics: River Hydrology and Hydraulics

The River Hydrology and Hydraulics course focuses on the application of fluvial geomorphology to an environmental river restoration effort on the College campus. With the large number of streams and rivers negatively impacted by human land-use and disturbance, a growing number of public agencies and private interest groups are focused on recreating, restoring or enhancing aquatic habitat. River restoration is an interdisciplinary field that combines ecological knowledge of aquatic habitat requirement from fisheries biologists, with design and implication work for instream structures from civil engineers and knowledge of the physical evolution of natural river systems form geomorphologists.

As geomorphologists we will need to understand how the local hydrology has influenced the shape and characteristics of the local channel systems through time. The aquatic habitat is best characterized by the physical creation and maintenance of a pool and riffel morphology and its importance in river restoration. An investigation of erosion and deposition within natural and anthropologenically-influenced stream channels is an integral part of these types of studies.

We will apply this understanding to help develop a restoration design for an incised channel on the Connecticut College campus. We will investigate a small channel that drains the northeast corner of the main campus and flows north of the College Athletic Complex to the Thames River. The channel has a serious erosion problem that has resulted in over 2 meters of vertical incision into the hillside and sedimentation of local wetlands. Students will produce a final report and channel design that may result in the implementation of a restoration project following the guidelines outlined in the student plan.

Course Goals and Objectives

Goals are learning outcomes—broad statements identifying the general educational outcomes you want students to display upon completion of the course (Woolcock, 1997 p.12).

Objectives are the concrete measures by which goals will be realized and are usually expressed as relationships between specific concepts. For example, one of the goals in a Political Science course might be to examine the role of the state in economic development in underserved communities. A corresponding objective might be to explore the conditions under which current state policies hinder or help economic growth (Woolcock, 1997 p.12).

In the vast majority of service-learning syllabi examined for this project, faculty simply conflated goals and objectives. While in many cases this was fine, confusion occurred when the combined goal/objective failed to delineate between outcomes and measures. For example:

COURSE OBJECTIVE

To encourage students to evaluate the strengths and weaknesses of welfare policies in American society.

The problem with this combined goal/objective is that it does not clarify for students what learning outcome will be measured. A more coherent approach would be to break down this goal/objective into a goal and a corresponding objective:

Goal: To encourage students to think critically about current welfare policies in the United States.

Objective: Students will critically evaluate the strengths and weaknesses of social and economic theories and arguments that inform current welfare policies.

This revised goal and objective alerts students that they will be evaluated on their ability to analyze particular theories and arguments that inform current welfare policies. Faculty can connect this objective to the specific assignment (evaluative measure) in the syllabus, thereby clarifying what they will measure and how they will measure it.

Another example of goals/objectives compressed to the point of confusion:

DANCE 200: OBJECTIVES

- To provide opportunities for students to bridge university experiences to the community through service work.

- To provide information about and practical experience in working with dance in the community.

- To provide a network of resources, people, and materials for linking dance to diverse community groups.

- To use community experience as a context for discussion and evaluation of individual and group projects.

The objectives above are more accurately described as goals. But when they are presented as objectives, one is left to wonder how students will be evaluated. And as there are no goals listed prior to the objectives one is left to wonder: "Why these?" "What's the purpose of the objectives?" and "Why include a service component?" When composing objectives, conceptualize them in a manner that reinforces the goals or outcomes you hope students will achieve.

A suggested revision of the first objective would be:

COURSE OBJECTIVE (REVISED)

Goal: To connect dance students to community arts organizations though service learning.

Objective: Students will demonstrate critical thinking in a 20 hour service placement.

Another inconsistency I found in the presentation of goals and objectives was the tendency of faculty to focus on the learning process (teaching activity) rather then the learning outcome (Gronlund, 1970 p.7). For example, one syllabus listed the objective, "To demonstrate to students an appreciation for the immigrant experience." This is not only a goal inaccurately expressed as an objective, but is conveyed in a manner that focuses on the instructor's role (the teaching activity), not the student's role (learning outcome). Presented to the student, the objective literally means that once the faculty member demonstrates an appreciation for the immigrant experience, the learning objective is met. I doubt this is what the faculty member had in mind. More likely she meant that upon completing the course she hoped students would exhibit some of the following competencies:

- Identify countries of origin and diverse ethnicity's represented in the communities in which students serve.

- Describe the steps involved in immigrating to the United States.

- List common social, cultural and economic issues immigrants encounter upon arriving in the United States.

- Demonstrate an understanding of skills needed to negotiate the US immigration system.

These four objectives clarify the initial goal of "demonstrating an appreciation for the immigrant experience." They are tangible to students, but more importantly, they specify measurable learning outcomes (products) not just the teaching activity (process). By focusing on the learning outcomes, you will ultimately focus on the teaching activity; for the extent to which students achieve the course objectives is the extent to which they realize the goals of the course—and this is a measure of teaching effectiveness.

As a faculty member, I have often dismissed the debate surrounding goals and objectives as hair-splitting. But the process of examining over 900 service-learning syllabi has convinced me that there is real value in delineating goals and objectives, if only for the sake of distinguishing between outcomes (goals) and measures (objectives) for students. The process of making this distinction can be an opportunity for faculty to think deeply about the service component and its relationship to course content—to once again reflect upon how to structure the service component and why this service activity is being utilized in this course.

The best way for faculty to begin formulating course goals and objectives in a service-learning course is by asking themselves:

- What educational outcomes do I want students to display upon completing this course?

- How can service-learning effectively help them attain that mastery?

- What student behavior will serve as evidence that this mastery has been achieved?

Faculty will be in a better position to evaluate leaning outcomes if they begin their course objectives with action verbs (Gronlund, 1970 p.12). For example:

- Identifies populations at risk

- Describes the characteristics of the progressive era

- Lists social service organizations that address domestic violence

- Contrasts current welfare policies to current economic trends

- Appreciates the complexity of the Weikwa River ecosystem

- Synthesizes community histories

- Evaluates the effectiveness of current neighborhood literacy programs

WHAT EXACTLY ARE WE MEASURING?

One of the more intimidating aspects of service-learning pedagogy is the assumption that faculty must measure student behavior (e.g. compassion). It is more accurate to say that particular student behaviors, like compassion, will serve as evidence that a course goal has been met or that a student is approaching a course goal. But it is this assumption that student behavior must be measured that makes many faculty uncomfortable with and resistant to service-learning pedagogy. After all, measuring student behavior in community settings raises larger questions about objective assessment (e.g., Is all service work measurable?). The problem lies not in measuring student behavior, for faculty are always evaluating behavior in some form. Rather, the concern is with the measure.

Consider the following objective: "Students will complete 13 hours of service at a local shelter." The problem with this objective is that some students will focus primarily on the measure to the detriment of the service activity. The objective gives students the license to believe that once they have achieved the stated measure of 13 hours their relationship with the shelter is over. Narrowly stating the objective as "Completes 13 hours" invites ambiguity as it fails to clarify what a student is to learn and how learning outcomes will be measured. To avoid this problem, the instructor should consider why 13 hours at the shelter placement is important. Is it to help students distinguish between facts and opinions about homelessness? To identify factors that lead to homelessness? To identify populations at risk for homelessness? If these are the goals for the service experience, the faculty member should state them as such under the larger heading, "Demonstrates critical thinking in a 13 hour service placement." This type of clarity tells students what is expected of them and reminds faculty what it is they need to measure.

Evaluating student behavior in a community placement inevitably leads faculty to judge specific human qualities. Many of the qualities we hope service will engender in our students are difficult to articulate in a syllabus because they are attitudes or appreciations. This should not discourage faculty from stating these goals. If you think it is important for students to serve in an adult tutoring program in order to grasp conversational Spanish and to gain an appreciation for the struggle of recent immigrants, then you must say so. If constructing a house with Habitat for Humanity serves to help students appreciate the complexity of neighborhood organizing, state that as an objective. If you hope that measuring the impurities in the water from Boston Harbor will help students gain a sense of awe for the wonders of an ecosystem, then say so. While there are no demonstrable measures of "love," "wonder," and "awe" there is the faculty member's professional judgement (Woolcock, 1997 p.13). And once again, the language of our goals has no meaning without clear objectives (standards) that permit judgement as to whether or not the goals have been achieved and what particular student behaviors will serve as evidence to faculty that a student is approaching a course goal.

Moreover, it is important that faculty craft goals and objectives in such a manner that they demonstrate to students the academic "rigor" of service. Goals and objectives should convey to students and community partners that a level of quality cannot and will not be compromised or obscured. The best strategy may be to incorporate a range of qualitative and quantitative objectives that combine to convey a holistic, thorough set of expectations.

Example: WS/IDS 350 - The Public Specter
Feminist Representations of the Afterlife

Course Goals

Students who have successfully completed this course should be able to demonstrate their understandings of:

- The Spiritualism movement in America in the late 19th and early 20th centuries.

- Ghost stories as allegories for the social, political, economic and cultural concerns of women.

- The ways a feminist perspective can inform images of the afterlife.

- The literary tools women authors have used to convey the psycho-social importance in ghost stories.

- How women's community history is conveyed through monuments at The North Providence Burial Ground.

- Cemeteries as public spaces that contribute to the health of a community and serve as sites that illustrate the social, political, economic and cultural concerns of women.

Course Objectives

Students who have successfully completed this course should be able to:

- Identify and analyze the cultural tensions between material and spiritual conceptions in late 19th century America and how those tensions gave rise to the Spiritualism movement.

- Identify and analyze the social and cultural anxieties evidenced in course assignments.

- Identify and analyze representations of women evidenced in readings, lectures, service and related assignments and how those representations continue to resonate and influence contemporary images of women.

- Identify, define and utilize metaphor, religious iconography and motif.

- Describe specific community events that impacted women in Providence as evidenced in the North Providence Burial Ground.

- Explain the history of cemeteries as public space.

Ways students will demonstrate Objectives 1–6:

- **Objective 1:** Research paper in which students research and analyze the Spiritualism Movement.

- **Objective 2:** Students will address this competency as part of a large service and research project. The project will include a writing component and a presentation.

- **Objective 3:** Students will keep a weekly journal in which they reflect upon representation of women in course assignments.

- **Objective 4:** Students will be asked to identify and interpret literary tools in class discussion and in weekly journal assignments.

- **Objectives 5 and 6:** Students will address through a negotiated, community-based, action research project.

Course Content: Required Readings and Sequencing

Once faculty have a clear sense of course goals and objectives, they must chose the materials that will best facilitate the realization of those goals and objectives and promote the needs of the service placement. Many faculty report that in the process of examining potential course material in relation to the intended service experience, they find that their original course objectives are inappropriate, a poor fit, or poorly specified. If this is the case, don't get discouraged. This is an opportunity to reflect on course construction and to make some necessary adjustments. Moreover, this is a good opportunity to connect course materials and assignments to course goals and objectives.

After deciding upon the appropriate course content, namely the readings and the service placement, the next step is to work out the order in which you present the material. This is a difficult task—one that requires faculty not only to project the kinds of students who will be in the course but also to prepare for the questions those students will raise throughout the service experience.

As faculty, we generally understand that the goal of introductory courses is to present a broad range of material throughout the semester, most of it equally challenging. The goal of upper division courses on the other hand is to progressively increase the degree of difficulty by building upon concepts and "to demonstrate to students the natural affinity different concepts have with one another" (Woolcock 1997 p.17). When thinking about the order or progression the course will take and how the service experience progressively serves the course goals, faculty should consider the level of disciplinary sophistication and engagement that the course requires from students. Introductory courses require a different ordering than do upper level classes (Woolcock 1997 p.17).

Our attempts to lay out the order of our courses are expressed for students as the weekly schedule, often the last two or three pages of the syllabus. In the weekly schedule, faculty often give their lectures interesting titles, remind students of impending assignments, caution students to be careful, or remind them to have fun on scheduled breaks. The weekly schedule is often the most interesting and relevant part of the syllabus for students. It is the script or the contract they adhere to, and it is the part of the syllabus they are most likely to challenge. What faculty member has not felt the wrath of a student for trying to change a date in the weekly calendar? When preparing the weekly calendar remember that this is your presentation of the order of events and, as such, it reflects how you envision the progression of knowledge for the course. The service component must be integrated into the weekly schedule in the same manner you would present a difficult text—guiding students through a progression from basic knowledge to more difficult concepts.

In a perfect academic world, faculty would have the opportunity to mull over course goals and objectives and the service component before choosing books and assignments. But the reality is far different. The bookstore begins calling midway through a busy fall semester—asking for book orders for spring semester courses. In a rush, many instructors choose books with the intention of building course goals and objectives around those texts, hoping that existing syllabi will serve as a template for a new course. Similarly, hurried instructors often treat the service component in a secondary fashion, choosing the placement or project and then constructing the course goals and objectives around the placement. Instead, like a seminal text, the service placement should be chosen or constructed because it enhances existing course goals and objectives, not because it fits a time constraint.

An overview of course assignments

After establishing the educational outcomes you hope students will achieve and the specific content that will best facilitate that outcome, you must decode what assignments will best measure students' progress. The majority of service assignments in the syllabi I examined were written papers, most often 3 papers. While service does provide a wonderful platform for student writing, faculty should not dismiss the importance of designing an appropriate range of measures for students (papers, tests, presentations, reports, reviews, performances).

In addition to listing assignments, faculty should discuss the respective weight of each assignment, which should directly reflect the course objectives. (When discussing the weight of each course assignment, faculty should refer to the course objective(s) that corresponds to the assignment.) The syllabus should also include due dates for each assignment, including where it should be submitted, what form the submission must take, who will be grading the assignment, when students can expect their work returned, and where to find grievance procedure policies.

An overview of the grading policy

When using service-learning, faculty do not evaluate students on the service placement, rather students are evaluated on the learning outcomes that flow from the service (materials they produce that are inspired by the service). The grade or weight that faculty allocate to the products of the service experience and related non-service assignments should accurately reflect the course objectives. The most common allotment is 100 points, with each assignment allocated a percentage of the 100 points. The points should be distributed in such a manner that they accurately reflect the value of the assignment as well as the time and effort faculty expect students to invest. Before assigning a final paper 50 percent of the course weight, faculty must ask, "Does this reflect my hopes for student learning outcomes?" And "Does this reflect a coherent progression of knowledge?" (In the syllabi I reviewed, faculty rarely referenced course objectives when describing the allocation of percentage points; thus, the syllabus failed to offer a clear connection between the objectives and the allotted points.) Additionally, faculty should provide a clear and concise description of who will evaluate the students' community work (e.g., Will a community partner evaluate student work?) and what is the relative weight of that evaluation.

A supplemental or recommended reading list

Service-leaning often elicits a real hunger in students for additional information. In my own experience, students expressed an appreciation for recommended reading lists more often in my service-learning courses than in courses I taught that did not utilize service. I found it helpful to categorize recommended readings under a number of different headings such as historical, contemporary theory, narratives, essential reads, web links, articles, books, movies, etc. and it was also useful to have students add to the list throughout the semester.

DESCRIBING THE SERVICE ASSIGNMENT

(by Dr. Richard Cone, Executive Director, Joint Educational Project, College of Letters, Arts and Sciences, University of Southern California)

Many syllabi include additional materials for students that are specific to the service assignment. These related materials are often constructed as informational resources, student contracts, or "frequently asked questions." The materials should alleviate the anxiety many students feel toward service by answering the following concerns:

Is the service optional or mandatory? If it is mandatory, what are the options for students who cannot fit community service into their schedule? Must they drop the course or are there some alternative paths? If it is optional, is the service extra credit? Does it work in lieu of a paper or some other requirement? Or is it merely an alternative way of gathering data for an end-of-semester paper?

There is a continuing controversy about mandating service. Often, students and less knowledgeable colleagues will snicker at the notion of mandating volunteerism. I believe it is important to address those misconceptions. Service-learning is not forced labor; it is a pedagogy. Faculty who utilize it are utilizing an alternative mode of teaching and learning. Just as instructors should not have to explain why they require term papers or class projects, they should not have to justify student work in the community, as long as they can justify the learning that ensues.

How many hours of service are students required to complete? (How many hours per week for how many weeks?)

If students are to make informed decisions, they must understand the commitment in relation to their other requirements. This becomes even more important as increasing numbers of students are working to cover the costs of higher education. When presenting the service component, the estimate should include service hours, transportation to and from the service placement, and an approximation of time needed for reflection.

What does the timeline for the semester look like? What is the deadline for finding a service site? When should community assignments be completed? When are assignments due?

To the greatest extent possible, these elements should be integrated into the syllabus so that for any given week, students can see what course readings, service requirements, and assignments are due.

Specific information about service placements

Faculty should include a section in the syllabus that addresses what type of service placements students will be expected to undertake. Are students required to find their own placement and, if so, what requirements must a site meet to be an appropriate placement? Will students select a site off a list and, if so, how do they make an informed decision about which site might be best for them? If the course does require students to choose from a list of approved sites, the syllabus should include a brief description about the site/agency and the type of work that students will be doing. If there is an office on campus that will assist students in making the link with the service site, the syllabus must tell students how they can contact the office. This information is critical, not only in helping students initiate the placement process, but also in alleviating the fear that service can inspire in students.

If students must assume responsibility for finding their own site or a site off a list, how do they go about informing their faculty member of their chosen site, their specific assignment, and the name and contact information of the person responsible for supervising their work? The syllabus should include any and all contracts or work agreements that students fill out with faculty and site supervisors. This allows the student, the faculty member, and the site supervisor to have copies and increases the likelihood that there is common understanding.

When must students begin? Create a firm deadline for getting situated. Remember "student time" is often unique. Students can and will take half of the semester getting located, resulting in little time for service and/or stacking service hours in the latter half of the semester thereby reducing the time available for reflection. With few exceptions, sixteen hours of experience in the community spread over eight weeks promises a better educational experience than sixteen hours done on two successive Saturdays. Moreover, goals and objectives depend upon the ability to measure steady progress over the course of the semester. Each trip to the community is an opportunity to provoke new thoughts, promote deeper understanding, and lead students toward the realization of course goals.

Requirements for the reflective component

Nothing is more central to the experiential learning process than the process of reflection. Expectations about reflection should be conveyed clearly and prominently in the syllabus. The weekly schedule should address the extent to which written reflection will be required, whether there is an oral reflective process, and how that process will take place.

Many experienced service-learning faculty embed reflection into the syllabus in the form of questions. These questions are generally designed to help students integrate readings, class discussions, and new concepts with their observations and experiences in the community. These questions may require a written response or the syllabus may indicate that the questions are to be addressed in class discussion or discussion sections. Some faculty members also use reflective questions on the syllabus as the basis for semi-formal or formal presentations based on student service work. It is important that the weekly schedule includes these questions and allows students to see that the learning progression is designed to parallel the course goals.

EXAMPLE: JOURNAL ENTRIES FOR WEEK 2

Reading: Sara Mosle, "The Vanity of Volunteerism"

- According to the author, why is it that volunteerism doesn't work?

- In what ways is the author's experience as a volunteer similar or different from your own?

- If we accept the author's argument, what would have to change to make volunteerism "work"?

Reading: Nina Eliasoph, *Avoiding Politics*

Based upon you experience in community service, in your home community, in your education, reflect upon the reading by addressing the following questions. Bring your written journal response to class.

- What is the author's analysis?

- In what ways is it consistent or inconsistent with your experience?

- What relevance does it have for this course? (consider the full dimensions of the course)

SAMPLE SYLLABI (SORTED BY MODELS)

Model Syllabi: Pure Service-Learning (One of Three)

SYLLABUS SLR 105: SERVICE LEARNING I

DEPARTMENTAL GOALS OF SERVICE LEARNING AT WAYNESBURG COLLEGE
The goal of Service Learning is to provide a laboratory in which learning experiences address human and community needs and provides the necessary time for reflection on those experiences. Service opportunities are structured to promote student learning and development. Desired learning outcomes include: acquiring a sense of civic and social responsibility, gaining exposure to cultural and socioeconomic differences, applying classroom learning and learning new skills. No more than four credits of service learning will be applied toward the baccalaureate degree.

CATALOGUE COURSE DESCRIPTION
Students will complete at least thirty hours of pre-approved, unpaid service experience. The service must be performed in the same semester in which the student is registered for the course. Learning activities that fulfill requirements for other courses or complete degree requirements cannot be used to fulfill the requirements of this course. Students will reflect upon their experience, its current and future impact, and the implications for life-long learning through the writing of reflection papers, other brief writing assignments, and a final paper. Students are strongly encouraged to complete the first level course early in their academic programs. A student may repeat SLR 105 once for additional credit when the service is performed at a site different than the site where the first credit was performed.

COURSE REQUIREMENTS
Students must:

1. Attend the Service Fair and the Orientation Session to SLR 105-305.

2. Submit the Student/Service Site Agreement and Student Orientation Guidelines prior to the beginning of the service experience proper (forms attached). These documents are due to the mentor two weeks after the service fair. If they are not turned in by that date, the student will need to withdraw from the course immediately or will be at risk of failing the course.

3. Attend five small group mentoring sessions: one absence is permitted, and the absence will be compensated by the student's writing an additional seminar paper #3 (attached).

4. Document the completion of thirty hours of community service for a non-profit agency.

5. Write a minimum of four 250–300-word reflection papers. Reflections must include both (a) personal growth reflections that focus on individual development and (b) academic reflections

that connect classroom learning with the service performed. These reflections will be word-processed. These are worth 40% of the final grade.

6. Write four seminar papers to be submitted by the student on the days when they are discussed in small group (assignments attached). These are worth 20% of the final grade.

7. Compile a photo essay/pictorial representation/record with written reflections to accompany the pictures and compile other products of the experience (brochures, letters, advertisements, etc.) into a portfolio. All other written materials for the course may be included in the portfolio. This is worth 10% of the final grade.

8. Compose a 1,250 word take-home final exam paper that utilizes at least two print resources and addresses the issue of the public and/or private funding of social service agencies (assignment attached). This is worth 30% of the final grade.

9. Students will receive a traditional grade for the course.

Course calendar: to be negotiated between mentors and students.

Model Syllabi: Pure Service-Learning (Two of Three)

Syllabus SLR 205: Service Learning II

DEPARTMENTAL GOALS OF SERVICE LEARNING AT WAYNESBURG COLLEGE

The goal of Service Learning is to provide a laboratory in which learning experiences address human and community needs and provides the necessary time for reflection on those experiences. Service opportunities are structured to promote student learning and development. Desired learning outcomes include: acquiring a sense of civic and social responsibility, gaining exposure to cultural and socioeconomic differences, applying classroom learning and learning new skills. No more than four credits of service learning will be applied toward the baccalaureate degree.

CATALOGUE COURSE DESCRIPTION

Students will complete the requirements for SLR 105 in this course. In addition, they will perform an additional 30 hours of community service, for a total of sixty hours, and they will compose an additional research paper that investigates a problem encountered at the service site. This problem may relate to issues of providing service, agency structure and/or finding, individual psychological, sociological and/or public policy causes of the needs that the agency intends to meet, etc.

COURSE REQUIREMENTS

Students must:

1. Attend the Service Fair and the Orientation Session to SLR 105-305.

2. Submit the Student/Service Site Agreement and Student Orientation Guidelines prior to the beginning of the service experience proper (forms attached). These documents are due to the mentor two weeks after the service fair. If they are not turned in by that date, the student will need to withdraw from the course immediately or will be at risk of failing the course.

3. Attend five small group mentoring sessions: one absence is permitted, and the absence will be compensated by the student's writing an additional seminar paper #3 (attached).

4. Document the completion of sixty hours of community service for a non-profit agency.

5. Write a minimum of four reflection papers. Reflections must include both (a) personal growth reflections that focus on individual development and (b) academic reflections that connect classroom learning with the service performed. These are worth 40% of the final grade

6. Write four seminar papers to be submitted by the student on the days when they are discussed in small group (assignments attached). These are worth 20% of the final grade.

7. Compile a photo essay/pictorial representation/record with written reflections to accompany the pictures and compile other products of the experience (brochures, letters, advertisements, etc.) into a portfolio. All other written materials for the course may be included in the portfolio. This is worth 10% of the final grade.

8. In lieu of the SLR 105 paper, compose a research paper of at least 2,500 words that investigates a problem encountered at the service site. This problem may relate to issues of providing service, agency structure and/or funding, or the individual psychological, sociological and/or public policy causes of the needs that the agency intends to meet, etc. The format of this paper will be negotiated between the student and the mentor. This is worth 30% of the final grade.

9. Students will receive a traditional grade for the course.

Course calendar: to be negotiated between mentors and students.

Model Syllabi: Pure Service-Learning (three of three)

SYLLABUS SLR 305: SERVICE LEARNING III

DEPARTMENTAL GOALS OF SERVICE LEARNING AT WAYNESBURG COLLEGE

The goal of Service Learning is to provide a laboratory in which learning experiences address human and community needs and provides the necessary time for reflection on those experiences. Service opportunities are structured to promote student learning and development. Desired learning outcomes include: acquiring a sense of civic and social responsibility, gaining exposure to cultural and socioeconomic differences, applying classroom learning and learning new skills. No more than four credits of service learning will be applied toward the baccalaureate degree.

CATALOGUE COURSE DESCRIPTION

Students will complete the requirements for SLR 205 in this course. In addition, they will perform an additional 30 hours of community service, for a total of ninety hours, and they will compose an additional research paper that identifies possible short-term and long-term solutions to the problems identified in the SLR 205 research paper. Students will also make a public, oral presentation of the findings of the research.

COURSE REQUIREMENTS

Students must:

1. Attend the Service Fair and the Orientation Session to SLR 105-305.

2. Submit the Student/Service Site Agreement and Student Orientation Guidelines prior to the beginning of the service experience proper (forms attached). These documents are due to the mentor two weeks after the service fair. If they are not turned in by that date, the student will need to withdraw from the course immediately or will be at risk of failing the course.

3. Attend five small group-mentoring sessions: one absence is permitted, and the absence will be compensated by the student's writing an additional seminar paper #3 (attached).

4. Document the completion of ninety hours of community service for a non-profit agency.

5. Write a minimum of four reflection papers. Reflections must include both (a) personal growth reflections that focus on individual development and (b) academic reflections that connect classroom learning with the service performed. These are worth 40% of the final grade.

6. Write four seminar papers to be submitted by the student on the days when they are discussed in small group (assignments attached). These are worth 20% of the final grade.

7. Compile a photo portfolio of the service performed (assignment attached). This is worth 10% of the final grade.

8. In lieu of the SLR 105 paper, compose a research paper of at least 3,750 words that identifies possible short-term and long-term solutions to the problems identified in the SLR 205 research paper. The student and the mentor will negotiate the format of this paper. This is worth 30% of the final grade.

9. Give a public oral presentation of the findings of the research.

10. Students will receive a traditional grade for the course.

Course calendar: to be negotiated between mentors and students.

Service-Learning Defined

- Service-Learning (SL) involves students in real-life settings where they apply academic knowledge and previous experience to meet real community needs.

- SL builds on the effective use of experience as an integral part of education in order to empower learners. Students should view the service as a "lab" experience for the integration of learning from past and present classroom experiences.

- SL makes a critical link between student's service "practice" with classroom-based 'theory' by drawing clear connections between knowledge based in an academic discipline and the lessons and challenges presented by students' SL experiences

- SL develops key leadership competencies-communication, Critical thinking, values clarification, imagination, discern social and individual differences. Students come to understand the needs of others, appreciate the difficulty of social change, and better understand their own competencies. SL provides the context for students' personal transformation.

- SL links service to academic learning; it puts students in the context to perform service that makes a genuine contribution to the community.

- SL, community service and volunteerism are not synonymous. Community service and volunteerism become SL when there is a deliberate connection between service and learning opportunities, and when that integration is accompanied by thoughtfully designed occasions to reflect on the service experience.

- The college gives academic credit for SL on the basis of the learning that students demonstrate, not merely for the service performed, though that same service has intrinsic moral/Christian value consistent with the mission of the College.

THE INSTITUTIONAL AND COMMUNITY IMPACT OF SERVICE LEARNING

- SL helps the College to fulfill its civic mission by creating community-college partnerships that educate students in the essentials of an informed, engaged, democratic public.

- Through SL the College prepares an educated citizenry for service to society, but also makes a deliberate contribution to helping solve significant social problems. SL provides the occasion for the dedication of the College's resources to meet the pressing civic, social, and economic needs of the region.

- The campus moves beyond a "volunteer-provider" relationship with communities into collaborative, longer-term relationships that involve direct service and other forms of public participation (e.g. community and economic development, neighborhood organizing, or public policy development).

1) Preparation

This is the linking of SL to specific learning outcomes and preparing students to perform the activities.

Students are provided with a clear sense of what is to be accomplished and what is to be learned during each SL activity. They learn how to do the work, who will be served, the social contexts related to the service, information about the service site, and what problems that may arise. They understand how sites are selected, how coordination and supervision will be achieved, the agency's and the Colleges understanding of each other's expectations and responsibilities, and how students are placed, trained, supervised, evaluated, and provided with opportunities for reflection.

2) Service

The experience should be challenging, engaging, and meaningful to students. Service performed should address a real need so that students perceive the activity and their participation as relevant and important.

Such service falls into three general categories:

> *direct service:* one to one, individual, personal contact;

> *indirect service:* the channeling of resources to solve problems; the student does not provide direct contact, but becomes part of a larger community effort, a kind of service that is often "high energy" and creates enthusiasm for those who serve; and

> *civic action:* active participation in democratic citizenship; informing the public about problems to be addressed and working toward solving problems; the format for civic action can be either individual or group.

3) Reflection

This is the means by which students come to understand the meaning and impact of their efforts. They link what they have learned about themselves and the academic disciplines to what they have done in service to others. Reflection is the active, persistent, and careful consideration of the service activity. Students ask, "What am I doing and why? What am I learning?" Reflection leads to self-assessment; hence, students become more independent learners. Areas of possible academic reflection are: morality, theology, race, class, gender, ability/disability, economics, public policy, civic responsibility, psychology, and sociology. Possible personal reflections include: What am I feeling? Why did I react the way I did? How might I react differently next time? What am I discovering about myself that I didn't know before? Can I make a change at this site? Without reflection, students simply go through the motions of service remain cognitively unaffected by the experience, and left with their personal ignorance and biases reinforced or unexamined.

4) Celebration

This is the sharing across systems, organizations and among individuals involved in SL. Included is the ritualization of the learning, achievement acquisition and application of knowledge gained during the semester. This final step also involves the recognition and evaluation of the partnerships between the College and community agencies. Community change is named and celebrated at transitional moments.

EXAMPLES OF REFLECTION PAPERS

An academic reflection (two of your reflections must be academic)

I answered phones today, because the kids I usually work with couldn't make it to the agency. I talked to a woman who needed food for her baby, and I talked to an elderly woman who needed a handicap accessible ramp at her house. She had fallen and broke her hip and needed a way into her house. I also helped some women pick out paint for the exteriors of their homes.

As I was helping these people, I wondered why these phone calls were necessary. Why weren't their families helping? This phenomenon illustrates an issue we discussed in sociology. Before the emergence of industrial societies, family members took care of and depended on one another. If an older member of the family needed something, they could look to their children to provide. That kind of value placed on family is rare today. There are people leaving their parents in hospital ERs and nursing homes today so they don't have to take care of them. They don't leave them for a few hours and come back but they abandon them there. You also have many single parent families. If that single parent isn't dedicated, or doesn't have a helpful family, they'll have trouble giving their children the attention they deserve. The agency at which I am serving is trying to provide the solution for this decrease in family value. Perhaps they are taking the place of family for many of the clients of this agency.

It's very interesting to see the concepts that I've learned in the classroom actually exist in the real world. It is also very sad. I think that we need to make "FAMILY" a more important part of American society today. People who live in our industrial society must make changes to that family members will get the care and support that they need.

A personal reflection (two of your reflections must be personal)

Most of my work at the soup kitchen is pretty routine: preparing food (chopping vegetables, making cookies, etc), serving the food and bussing tables. After ten hours at my site, I can practically do these tasks without thinking about them.

But my personal exchanges with the clients are anything but routine. I have discovered that the people I serve are really quite amazing. By spending time with them, serving them food and bussing their tables, I have had a chance to hear some of their stories. My encounters with them have "blown away" my prejudices about the poor. I thought that all those "Hoopies" who sit on the wall in front of the Greene County Courthouse were lazy people, taking advantage of the welfare system. But I have discovered that they have "sad songs that they sing" to others who lend them an ear, "songs" about how they have been victims in life. Now I realize that these folks can be manipulative and that these "songs" they sing can be disabling. But by listening to their stories, I have discovered that I have more in common with the recipients of my service than I ever imagined! I am more like them than different from them! I have my "songs" too, I realize. But I also realize that my previous explanations for poverty, unemployment and welfare are simplistic and disconnected from the real experiences of people.

Having discovered that, I have a new attitude toward the poor in this area. I can listen to them and see them with more compassion. I now get angry with others who voice the prejudices I used to hold about the people who I now consider my friends ... even sisters and brothers. My service has changed me and I am incredibly grateful for this opportunity.

SEMINAR PAPER ASSIGNMENTS

Seminar Paper #1; What is service?

Take some time to think about an instance when you were the recipient of service—a time when someone offered you help. In a paragraph of 100–150 words, describe the situation that required the service of the other person, who assisted you, and how they provided service. Remember how you felt when you were in need and how your feelings changed once you were served.

Now, write a second paragraph of similar length, write of another experience in which you provided a service for another person.

Then, reflecting on both circumstances, give your definition of service.

Seminar Paper #2; You and your service site

In a paragraph of 200–250 words, describe your service site and write of some of your initial experiences. Describe your service activities in some detail. Is there a particular early experience that has made an emotional or cognitive impact on you? Describe that experience and reflect on your feelings or thoughts about it. Do you think that you are making a difference at the site and in the lives of the people you serve?

Seminar Paper #3; Current issues related to service

Locate an article in a journal, magazine or newspaper that reflects on an issue encountered at your service site. (This probably will not be an article about your agency per se, unless the piece investigates in a critical way a particular problem at your site.) In your seminar paper, describe the relationship between the content of the article and what you have learned first hand at your service site. Think and write critically about the article: Does the information in the article accurately depict the situation at your service site? Your seminar paper should be 250–300 words. (EBSCOHost is a great way to locate such articles. When you use this Internet site, you can use as key words your type of service site or you may think of a problem that you have encountered at your service site.)

Seminar Paper #4; Learning through service

Spend some time reflecting on your overall experience at your service site. Identify what you have learned about yourself (especially if you are "strange" to this kind of site or to the kinds of individuals you are serving), what you have learned about your agency, and what you have learned about the clients you have served. Identify any of the skills or knowledge you have gained in previous or current classroom experiences and applied at your service site. This seminar paper should be 250–300 words long. You should write a sentence or two to reflect on each of the kinds of learning you have gained this semester about yourself your agency, and your clients, as well as the skills and knowledge you have applied.

SLR 105 Final Paper Question

The assignment is intend to provide students with the opportunity to think and write critically about their service learning experience and how that experience intersects with some of the larger issues in American society. There currently exist two dominant schools of thought regarding meeting human need in American society. One view espouses that federal, state and local government should allocate and spend tax dollars to fund professional social agencies that would, in turn, meet the needs of their communities. The other position states that the burden for social agencies would be placed on individual citizens and agencies that choose to serve those in need by giving of personal time, money and skills.

With at least 1,250 words, and utilizing at least two print resources, discuss the pros and cons of each position.

- How does your service learning experience support and/or challenge each position? Cite specific examples from your experience.

- How would your agency you have served be affected by each position?

- Given that both positions "cost" something of individual citizens, which position do you support and why?

How does the position you now claim compare with your definition of service you stated at the beginning of the semester? Has your definition of service changed? Identify specific experiences that have contributed to the change in you.

Model Syllabi: Discipline-Based Service Learning

PSYCHOLOGY P425
Emotional & Behavioral Disorders of Childhood & Adolescence

Professor:	Dr. Randall E. Osborne
Office:	Indiana University East
	Middlefork Hall #352
	2325 Chester Blvd.
	Richmond, IN 47374

Class Time: TR 9:30 - 10:45 a.m., ML Rm. 322

Text: *Developmental Psychopathology (3rd Edition)* by Charles Wenar

Service Learning Coordinators: Jim Penticuff & Ken Weadick

The purpose of this course is to study the development, classification, intervention and treatment of classic childhood behavioral and emotional disorders. Although the title of this course is Behavioral Disorders Childhood and Adolescence, we will also spend considerable time discussing emotional disorders and their effects on the child and adolescent. We will discuss such issues as causal factors that lead to or promote such disorders, problems in classifying the disorders, methods of treatment, and the advantages and disadvantages of particular treatment strategies. As time in the course permits, we will discuss case histories, and use examples to illustrate key points whenever possible. The issues involved in understanding emotional and behavioral disorders are quite complicated and the issues get further muddied when children and adolescents are involved. Factors within society, families and even the school system foster and perpetuate these problems and these causal issues will be discussed in-depth early on in the course. Once causal factors are understood, then, and only then, can we begin to address issues related to diagnosing and treating the disorders.

CAMPUS LEARNING OBJECTIVES

Indiana University East has established eight learning objectives for our students. These achievement goals are:

- An educated person should be exposed to a broad variety of academic fields traditionally known as the Liberal Arts (Humanities, Social Sciences, Natural Sciences).

- An educated person should have achieved depth in some field of knowledge.

- An educated person should be able to express him or herself clearly, completely, and accurately.

- An educated person should be able to relate computational skills to all fields so that he or she is able to think with numbers.

- An educated person should be able to identify problems and to find efficient solutions to those problems in all areas of life.

- An educated person should develop the skills to understand, accept, and relate to people of different backgrounds and beliefs.

- An educated person should be expected to have some understanding of and experience in thinking about moral and ethical problems.

- An educated person should have conceptual ability: i.e. the ability to think rationally, to develop informed opinions, and to comprehend new ideas.

Of course no single class could accomplish all of these goals. This course is specifically designed to enhance your skills and abilities in achieving learning goals numbers 2, 3, 5, & 6.

SPECIFIC CONTENT LEARNING OBJECTIVES

There are many key points that you will be expected to know in this course. To help you to understand those points, I have summarized many of them into categories of learning objectives. These objectives will provide you with a summary of some of the major issues that will be discussed & that you will be expected to know as we progress through the course. We will use exams, quizzes, and other assignments to reinforce the following objectives in the course:

1. Understands the Difference Between "Emotional" & "Behavioral" Disorders

1.1 defines "abnormal"

1.2 explains the difference between "developmental" & "societal" norms

1.3 explains the importance and problems of using definitions

1.4 describes the criteria used to classify "emotional" disorders

1.5 describes the criteria used to classify "behavioral" disorders

1.6 explains the current National Mental Health and Special Education Coalition definition for "seriously emotionally disturbed"

1.7 describes the improvements of this definition over previous ones

2. Understands Basic Approaches to the Problems Discussed

2.1 explains the Biogenic model

2.2 explains the Psychodynamic model

2.3 explains the Psychoeducational model

2.4 explains the Humanistic model

2.5 explains the Ecological model

2.6 explains the Behavioral model

2.7 describes the strengths & weaknesses of each approach

3. Understands the Issues Involved in Screening & Classification

3.1 explains the issues that complicate screening

3.2 describes the reasons that screening is so important

3.3 explains the criteria used in selecting a screening procedure

3.4 briefly describes the major screening methods

3.5 describes the behavior rating profile

3.6 describes the test of early socioemotional development

3.7 describes the social-emotional dimension scale

3.8 describes the child behavior checklist

3.9 describes the systematic screening for behavior disorders

3.10 describes the school archival records search

4. Understands the Causal Factors that Create & Perpetuate The Disorders

4.1 describes the biological factors

4.2 describes the family factors

4.3 describes the school factors

4.4 describes the cultural factors

4.5 explains the possible interactions between these causal factors

5. Understands Each of the Disorders Discussed

5.1 explains Infantile Autism

5.2 explains Childhood Schizophrenia

5.3 explains Depression

5.4 explains Attention & Activity Disorders

5.5 explains Conduct Disorder

5.6 explains Delinquency & Substance Abuse

5.7 explains Anxiety-Withdrawal Disorders

5.8 explains Psychotic Disorders

5.9 understands the connections among these disorders

6. Understands Possible Interventions & Treatments for Each Disorder

6.1 describes interventions and treatments for Autism

6.2 describes interventions and treatments for Schizophrenia

6.3 describes interventions and treatments for Depression

6.4 describes interventions and treatments for Attention/Activity Disorders

6.5 describes interventions and treatments for Conduct Disorder

6.6 describes interventions and treatments for Delinquency & Substance Abuse

6.7 describes interventions and treatments for Anxiety-Withdrawal Disorders

6.8 describes interventions and treatments for Psychotic Disorders

6.9 explains unresolved issues for each disorder

7. Applies Course Principles to Service-Learning Projects

7.1 describes relationship between course material and service-learning agencies

7.2 describes specific "problem" being addressed with service-learning project

7.3 explains course content that relates to possible solutions to service-learning "problem"

7.4 describes proposed solution to agency for possible implementation

SERVICE-LEARNING PROJECT

Since a significant part of this course is devoted to understanding individuals suffering from emotional and behavioral disorders, it is especially important that we avoid the temptation to assume that the disorder defines the person. In order to truly understand the impact and significance of these disorders for the lives of those affected, students will work in groups and work in agencies that work with children and adolescents. Specifically, student work groups can choose between a variety of projects at The Mental Health Association in Wayne County or Townsend Community Center in Richmond. Both of these agencies work closely with child and adolescent populations and have worked with us to create projects that will allow student work groups to gather information, volunteer in the agency and work to solve a real problem facing the agency and the population being served.

Each student must volunteer in the assigned agency for 10 hours during the course of the semester. These hours can be completed alone or groups may choose to work their hours together as they work to help the agency complete a task, solve a problem, etc. that is specifically related to emotional and/or behavioral problems of children and adolescents. Students will also be expected to do library research gathering information about the population they are working with and the specific problem they are addressing for the agency. This information, along with any proposals they may arrive at after completing the volunteer hours at the agency, will be compiled in a group project course paper. A copy of this paper will be turned in for grading, one copy will be turned in for course files and another copy will be provided for the agency in which the placement took place. Groups will also do brief presentations of their experience to the rest of the class.

These papers need to be a minimum of 10 pages (with at least 15 references) and need to be written in APA style. Please see me if you need help with APA style writing.

Presentations must be a minimum of 20 minutes long and include at least 2 handouts for the other students in the class.

Students will work in 5 person (maximum) work groups. Although student work groups can choose which of the 2 agencies they would like to work for, a maximum of 3 groups can work for either agency. Agency assignments (and project assignments within agencies) will be on a first come, first serve basis.

Ken Weadick will serve as the Service-Learning Coordinator for the Mental Health Association in Wayne County. Ken will work with groups who choose this agency to decide on a project, make initial contact with the agency, plan the service-learning project (i.e., what the group will attempt to do for the agency), help to solve any problems that might arise, coordinate and provide materials for completion of the project (i.e., office type supplies), advise groups during the writing of the project paper, and attend an exit meeting with the group, myself, and the agency sponsor to complete the project (or update the agency on project progress).

Jim Penticuff will serve as the Service-Learning Coordinator for the Townsend Community Center in Richmond. Jim will work with groups who choose this agency to decide on a project, make initial contact with the agency, plan the service-learning project (i.e., what the group will attempt to do for the agency), help to solve any problems that might arise, coordinate and provide materials for completion of the project (i.e., office type supplies), advise groups during the writing of the project paper, and attend an exit meeting with the group, myself, and the agency sponsor to complete the project (or update the agency on project progress).

The Mental Health Association in Wayne County is a not-for-profit agency whose mission is defined as "working for America's Mental Health and Victory over Mental Illness." The Association sponsors many support groups including depression, attention-deficit disorder, incest survivors, Tourette's Syndrome, anxiety and depression screenings, and others. Prior placements for students have included helping to conduct the "I'm Thumbody" self-esteem program conducted in 3rd grade classes in the county, and various other advocacy programs. The MHA is located at 830 Sim Hodgin Parkway (across from Reid Hospital).

The Townsend Community Center provides individuals in the community with programs and services geared specifically toward at-risk children and adolescents. Students may work to establish new programs for youth, may be asked to conduct a community needs assessment, work to create and conduct a community self-esteem presentation, etc. The Center is located at 855 North 12th Street in Richmond.

POTENTIAL PROJECTS

Projects at the Mental Health Association include:

1) "I'm Somebody" Self-Esteem Program

2) BABES—Children and Adolescent Alcohol Awareness Program

3) Create & conduct a Junior Mental Health Needs Assessment

What junior mental health needs exist in the community? What programs are currently in place to address those needs? Which needs are not being fulfilled? Suggestions for new programs and/or changing existing programs to fulfill those needs.

Projects at the Townsend Community Center include:

1) Changing the Child's Perception of Authority Figures person?" role-playing in authority positions - "what's it like to be this

2) Evaluating the effect of "fee for services" programs. Is it effecting utilization? Is there a psychological impact? Does it hinder involvement? How does this influence staff perceptions of the program? What are the problems if exceptions to fees are allowed?

3) Structured programs for high school age youth. What would it take to get this age group involved? What programs are they interested in? Why have past efforts to get this age group involved failed?

REFLECTING LEARNING FROM THE SERVICE PROJECTS

I am a firm believer that students gain a significant amount of understanding by reflecting on course content in a variety of ways. This is also particularly important given the applied nature of the service learning projects. For this reason, you will be given multiple opportunities to reflect on what you are learning from the service learning project and how it integrates with what you are learning from the content discussions in this course.

Some of these points are "individual" points, meaning each student does the reflection and each student earns his/her own points for that reflection.

Other reflection points will be "group" points meaning the reflection is completed as a group and each group member receives the number of points that reflection earns.

Please note that there are no specific right or wrong answers in these reflections. You are being asked to engage in critical thinking about the service projects and how the major concepts from this course (the ones you feel are relevant to your project) relate to the project you are conducting and the product you are developing for the agency.

Specific reflection assignments and point values are as follows:

Individual Reflection Assignments

1) *Exit Cards*—At the end of each class period (once projects have started), you will be asked to take a few moments and reflect on the content currently being covered in the course. In particular, you will be asked to answer the following question, "How does Information from today's class period relate to your service project/experience?"

3 points each x 21 class periods = 51 points maximum.

NOTE: An exit card can ONLY be turned in for class periods in which you are physically present.

2) *Thought Papers*—throughout the semester you will be asked to complete four one-page "Thought Papers." I call these thought papers because I want you to discuss with me some aspect of the course and/or the service project that has stimulated your thinking. Be sure and include answers to the following questions:

—How has this situation/information challenged or changed your way of thinking?

—What might you do differently now that you have confronted or encountered this issue?

3) *Essay Question(s) on Exams*—At least one essay question will appear on each of the three exams. These questions will ask you to consider a dominant issue from the current section of material and discuss that issue as it relates to the service project you are doing. These will be worth a varying amount of points on each exam but at least 15 out of the 100 points.

Group Reflections

1) *3-minute Updates*—Once each month, groups will take about 3 minutes of class time and give a very brief update or progress, obstacles, goals, etc. You will need to choose a spokesperson for each of these and a given student can only give one of these updates. Each group member present during the update class periods will earn 5 assignment points for the update given by their group member.

2) *Final Updates*—Groups will schedule and present a final project update during final exams week (note we do not have a regular final exam). Each group member must be involved in this presentation and a copy of the final project product must be turned in to the instructor at the completion of this presentation. Except in extreme circumstances, only those group members present during the presentation can earn Final Update points. Final Updates are worth up to 50 points and should include expanded coverage of the same items requested in 3 minute updates plus strong integration of course content.

3) *Project Products*—These are the culminating event for the course. These products should illustrate what you did for the agency, your resolution to the agency's problem or stated need, an analysis of major course content as it applies to the work you did, applicable references (minimum of 15), and individual reflections from each group member about the experience and specific ways the project effected their learning. These products will be graded as a group and are worth up to 100 points.

NOTE: All group members will be asked to turn in evaluation forms for all group members in a sealed envelope. I will use these evaluations to determine relative contributions from each group member and may adjust certain student grades accordingly, if necessary, after having consulted with those students.

NON SERVICE-LEARNING PAPER OPTION

Students who do not wish to participate in the service-learning project are not required to do so. Those students who decide not to do this project, however, must complete the following option. This requirement involves choosing one of the disorders covered in the course, doing a search of the relevant literature (psychology journals, medical journals, education journals, etc.) and summarizing what is known about:

1) Potential causes of the disorder

2) Significant symptoms

3) Treatment strategies

In addition, students are expected to interview at least 2 persons who work with individuals with this disorder (e.g., a school counselor, a physician a therapist, someone at the Mental Health Association, etc.) to get practical information about this disorder. Excerpts from these interviews MUST be included in the paper. These papers need to be a minimum of 10 pages (with at least 20 references) and need to be written in APA style. Please see me if you need help with APA style writing.

Students choosing this option will still do an in-class presentation. This presentation, however, will focus on their findings related to their chosen disorder rather than on an agency project. Presentations must be a minimum of 20 minutes long and include at least 2 handouts for the other students in the class.

POINTS FOR THE COURSE

2 Hourly Exams X 100 points each . . . . 200 points

Highest Quiz Score X 30 points. . . . . 30 points

In-class, Take-home Assignments, Exit Cards . . . . 100 points

Agency Project/Paper. . . . . 100 points

In-Class Presentation . . . . 50 points

Final Exam . . . . 100 points

Total. . . . . 580 points

AGENCY PROJECT/PAPER

This paper (8–10 pages) is meant to allow you to explore in-depth some aspect of an agency that works with children and adolescents. You will be randomly assigned to a group then your group will be asked to choose one of the two agencies sponsoring the service-learning component of this class (Townsend Community Center & The Mental Health Association in Wayne County). After deciding which agency the group would like to work in, groups will choose from a short list of potential projects designated by the agency as addressing problems relevant to the populations being studied in this course. This paper will be due prior to the end of the semester so I encourage you to start your service-learning project early in the course. Students can meet with the service-learning coordinators or myself at any time to discuss the project, the "problem" they are addressing for the agency, etc.

Although some in-class time will be used for preparing groups to conduct the service-learning project, the majority of the work will be done while students are volunteering in the agency. The Service-Learning Coordinators will be available to help work groups make contact with the agency, establish a project goal, problem solve if problems arise, and coordinate volunteer hours. *It is extremely important that you think about the course learning objectives as you write your project paper. You must consider how the experiences you are having as you conduct the project relate to the learning goals spelled out for this course.*

For example, you might consider how your service experiences have influenced your perceptions of what is "normal" or "abnormal."

EXIT CARDS

You need to purchase a package of note cards for this course. At the end of each class period I will ask you to fill out an exit card as described earlier. On this card you are also encouraged to comment about the class, the material being covered, ask questions, ask for clarification, make connections to other material in the course, ask for advice, let me know what you think is working particularly well in the course, or let me know what things you think are not working well. This is an attempt on my part to make you—the student an active partner in the class. It also provides you with a non-threatening way to ask questions and comment on the class.

Another important function of the exit cards is to provide opportunities for you to reflect on how the content from any given class period relates to the experiences you are having in your service projects.

These allow me to keep a finger on the pulse of the class and respond to your needs. I will read these exit cards after each class period, write a personal response to each one, and give you three points toward your assignment point total needed of 100 points. You can earn up to 51 of the 100 points this way That would be turning in 17 of the exit cards out of a possible 22 lecture periods (not counting exam and presentation days).

STUDENT ASSESSMENT GROUP

As a part of my ongoing efforts to make this class as good as it can be, I would like to ask five or six (or even more of you if you're willing) to form a student assessment group that will meet with me about every 2nd or 3rd week to discuss the course, how things are going, any perceived problems, any compliments, etc. This group will meet for about 20 minutes either before or after class (whichever fits students schedules the best). I will take notes from these meetings and use them to make necessary changes to the course to maximize the learning that takes place. I will also ask you to submit a short written summary at mid-term and the end of the semester summarizing your feelings about the group, the course, my teaching style, the lectures, the assignment, etc. These will be used by me to make the course even better the next time that I offer it. This group will be invaluable to me and the other students because only feedback from students can let me know what I am doing right or what I could improve to enhance the quality of my instruction and the success of the learning environment in this class.

LECTURES AND ASSIGNMENTS

Week 1: Introduction to Course & The Problem of Emotional & Behavioral Disorders. First Discussion of Service-Learning Projects.

Read Chapters 1 & 2 in text.

Week 2: Approaches to the Problem. Screening & Classification. Follow-up Discussion of Service-Learning.

Projects and initial group work activity. Read Chapter 3 in text.

Week 3: Causal Factors. Read Chapter 14 in text. Initial Orientation at Agencies. Ken & Jim will coordinate a trip to each agency.

Thought Paper 1 Due.

Week 4: Causal Factors (conclusion). Exam 1 Review distributed.

Week 5: Exam 1. Service-Learning Projects Begin.

Week 6: Autism. Schizophrenia. Read Chapters 4 & 10 in text.

Week 7: Depression. 3-minute Project Updates. Read Chapter 7 in text.

Thought Paper 2 Due.

Week 8: Attention & Activity Disorders. Read Chapter 6 in text.

Week 9: Conduct Disorder. 3-minute Project Updates. Read Chapter 9 in text.

Week 10: Spring Break (Have Fun & Be Careful!).

Week 11: 10-minute Service-Learning Project.

Exam 2 Review distributed. Exam 2.

Week 12: Delinquency & Substance Abuse. Read Chapter 11 in text pages (310–326).

Thought Paper 3 Due.

Week 13: Anxiety-withdrawal disorders. Read Chapter 8 in text.

Week 14:   Psychotic Behavior.
           Thought Paper 4 Due.
Week 15:   Exam 3 Review distributed. Exam 3.
Week 16:   Formal In-class presentations of Service-Learning Projects. Project Papers Due.

Model Syllabi: Problem-Based Service-Learning

COLLOQUIUM ON COMMUNITY DEVELOPMENT: POLITICS 348
Prof. Preston Smith
Mt. Holyoke College
Fall 1999

The purpose of this course is to engage students in the various ideas, debates and strategies regarding the development of inner city communities. You will hear speakers and discuss readings that will introduce you to the field of community development. You will examine the assumptions about community, agency, efficiency, equity and political efficacy that underlie discussions of community development. You will grapple with debates that animate the study and practice of community development. You will also engage in hands-on research that will assist the objectives of a local community-based, nonprofit organization.

Is there an effective "third sector" that is more fair and humane than the market, but more efficient than the state? What assumptions about public action are embedded in the notion of "community development?" Is the agency of poor, disenfranchised residents nurtured in grassroots efforts to revitalize inner city neighborhoods? Just how democratic is the organization and practice of locally controlled community development? Should inner city neighborhoods be abandoned and their residents disperse to more affluent neighborhoods in the metropolitan area? Should we invest in people rather than places? Lastly, can locally based action adequately respond, resist and transform communities that have been ravaged in the global marketplace?

This course will feature people who study, practice and regulate community development. There will be a particular focus on poor neighborhoods in Holyoke and Springfield.

COURSE REQUIREMENTS

Class participation and attendance; Required readings; One Reflection paper; Research project. (Detailed instructions will be handed out in class).

I will take into account how well you have expressed your ideas in written form. It is difficult for me to credit good ideas and arguments if they are written poorly. Please proofread your work or it will affect your grade.

You are expected to do your own work and properly credit the work of others. I expect that you will adhere to the college's Academic Honor Code specified in *Mount Holyoke College Student*

Handbook. Use the *Guide to the Uses and Acknowledgment of Sources* for assistance on the way to properly credit the work of others. If you have any questions please don't hesitate to ask me.

The following texts can be purchased at the Odyssey Bookshop:

John Charles Boger and Judith Welch Wegner, eds., *Race, Poverty, and American Cities.* Chapel Hill, NC: University of North Carolina Press, 1996.

Thomas D. Boston and Catherine L. Ross, eds. *The Inner City: Urban Poverty and Economic Development in the Next Century.* New Brunswick, NJ: Transaction Publishers, 1997.

Rhoda H. Halperin, Practicing Community: *Class Culture and Power in an Urban Neighborhood.* Austin, TX: University of Texas Press, 1998.

Robert Halpern, *Rebuilding the Inner City: A History of Neighborhood Initiatives to Address Poverty in the United States.* New York: Columbia University Press, 1995.

W. Dennis Keating, Norman Krumholz, and Philip Starr, eds. *Revitalizing Urban Neighborhoods.* Lawrence, KS: University Press of Kansas, 1996.

*This designates readings that are in a Xeroxed course packet that you may purchase from the Politics Department office at 222A Clapp. Most of these readings, and assigned films are on reserve at the library.

CLASS SCHEDULE

9/14   Introduction

9/21   Community Development: Ideology, Politics and Policies

            Discussion

            R. Allen Hays, "Power, Ideology, and Public Policy," and "The Ideological Context of Housing Policy," pp. 1–56 in *The Federal Government & Urban Housing: Ideology and Change in Public Policy.* Second Edition. Albany, NY: State University of New York Press, 1995.

            *Nicholas Lemann, "The Myth of Community Development," *New York Times Magazine,* January 9, 1994, Section 6.

            *Michael Katz, "Intellectual Foundations of the War on Poverty," chapter 3 in *The Undeserving Poor: From the War on Poverty to the War on Welfare.* New York: Pantheon, 1989.

            *Harvey A. Goldstein, "The Limits of Community Economic Development," pp. 40–53 in Pierre Clavel, John Forrester, and William W. Goldsmith, *Urban and Regional Planning in an Age of Austerity.* New York: Pergamon Press, 1980.

9/28   Community Development in Holyoke & Springfield

            Meet with Community Liaisons

10/5   National Urban Policy, the Urban Crisis, & Community Development

	Discussion
	John Charles Boger and Judith Welch Wegner, eds., *Race, Poverty, and American Cities,* Parts I & 2, pp. 3–269.
10/12	Semester Break
10/19	Neighborhood-Based Services and Community Development *Speaker: Yamira Moreno, Director of After-School programs for Girls Inc., Holyoke.*
	Robert Halpern, *Rebuilding the Inner City: A History of Neighborhood Initiatives to Address Poverty in the United States.* New York: Columbia University Press, 1995.
10/26	Inner-City Neighborhood Revitalization
	Discussion
	W. Dennis Keating, Norman Krumholz, and Philip Starr, eds. *Revitalizing Urban Neighborhoods.* Lawrence, KS: University Press of Kansas, 1996.
11/2	Housing and Community Development
	Speaker: Nellie Bailey, President of the Board of Harlem Tenants Council, New York.
	Boger & Wegner, eds. *Race, Poverty and American Cities,* Part Three, "Residential Mobility: Effects on Education, Employment, and Racial Integration," pp. 273–431.
	*Jason DeParle, "The Year That Housing Died," *New York Times Magazine.* October 20, 1996. Section 6.
	*Larry Bennett and Adolph Reed, Jr., "The New Face of Urban Renewal: The Near North Redevelopment Initiative and the Cabrini-Green Neighborhood," in Adolph Reed Jr., *Without Justice for All: The New Liberalism and Our Retreat from Racial Equality.* Boulder, CO: Westview Press, 1999: 175–211.
11/9	Community Development: Case Study
	Discussion
	Rhoda H. Halperin, *Practicing Community: Class Culture and Power in an Urban Neighborhood.* Austin, TX: University of Texas Press, 1998.
11/16	Community Organizing and Community Development
	Discussion
	Karen Paget, "Citizen Organizing: Many Movements, No Majority," *The American Prospect,* No. 2. Summer 1990:115–128.
	*Steven Rathgeb Smith and Michael Lipsky, "The New Politics of the Contracting Regime," pp. 171–187 in Nonprofits for Hire: The Welfare State in the Age of Contracting. Cambridge, MA: Harvard University Press, 1993.
11/23	Inner-City Economic Development
	Discussion
	*Michael Porter, "The Competitive Advantage of the Inner City," *Harvard Business Review* (May-June 1995): 55–71.

Thomas D. Boston and Catherine L. Ross, eds. *The Inner City: Urban Poverty and Economic Development in the Next Century.* New Brunswick, NJ: Transaction Publishers, 1997: Part 1.

Reflection papers due in class.

11/30   State Politics and Local Economic Development *Speaker: Carol Harper l'84, Program Manager, Massachusetts Community Development Action Grants, Division of Community Services, Executive Office of Communities & Development, Massachusetts Department of Housing & Community Development, Boston.*

Thomas D. Boston and Catherine L. Ross, eds. The Inner City: Urban Poverty and Economic Development in the Next Century. New Brunswick, NJ: Transaction Publishers, 1997: Part II.

12/7   Presentation practice

12/14   Presentations

Research projects due December 17.

COMMUNITY DEVELOPMENT PROJECTS

Mobility study

Sponsors: Hampden Hampshire Housing Partnership, Inc. (HAP) *Liaison:* Wendy Tydenkevez, Director of the Regional Counseling Program for Section-8 recipients.

The purpose of this project is to evaluate the housing satisfaction of local low-income residents of Springfield metropolitan area. Last year Mount Holyoke students created a database of 100 households (5% of the program participants) who have received section-8 certificates from the Hampden-Hampshire Housing Partnership (HAP, Inc.). These students evaluated how often the recipients moved, and the housing-type and neighborhood conditions of their residences. In addition, they secured census data on the economic, housing, and racial characteristics of the census tract and/or block where the residence is located. Last year students worked on constructing the database. 100 recipients had been coded and entered into the database (Microsoft Access).

Site Visits

Last fall a subgroup of students conducted 25 site visits involving 9 households in order to get a fuller description of the housing characteristics and neighborhood conditions. We would like to expand on the number of households whose residences we want to analyze. This group of students created a windshield survey tool that you can modify (if necessary) and use for your site visits.

Interviews

This semester we would also like to begin some in-depth interviews of the residents of the sites you will visit. The previous levels of analysis—census data and site visits—can provide some information, but in order to understand the decision-making of different households we need to see why people move from a particular residence. If we are finding that people are not moving to the suburb, we need to try to understand why? Is it discrimination or cultural unfamiliarity? Does it have to do with isolation and the lack of transportation? Your group will evaluate trends in order to formulate findings about the patterns of movement, characteristics of the housing and neighborhoods chosen, and decision-making process by section-8 recipients.

Credit Union Feasibility Study

- *Sponsors:* Nueva Esperanza

- *Liaisons:* Carlos Vega, Executive Director

- *Contact:* Nueva Esperanza

The purpose of this project is to determine whether a community-based credit union is feasible for the inner-city wards of Holyoke. Last year Mount Holyoke students conducted a survey of the people, who live, work or get services in South Holyoke and the Flats, two low-income, predominantly Puerto Rican neighborhoods. The survey results suggest that the participants use formal banking. The students then concentrated using last year's research on the inconvenient location of formal banks, and the unavailability of automated teller machines (ATM). Last year students researched the history and current status of banking services in South Holyoke and the Flats. Students presented: a history of how banking mergers have affected banking services in the area; a socioeconomic profile of the target population using census material; a map with the location of both formal and informal banking facilities; and a study of the what kind of credit union would fit the needs of the community. This study commented on the accessibility, both physical and cultural, of formal banking services in the neighborhoods.

This semester you determine what it will take to create a community development credit union in South Holyoke. You will study the regulations for creating a credit union to see what steps need to be taken. You will study examples of credits union in similar locations to understand their successes and failure. This may include hearing from people who have built successful credit unions.

Once you have the model of what will work in Holyoke you are to write a planning grant so that the plan can be implemented. You will need to identify funding sources. The first task of implementation is to create educational workshops co-led by Holyoke residents and Mount Holyoke students on the benefits of a community-based credit union in South Holyoke.

Community Gardening Output Study

- *Sponsor:* Nuestro Raices, Holyoke

- *Liaison:* Daniel Ross, Executive Director

The objective of this research project is to measure the agricultural production of community gardeners in Holyoke. After you have collected information on agricultural production, you are to write a report on the benefits of community garden for Holyoke that will go to the Mayor of Holyoke, City Council, and Department of Community Development and Planning.

Last semester students interviewed 10 gardeners and measured their output. They researched how much of the food is used for consumption by the household and how much is sold or given away. They determined that each household saved approximately $540 a season. In addition to the interview tool, a subgroup of students created a price survey of supermarkets and bodegas that service the inner-city neighborhoods in order to assign prices to the goods produced. They were also able to compare the quality and price of food among these options and with stores in the white and more affluent wards. In addition the report also includes the cultural and social benefits derived by Puerto Ricans in community gardens.

This semester you will continue to use (perhaps modify) this tool in order to interview more gardeners. There are 84 gardeners in total and we would like to interview as many as possible. The survey tool may need to be revised to be used this upcoming season to record gardeners' output on a daily or weekly basis.

Mortgage Lending Discrimination Project

- Sponsor: Housing Discrimination Project (BDP)

- Liaison: Marian Kent, Acting Executive Director and Tamari Cox,

See separate confidential sheet

Note: Participation on this project will take the utmost confidential discretion because of the sensitivity of the data and consequences of the research.

Model Syllabi: Capstone Courses

WOMEN'S COMMUNITY EDUCATION PROJECT
Portland State University
In Other Words
Summer 2000
Melissa Kesler Gilbert

DESCRIPTION

In this course, we will be working with our community partner, the local nonprofit feminist bookstore IN OTHER WORDS and their sister organization, The Women's Community Education Project. Our project this term is to coordinate a series of *rap sessions* with local teen girls about current issues in their lives. We will use these group conversations to encourage the girls to become a part of our ZINE project—where they will write, edit, and publish a grassroots, mini-magazine with our class. Please take a look at the enclosed outreach plan for more detailed objectives. In preparation for this project, we will read feminist scholarship on women's organizations, feminist bookstores, and teenage girls as well as focus group and zine publishing methodologies.

COURSE STRUCTURE AND OBJECTIVES

This CAPSTONE course is designed as an advocacy project-in-progress: We are building a bridge between women's studies scholarship in the academy and praxis in our community. team, we will design our project with the following objectives in mind: As an interdisciplinary research team, we will design our project with the following objectives in mind:

1) A TEAM APPROACH: To work together as a collaborative research team—learning to value, respect, and incorporate our different standpoints.

2) FROM THEORY TO PRAXIS: To apply women's studies scholarship (and the expertise you bring from your own discipline) to contemporary women's issues in our community.

3) A BRIDGE TO THE COMMUNITY: To encourage you to become an active member of your community by introducing you to a network of women involved in grassroots organizing, feminist community building, and women's educational resources.

4) A CRITICAL PIECE OF THE PIE: To enhance your ability to think experientially, analytically, and critically about girl's/women's everyday lives as they are experienced in your community.

5) FINDING A VOICE: To assist you in reflecting and interpreting the complexities of girls'/women's experiences, resulting in a variety of opportunities for oral, written, and graphic communication.

TEXTS

Francesca Lia Block & Hillary Carlip. *ZineScene: The Do It Yourself Guide to Zines.* GirlPress. 1998.

Hillary Carlip. *GirlPower:Young Women Speak Out.* New York: WarnerBooks. 1995.

Brown. *Raising Their Voices.*

Pipher. *Reviving Ophelia.*

GirlPOWER! Capstone Workbook. Available at Clean Copy.

Selected research articles and agency literature to be distributed in class and/or on reserve in the women's studies office (CH401). Please note that the office is open from 9–3:00 M–F

REQUIREMENTS

SCHOLARLY & PERSONAL REFLECTIONS: 100 POINTS

A *third* of your grade will be based on your reflective VOICE in this course—evidenced in a written response journal due each week. The following are required:

1) Portfolio Assignment (not-graded, but required: 20 points see handout)

2) Research Reflection journal (see handout) (EMAIL is required)

10 points per journal x 8 weeks = 80 points total

COMMUNITY WORK: 100 POINTS

A third of your grade in this course will be based on your *informed community* work as part of our research team. This work will take place both in and outside of the classroom and is dependent on the design of our project. This portion of your grade includes both primary and secondary tasks.

1) Primary Task: Rap Sessions & Publishing a Teen Zine (75 Points)

Your primary task for this course is to make contacts with teen advocates in the Portland area and to conduct several rap sessions with teen girls, encourage them to participate in our project, solicit submissions, and design our zine. Your "focus group" work may include the following:

> Background Reading
> Focus Group Guide Design
> Taped Focus Groups (rap sessions)
> Legal Release Forms
> Transcript (NOTE: 1 hour interview = about 10 hours transcribing. Plan ahead!)
> Editing Transcripts
> Editing Zine Submissions
> Running Zine Workshops
> Writing Zine Article(s)
> Research on books, movies, scholarship, internet sites related to Zine topics
> Presentation to *In Other Words*

Final Products: At the end of the term you will be responsible for depositing the following materials in the Women's Studies Program Oral Narratives Archives: tapes, transcript (on paper and disk), legal release forms & final papers. These materials will be a valuable source for future capstone courses.

2) Secondary Task: Of Your Own Design (25 Points)

You will negotiate a secondary task applicable to our project that you will be responsible for completing on your own with your mentor's & community partner's assistance. This task is your opportunity to use skills specific your major and should reflect your personal interest in an issue related to teen girls or the bookstore. It may or may not be directly related to the ZINE.

You will submit a proposal to your mentor and instructor on the second week of our class. We encourage these projects to be completed in small groups, but individual projects are also a possibility.

TEAM WORK—SOCIALLY RESPONSIBLE LEARNING: 100 POINTS

A third of your grade is based on evidence of your acting responsibly to each other and our community partner.

We are working as a group: We will move through this course together setting goals, designing projects, brainstorming, delegating tasks, negotiating expectations and setting deadlines. It is important that each of you is present and takes part in the decision-making process. The syllabus is here as a guide, but each of you has a voice in this agenda and may advocate changes as the course evolves. We are interdependent on one another to make our project work. Your BEING here is critical!

We are working with each other: Each of you will work closely with each other, your mentor, community partners, and the instructor. Each of us is responsible to the other members of our research team in meeting the expectations of the group. As members of both a research community AND a social community we need to appreciate the life choices of all of those involved in this project (from the person sitting next to you to the teen girls you will work with). I hope that this work will help us to practice our own capacities to engage in collective, ethical, interactive, and organizational challenges that mirror those in our local women's community.

Points: You will earn 6.25 points for each working class session in which you:

a) are in attendance in the classroom (or participate by a service/research task in the community during class time);

b) show evidence of careful preparation for our working session (including notes on readings, drafts, notes from research, etc.—you may be asked to turn these in);

c) contribute to class discussions, planning sessions, and small group work; and

d) confirm that you have carried out assignments on time and volunteer for additional research tasks when appropriate.

Please Note: The 16 sessions include all T/TH sessions (including holidays) and the final presentation.

Miss a Working Session?

If you miss a working class session, a community meeting, or other capstone-associated event it is up to YOU (not your instructor OR your mentor) to get notes from class, check on deadlines, retrieve materials passed out it class, and get up to speed with the project. If you know in advance that you will be missing class (an emergency, another priority, etc.) you should contact your MENTOR as soon as possible before the class and/or drop off material related to that working session. If you miss a class unexpectedly you should contact your mentor as soon as possible after the class session to explain your absence and arrange to pick up materials from the session. We understand that life is full of surprises and understand that everyday life may make demands on you that conflict with our work. If you keep us informed of unexpected events and make arrangements to complete your work, meet deadlines, and/or participate in some other agreed upon way, we will work with you.

GRADING

Your final grade for this course will be based on:

1) the completeness of the above requirements, as well as

2) the quality of your analytical thinking, reflection, writing, and oral presentation.

Your mentor and I will assign grades to your journals after consultation with the instructor. Mentors will also keep records of your class participation. Your mentor and instructor will assess final grades for your community work as the project evolves. In addition, you will be asked to assess your own work from time to time in this course. Please feel free to ask about the status of your work as the course progresses. You are encouraged to discuss feedback with us as often as possible.

Please note: You will not receive a grade for this course until you have returned all loaned equipment and turned in the final products listed above.

CAPSTONE PROJECT PLAN

Readings: With the exception of your texts, readings will be assigned as we move through the project (in order to make choices most relevant to the flexibility and design of specific content, issues, and methodologies). These readings will be on reserve in the Women's Studies Office (CH 401) where you may borrow them to photocopy or loan for a two hour period between 9 and 3.

Week One: Introductions

> T June 20: Introduction to Capstones, Mentor, and Your Collective
>
> What is a capstone? Issues of Confidentiality and Anonymity.
>
> Video clips from past GIRLpower! classes
>
> RESEARCH TASK: sign confidentiality agreements, fill out forms, and get to know each other, review assignments
>
> TH June 22 Starting Our Own Collective
>
> Reading: Articles on Reserve (Feminist Bookstore Movement Articles); Capstone Handbook
>
> RESEARCH TASK: A Group Process Exercise: How can we work together as a group? What kinds of ground rules should we establish as guidelines for our collaboration? Sharing Portfolios.
>
> √ Portfolio Due
>
> √ Short list of possible girl contacts from your own community
>
> Personal Research Tasks to Complete:

Week Two: Community Building

T June 27 Meeting Our Community Partner & Local Girl Advocates

GUEST: Catherine Sameh from In Other Words; The Girl's Initiative Network (GIN), et. al.

Reading: Articles on Reserve

Reviving Ophelia (Selected Chapters)

Zine Scene: CH. 1 & CH. 14

RESEARCH TASK: learning about local girls, setting group goals

√ Questions for Catherine and other GIRL advocates.

Personal Research Tasks to Complete:

TH June 29 Building Bridges with Community Contacts

Reading: Zine Scene: CH. 2–4

RESEARCH TASK: Laying out our constituencies, making preliminary contact assignments.

Reviewing contact protocol for phone calls to - -! Review Contact Sheets

√ Secondary Proposal (might include a BOOKSTORE activity)

Personal Research Tasks to Complete:

Week Three: Methodologies for Girl Talk

T   July 4   HOLIDAY: NO-CLASS

Personal Research Tasks to Complete:

TH July 6   THEME ONE- *The Ethics of Girl Talk*

Reading: *Raising Their Voices* (Selected Chapters)

Zine Scene, p. 41

RESEARCH TASK: Review oral history ethics, review consent forms for girls and parents, discuss legal issues: publishing work/distributing to teens, mandatory reporting, interruption skills training, handling flashbacks

√ a list of your concerns about this project, dealing with teens, publishing work, dealing with schools, teachers, agencies

√ FIELDTRIP to the Bookstore: Before class today you should make a trip to the bookstore. We will give you a list of questions to answer about the store and its resources. We encourage you to go with someone from class, take a friend, or a teen girl with you!

THEME TWO, *Learning to Listen to Myself: Personal Standpoints*

RESEARCH TASK: Applying ourselves to our work. How does my voice, my assumptions, my perceptions, and my inferences affect my role as a focus group facilitator?

√ Your Personal Identity Narrative

Personal Research Tasks to Complete:

Week Four: Getting Reading to Rap in The Girl Zone

PLEASE NOTE; YOU SHOULD TRY TO SCHEDULE YOUR FIRST RAP SESSION FOR THIS WEEK

T July 11: THEME ONE: *Framing our Rap Sessions*

Reading. Articles on reserve

Zine Scene: CHPS. 5-6;

Girl Power (Selected Chapters)

RESEARCH TASK: Brainstorm about possible rap session formats, share ideas

√ Bring a design for your rap session

THEME TWO, *A Session of Our Own*

RESEARCH TASK: Practice sessions, interruption, facilitating and using our equipment. We will run our own rap session in class - be prepared to rotate in as a facilitator.

Personal Research Tasks to Complete:

TH- July 13 TALKING BACK: Reflections on Rap Sessions Writing Girl's Voices ... From Tape to Paper

Reading: Articles on Reserve

RESEARCH TASK: Our session will consist of us talking about what we are learning from the girls, processing their words and thinking through new directions, for our zine project. We may want to come up with questions to ask across all of the sessions—or a specific writing or art piece we would like the girls to work on! We will also discuss transcribing.

√ Revised Rap Session Formats

Personal Research Tasks:

Week Five: Girl Talk

T July 18 TALKING BACK AGAIN: More reflections, revising, rethinking

Reading: Articles on Reserve

RESEARCH TASK: Talking more about what we arc learning from the girls, processing their words and thinking through new directions. for our zine project. Discuss analysis/thematic organization.

√ Thumbnail sketches

Personal Research Tasks to Complete:

TH July 20 TALKING MORE: Reflections on rap sessions

Reading: *Zine Scene:* CHPS. 7–10; Articles on reserve

RESEARCH TASK: Laying out what we have, what we still need. Scheduling follow-up rap sessions. Conducting more focus groups or follow-up sessions.

√ Interview Notes, Transcripts, Thumbnail sketches

Personal Research Tasks to Complete:

Week Six: Zine Sheen

T July 25 NAME THAT ZINE & FORMAT IDEAS—Our Own Look

RESEARCH TASK Making format decisions, collecting submissions, deciding on a table of contents, identifying themes in our work, assigning sections

√ examples of zine submissions, freewrites, artwork, and a list of themes from YOUR sessions

Personal Research Tasks to Complete:

TH July 27 FORMAT IDEAS

RESEARCH TASK Making more format decisions, collaborating in writing teams, prioritizing work and dividing tasks. How will the GIRLS be involved in the ZINE editing? How to WRAPUP with the girls—saying goodbye?

√ envelopes with quotes, freewrites, transcripts, artwork for each theme section

Personal Research Tasks to Complete:

Week Seven: Getting it on Paper

T August 1 Writing & Editing

Reading: *Zine Scene:* CHPS 11–13

RESEARCH TASK: Edit sections, Invitations out to people for our FINAL PRESENTATION!

√Drafts of submissions

Personal Research Tasks to Complete:

TH August 3 Writing & Editing

RESEARCH TASK: Edit sections

√ Drafts of your zine sections

Personal Research Tasks to Complete:

Week Eight: Glue

T August 8 Layout, paste-up sessions & photocopying

RESEARCH TASK: Editing final copies, laying out pages; Organizing the final presentation—How will we present this to the community, the teens, teen advocates, agencies, and the university? What do we need to do in order to prepare? Follow-up phone calls. How do we want to celebrate privately? How to wrap-up?

Getting the Zine to the GIRLS! Making Distribution Plans

√ Final Submissions

Personal Research Tasks To Complete:

TH August 10

Final: Sharing Our Work with the Community

Invite your friends, family, teen girls, advocates, etc. to our presentation. Please note that you are required to present for this presentation—so plan your schedule ahead of time! This counts as your final for the course.

Personal Research Tasks to Complete:

Model Syllabi: Service-Learning Internship

UC 312: COMMUNITY PROJECTS IN THE ARTS AND HUMANITIES

University of Michigan

Instructor:	David Scobey
Projects Coordinator:	Rebecca Poyourow
Seminar meetings:	W 2-4
Seminar room:	Reader Center
Phone:	(Architecture) Nichols Arboretum
	(Arts of Citizenship)

This course is an experiment in community-based teaching and learning. On the one hand, it is a Practicum for collaborative public projects in the arts and humanities; on the other hand, it is a seminar that explores the significance of culture in community life and the promise and problems of collaboration between universities and communities to create new cultural goods.

THE PROJECTS PRACTICUM

The course will sponsor eight projects, all organized or supported by the UM Arts of Citizenship Program. Each of you will work on one project of your choosing for the whole term; project teams will typically have from two to five students on them. All the projects have faculty supervisors or project coordinators, and most have both. In addition, Rebecca Poyourow will help me to coordinate the logistics of all the projects in the course. All the projects bring student teams together with community or professional partners, and many involve graduate student and staff co-workers as well. Although the projects are varied in their partners, themes, and products, all of them involve the collaborative creation of cultural resources: new K-12 curricula, radio documentaries, historical exhibits, dramas, Websites. Your project work will require you to combine various academic skills—research, teaching, writing, interviewing, design—to create public goods useful to the larger community. Nearly all the projects will require you to travel to off-campus sites, but you do not need to have a car or van-training to take the course. The projects are described in the last part of this syllabus.

THE WEEKLY SEMINAR

The course will also meet as a whole for a two-hour weekly seminar; the seminar is essential to the goals of UC 312, and your attendance and participation are required. These meetings will both reflect on the larger themes of community-based cultural work and discuss the progress and problems of the projects. You will have short assigned readings for the seminar meetings, and the teams will occasionally be asked to report back on their work.

CREDIT-HOURS AND WORK EXPECTATIONS

You may take UC 312 for either three or four credits, and my expectation is that you will commit three hours a week of work time (including seminar meetings and readings) for each credit-hour. With two hours a week in seminar, and one-two hours a week of class reading and writing, my expectation is that you will be working on projects for 5–9 hours a week, depending on your level of credit-hours.

READINGS

The seminar readings average 50–75 pages a week; they are meant as brief but significant explorations of the themes of the course. Please come to class having read and thought about them and prepared to talk about them. The readings include four books available at Shaman Drum bookstore:

- Jane Addams, *Twenty Years at Hull-House*

- Harry Boyte and Nancy Kari, *Building America*

- Dolores Hayden, *The Power of Place*

- Nadia Wheatley and Donna Rawlins, *My Place*

Other reading assignments include Website materials and photocopied materials that will available at the Arts of Citizenship office, 232C West Hall.

In addition to the seminar readings, each project will have some reading of its own. All project teams will receive an introductory packet of materials in the first weeks of the term, and Julie Ellison's Poetry of Everyday Life project has two additional required books available on the UC 312 shelf at Shaman Drum.

PROJECT AND SEMINAR WRITING

UC 312 asks you to do two, equally valuable types of writing. First of all, each project is oriented toward the collaborative production of some sort of publicly useful product: for instance, a curriculum guide for a third-grade environmental education unit; a traveling exhibit on the history of the Underground Railroad; or a script for a radio piece on coming of age in Detroit in the 1960s. At the same time, I would like you to keep a course journal in which you write reflectively about your experience on your project and your engagement with the themes of the course. The journal will work best for you as a tool for exploration if you make the writing straightforward but analytically serious, neither 'academic' nor casual: think with it. You will be required to complete and submit four 2–3 page journal entries over the course of the term—although you may write as much as you like, of course—and to culminate the journal with a 6–8 page "think piece" analyzing and assessing your project work at the end of the term.

GRADING

Both your project work (60%) and seminar work (40%) will be taken into account in your grade. My assessment of your project work will include the effectiveness of your work with your team, your collaboration with other project partners, and the quality and timeliness of the product you create. My assessment of your seminar work will include both your journal and your class participation.

WEEKLY SEMINAR

Sept 6:   Introductions

Sept 13:   Community, Culture-Making, and Place: A Model
            Nadia Wheatley and Donna Rawlins, *My Place*
            By the end of this week, you should be firmly committed to a project team

Sept 20:   How? Community Projects as a Way of Learning
            Introductory reading packets for project teams

Sept 27:   Why? The Crisis of Public Life
            Harry Boyte and Nancy Kari, *Building America*, 1–32, 78–94, 112–147
            By the end of this week, your project should have finished its orientation and training

Oct 4:   Who? Boundary Crossing, Social Change, and Personal Transformation
            Jane Addams, *Twenty Years At Hull-House*, 3–76

Oct 11:   Where? Building Bridges Between the University and the Public

"Wingspread Declaration on Renewing the Civic Mission of the American Research University" (http://www.compact.org/news/Wingspread.html)

David Scobey, "Putting the Academy in Its Place"

Oct 18:   Where? The Contested Terrain of Community Life

Addams, *Twenty Years At Hull-House,* 77–104

Dolores Hayden, *The Power of Place,* 14–43

Oct 25:   Works in Progress

Reports from project teams about progress and problems

Nov 1:   How? The Politics of Collaboration

Guest speaker: Liz Lerman, Artistic Director, Liz Lerman Dance Exchange

Nov 8:   Projects: Community History and Research

Hayden, *Power of Place,* 139–87

By now your project team should be planning or working on your final term products

Nov 15:   Projects: Writing With and For the Public

Guest speaker: Tamar Charney, reporter, Michigan Radio

Nov 29:   Projects: Community-Based Teaching With Younger Students

Website, West Philadelphia Landscape Project (www.upenn.edu/wplp/)

Dec 6:   Project forum

Dec 13:   Project forum

PROJECTS

1) The Underground Railroad in Washtenaw County: This project explores the history of the Underground Railroad, antislavery activism, and African-American community life in the Ann Arbor/Ypsilanti area. Students will join a university/community research team, work in research archives at the Bentley Historical Library, Eastern Michigan University, and the Ypsilanti Historical Society, and help to create a traveling exhibit to be displayed in February in conjunction with a play about the Underground Railroad by Wild Swan Theater.

Faculty Supervisor: Joyce Mier; Project Coordinator: Carol Mull

2) Emerging Voices: Life Stories and Youth Theater: This partnership with Detroit's Mosaic Youth Theater, the Charles H. Wright Museum of African-American History, and the Residential College explores what it has been like to come of age in Detroit over the past several generations. Students will help Mosaic Youth Theater create a play about growing up in Detroit in the 1940s, do interviews and research to provide supporting materials, and write an accompanying curriculum guide. Mosaic's play will be performed in summer, 2001 as part of the Detroit 300 civic celebration.

Faculty Supervisor: David Scobey; Project Coordinator: Pilar Anadon

3) Emerging Voices: Creating a Radio Documentary: In addition to the drama project, Emerging Voices will work with Michigan Public Radio to create two radio documentary pieces about coming of age in Detroit during the era of the 1967 riot. Students will work the public-radio professionals to do interviews, research, and script-drafting for the pieces, which will be broadcast in Winter Term, 2001.

Faculty Supervisor: David Scobey; Project Coordinator: Pilar Anadon

4) Southwest Detroit: A Multicultural Community: Part of a longer-term community project on the history and culture of Southwest Detroit, the city's most ethnically diverse area, this group will do archival and oral-history research on the history of the neighborhood.

Faculty Supervisor: Robert Self

5) Students On Site: A Community History Curriculum (4-5 students): This team of UM students will teach a five-six week local-history curriculum to 3rd and 4th grade classrooms in the Ann Arbor schools, as well as helping to complete a curriculum guide for the unit.

Faculty Supervisor: David Scobey; Project Coordinator: Fiona Lyn

6) Students On Site: A Community History Website (3 students): This project will help to research, write, and complete an online collection of historical materials about Ann Arbor's community history. You can view the Students On Site Website in its current stage of development at www.artsofcitizenship.umich.edu/sos. No computer expertise is required.

Faculty Supervisor: David Scobey; Project Coordinator: Michelle Craig

7) Students On Site: The Poetry of Everyday Life (8 students): This project combines research into the role of poetry in everyday community life with a writing and art curriculum working with

4th-grade students at Bach Elementary School. The project team will create chapbooks and design an exhibit for display at the Ann Arbor District Library in January.

Faculty Supervisor: Julie Ellison

8) Environmental Legacies (4 students): This group will work Ann Arbor teachers and local environmental educators to revise and complete a 4-week pilot curriculum, aimed at 3rd graders in Ann Arbor, that combines local history with environmental education. Students will complete a curriculum guide and perhaps test the unit with a collaborating pilot class.

Faculty Supervisor: David Scobey; Project Coordinator: Erin Gallay

Model Syllabi: Undergraduate Community-Based Action Research

ECO 295 LEHIGH CORPS
Lehigh University
Regional Economic Development Practicum
Spring 1999
Todd A. Watkins
447 Rauch Business Center

This Lehigh Community Research and Policy Service course will. involve teams of students in community-oriented research projects. The twin purposes of the program are: I) to provide real-world, team oriented learning experiences to Lehigh students and II) to provide a resource for local governments and community organizations that would allow them to draw upon the expertise of our students as consultants in analyzing problems and formulating policy.

The students will participate in the design and execution of a specific research project identified by a Lehigh Valley development agency. A description of this years projects is attached. The results of this research project will be communicated both orally and in a written report to the agency. Your grade in this course will, be determined in consultation with the agency and will be based upon your written report, your presentations in class and to the agency and your team's research notebook. The research notebook win include copies of briefings, a weekly work record, an annotated bibliography of books, articles and other material used in your project and a copy of the presentation prepared for the sponsoring agency. This research notebook will also be presented to the agency. An outline for the final report is also attached. At term's end we will also ask each of you for a peer evaluation of other teammates, using the form attached here.

Even though this course has no assigned readings or tests, it remains a 3-credit course. We expect 3 credits worth of work from each of you. A typical 3 credit course meets 2.5 to 3 hours per week and faculty generally expect two to three times that out of class doing reading, homework, writing and so forth. This is roughly 10 hours of effort per student per week. Sustained effort at this pace throughout the semester is required by each member of a project team to provide your external client with a substantive, Lehigh-quality report.

We are scheduled to meet in Rauch 101 every Monday, Wednesday and Friday from 2–3 p.m. Please take note of the following scheduled meetings for the entire class. In addition to these scheduled meetings each team will meet with the instructors at least once a week. Any other meetings for the entire class will be announced before time.

1/13	Introduction, Summary of projects
1/15	Initial sorting of students into study teams
1/18	Assignment of teams to projects
1/22	Brief Statement of the Study Project after consultation with Agency
2/17 & 19	Presentation of a complete problem statement and proposed methodology
3/29 & 31	Mid-semester briefing on sections 11, 111, and IV (see outline) of the Report
3/31	Written draft of sections II, III & IV due
4/26-30	Dry run of team presentations
5/3	Final Reports Due
4/30-5/7	Oral presentation of results and submission of Final Report to Agency

RESEARCH PROJECTS IDENTIFIED BY DEVELOPMENT AGENCIES

1. Fresh Food Market Impact Project
Community Action Development Corporation of Bethlehem—Esther Guzman

This agency is interested in research to support an initiative to establish a fresh food market on the South Side of Bethlehem. One key element is a survey of consumer eating and shopping habits to help determine the need for new fresh food outlets. This survey would address the degree of shopping inconvenience currently facing South Side residents. A second element would be an assessment of the economic impact of a fresh food market on the community.

2. Profile of Tourists and Potential Tourists to the Lehigh Valley
Lehigh Valley Convention & Visitors Bureau—Mary Ann Bungerz

This project would develop and analyze the results of a mail survey of people who have received tourist information from the bureau. The survey would be designed to address questions related to: 1. The perceptions of the Lehigh Valley as a tourist destination; 2. The effectiveness of the bureaus promotional literature; 3. The development of demographic profiles of those who actually visit the area and those who requested information but didn't visit the area, and 4. The assembly of a data base on the spending levels and patterns of visitors. The starting point is an existing survey instrument developed by Muhlenberg College students.

3. The Impact of Tax-Exempt Properties on Lehigh Valley Cities
Lehigh Valley Partnership Strategic Planning Committee—Ed Yarrish

This project will collect data on the total assessed value and foregone tax revenue of properties that are exempt from property taxes in Allentown, Bethlehem and Easton. The data necessary for this project is available at the county administration centers in Allentown and Easton. The final report would be centered on a series of spread sheets that provide the information needed by the Strategic Planning Committee.

4. Transportation Barriers to Successful Welfare to Work Transitions
Council of Hispanic Organizations—Lupe Pierce

The Council is preparing a proposal for a transportation grant to improve the public transportation options open to inner-city residents. They would like research to document the extent to which women living in the inner city of Allentown are limited in their search for employment by the current configuration of bus routes. The study team would meet with LANTA planners to identify ways in which routes could be changed or new services developed to enhance the possibility of successful transitions from welfare to work.

5. A Structured Approach to Philanthropy
Lehigh Valley Community Foundation—Jan Surotchak

The study team would use existing methodology to survey and interview donors and potential donors to the Foundation. The purpose of this research is to assist the foundation in analyzing giving patterns and identifying potential donors by developing a database on the level of donations, the timing of donations and the motivation for donations by philanthropists.

6. The Vitality of the Local Entrepreneurial Environment
Bridgeworks Enterprise Center—Wayne Barz

This project would attempt to assess the vitality of the local environment for assisting people in starting businesses. Mr. Barz feels that the long dominance of large corporations in the local economy and the "nonrisk-taking" attitude in Pennsylvania German Society limit the local support for business development. One important element would be the collection of statistical data and other information to compare the Lehigh Valley with other similarly sized urban areas. Such a benchmarking study could serve as a way of "testing" Mr. Barz's hypotheses.

7. Lehigh County Reuse and Regeneration Center
Good Shepherd Work Services—Joe Schwindenhammer

Significant volumes of re-usable building materials and large furnishings and appliances are disposed of each year in municipal waste collection programs. A growing number of cities nationwide are opening refurbishment operations that entail retrieving these materials from the waste stream, refurbishing them and selling them through thrift-like retail establishments. Good Shepherd Work Services has developed a business plan for opening a Reuse and Regeneration Center in Lehigh County by April 2000. Its multiple goals include reducing the waste disposal volumes and costs for the County and providing work training for people with disabilities and (in conjunction with Lehigh County vo-tech) for young people from the County juvenile detention programs. They would like a projection of the economic costs and benefits of the Center for Good Shepherd and for Lehigh County, based on comparisons to the results at similar centers throughout the country. They have detailed information of five such centers, but would like more in-depth analysis and collection of a broader set of data.

REQUIRED TOPICS IN FINAL REPORT

The final reports should cover the following topics, discussed in more detail below.

I.   Executive Summary

II.   Introduction & Problem Statement

III.   Background Research

IV.   Methodology

V.   Findings & Analysis

VI.   Conclusions & Recommendations

VII.   References

You do not need to follow this specific outline—organize your reports to suit your project-but each report should address the broad topics.

The oral presentations should be summaries of the same topics. We encourage you to use overheads/computer projection and presentation software such as PowerPoint and make your presentations as professional as possible. Remember that we would like you to present your findings in an oral briefing at the end of the term to the client organizations.

I. Executive Summary

Write this last. In the final report please include an executive summary of your project.

Busy policymaker executives may, in fact, never read whole research project reports, so executive summaries are critical to effective use of your work. The executive summary should be able to stand alone (and include the title and your names). It is not an introduction (e.g. not "this report contains....") You should be able, if you wanted, to hand it out at a community meeting or pass it along to the mayor, and have it alone be useful and informative. It should contain the major questions you addressed, your methods and your main findings and conclusions, and essential supporting points for those conclusions. Think of the executive summary as a complete mini version of your report. After reading it, the mayor should be able to give her constituents or the local paper a cogent description of your main findings and how you arrived at diem. Shoot for approximately 500 words. [No need to do this for the mid-semester draft reports]

An effective executive summary:

- uses one or more well-developed paragraphs, which are unified, coherent, concise, and able to stand alone;

- uses an introduction-body-conclusion structure in which the parts of the report are discussed in order. purpose, methods, findings, conclusions, recommendations

- follows strictly the chronology of the report;

- provides logical connections between material 'included;

- adds no new information but simply summarizes the report;

- is intelligible to a wide audience.

To write an effective executive summary, follow these four steps outlined by the Purdue University Writing Lab:

1) Reread your report with the purpose of summarizing in mind. Look specifically for these parts: purpose, methods, findings, conclusions, and recommendations.

2) After you have finished rereading your report, write a rough draft without looking back at your report. Consider the main parts of the summary listed in step #1. Do not merely copy key sentences from your report. You will put in too much or too little information. Do not summarize information in a new way.

3) Revise your rough draft to:

- correct weaknesses in organization and coherence,

- drop superfluous information,

- add important information originally left out,

- eliminate wordiness, and

- fix errors in grammar and mechanics.

4) Type your revision and carefully proofread the typed copy. Reading aloud may feel silly but can often catch unclear or awkward written style. This also applies to the main body of the report.

II. Introduction & Problem Statement

What is the general problem area your project involves? What is the client organization and what, briefly, does it do? What, specifically, does the client organization want from the project, and what might be likely uses of your analysis once completed? What is known and what is unknown? In other words, overview what you are doing and why the client (or other readers) is interested in the findings in the first place. Do not assume the reader knows about the problem, or that the reader thinks it is an important or interesting problem. Also lay out the scope of your problem: when, where, what extent. State the "what and why" as specifically and concretely as you can, rather than generally and abstractly.

III. Background Research

The idea here is to spend some significant effort finding out what others know questions they've asked, and how they did it, so you are not starting from scratch or re-creating the wheel. You should discuss previous studies, research, papers, data, etc. that have addressed similar issues. What have those who looked into this area before already discovered? What other cities or agencies have done similar studies? What were their major findings and how (methodology) did they do it What were the major unanswered questions and why? How is the focus of your project similar or different? How has the previous research shaped what you did/are doing in your project? You should also here define any terms that may be unfamiliar to a general reader.

IV. Methodology

Describe in detail your research methodology. What information/data sources are you using? What, specifically, do they contain? How were they collected/put together? What is their scope? How will you be using that information, specifically? If you are collecting your own data, how and what, specifically A good methodology section would allow the reader to fully re-construct the steps you took if the reader wanted to repeat your study.

V. Findings & Analysis

Describe and present in detail your findings, your analysis of those findings, and fully discuss the implications of those findings for your client organization. Describe in detail each point of support for your main conclusions. Here is the key area where you establish the credibility of your work. Support all points by carefully selected relevant data. Acknowledge sources. Any table or chart should be numbered, fully explained in the text and also have a descriptive tide. It is appropriate here to discuss the strengths and weaknesses of your data, your methods and overall findings. Where data are not available, acknowledge the lack of support material and explain why you think as you do in spite of the information gap. [For the mid-semester drafts, in this section be as complete as you can at this stage. What have you found so far?]

VI. Conclusions & Recommendations

It is generally appropriate here to restate the general problem, and then summarize your main findings and major points of support for those findings. What is the central theme in this report? You also want to include your recommendations for how the client organization could use your findings. Also discuss questions/issues that remain unexplored and any areas for future work that your work uncovered. What concrete steps should the organization take based on your findings? Are there significant holes in policies or available information that the organization could remedy?

VII. References

Include a complete list of references and data sources you used. In the body of the text, cite references where appropriate. Use whatever citation style you are familiar with, but be complete. The reader should know which ideas are yours and which are someone else's. You should include in your citations and references any online information you used. A useful reference is the Modem Language Association's on-line citation style guide at http://www.mla.org.

Model Syllabi: Journal/Reflection Focused

ENGLISH 101 & 107 SYLLABUS
University of Arizona
English 101-24, MW/F 9:00 – 9:50 a.m., Harvill I I I
English 107-05, M/W/F 10:00 – 10:50 a.m., Harvill 232
Instructor: Adrian Wurr

REQUIRED TEXTS
• Prineas, Sarah, Lori Church, and Adrian Wurr, eds. *A Student's Guide to First-Year Composition.* 20th ed. Edina, Minnesota: Burgess International Group, 1998.

• Hacker, Diana. *A Pocket Style Manual.* 2nd ed. Boston: Bedford Books, 1997

• Miller, Thomas P., et al. *The University Book: An Anthology of Writing from the University of Arizona.* 2nd ed. Needham Heights, Massachusetts: Pearson Custom Publishing, 1999.

OTHER REQUIRED MATERIALS

• A pocket folder (for turning in journal and portfolio work)

• White, lined loose-leaf paper

• Copies of your work as needed for class and group discussions

*A college dictionary is also recommended

COURSE DESCRIPTION

First-year composition classes are designed to introduce you to university-level reading and writing. English 101 and 107 explore writing as a negotiation between writers and readers that is shaped by specific purposes, expectations, and situations. This course seeks to strengthen your skills as a reader and writer in different personal and social contexts by engaging you in a variety of literacy's and rhetorical situations, both in the classroom and in the local community. In addition to regular classroom activities, we will use service learning to expand traditional notions of reading, writing, and texts to include computer and civic literacy's, visual and living texts. You will be asked to write three major essays, two in-class timed essays, and a variety of shorter texts, as well as to volunteer about fifteen hours in the community group of your choice. Through hands-on learning, you will practice different strategies and literacy's to meet personal and professional goals while also helping others to do the same.

ASSIGNMENTS

Formal Assignments. You will write 4 out-of-class essays and 2 in-class essays. Your first essay will be the **Diagnostic Essay**, started in class on the first day, and finished out of class in the next day or two as homework. The first graded essay will be a rhetorical analysis essay, **Understanding How Arguments Work.** In this essay, you will analyze an essay written by a professional in a discipline of interest to you. The next essay (in-class) will be the **Midterm Essay,** in which you will analyze a text chosen by your teacher and/or other members of the class. For the fourth essay (out-of-class), **Creating an Argument,** you will choose an issue, research what has been written on this issue by other members of your chosen discipline, and frame your own argument in response to this issue. The fifth essay (out-of-class), the **Reflective Analysis Essay,** will serve as the preface to an **Inquiry Portfolio,** and will ask you to critically reflect on your best work over the semester as well as the various rhetorical situations in which it was produced. Finally, in the **Final Exam Essay** (in-class), you will synthesize from 0 you have learned over the semester to produce an essay addressing a text or texts chosen by the department.

The three graded out-of-class essays will be written through a process of at least two drafts and workshop analysis. Revisions should show significant changes in purpose, audience, organization, or evidence, according to feedback you receive from the workshop and from your instructor.

Informal Writing Assignment. These include short out-of-class writings, service-learning journal entries, email, and workshop evaluations. Many of these assignments, labeled "SW" for short writing assignment in the daily schedule below, are keyed to the formal essay you are currently working on. All informal writings assignments are due in class the day after they are assigned to receive credit. If you miss one or more of these assignments, the corresponding formal essay will not receive full credit.

Format. Final versions of the three out-of-class essays should be printed or typed, double-spaced, and titled. First versions must be double-spaced and legible. In-class essays must be handwritten, of course, but will be written in bluebooks, every other line, one side of the page. Informal assignments must also be typed unless otherwise specified. See Appendix B in the Student's Guide for a list of computing centers available free of charge to students.

COURSE POLICIES

Attendance. Regular attendance is critical to the learning process and your success in this class. Most of our classwork will involve class discussion, workshop, and in-class writing, all of which are critical to your understanding of the writing process and your development as a writer. If you miss more than three class sessions, I may drop you from the class. If you must miss a class, contact me before the missed class by calling my office, by calling the English Department and leaving a message, or by leaving a note in my mailbox. You are responsible for finding out about and making up any missed assignments, including in-class writing. See "Attendance—Yes, You Have to Be There" on p. 115 in the Students' Guide for the official departmental policy on attendance.

Conferences. I will schedule individual or small-group conferences several times during the semester. You should come to your conference prepared to discuss your current work. A missed conference counts as an absence. For more on conferences, see "Conferences and Office Hours" on p. 116 in the Student's Guide.

Grading. To complete this course successfully (i.e., with a grade of C or higher), you must attend class and all scheduled conferences; complete A assignments on time; prepare for class; and participate in class activities and discussions. You cannot receive a passing grade in this class unless you have submitted all major assignments and completed the final exam. To receive full credit, all written assignments must be submitted on time, in the proper format, and with the required supporting materials (i.e., all drafts, journal entries, etc., associated with that particular assignment). I will not grade a final draft unless I have previously read at least one rough draft and unless that draft accompanies the final draft. Please note that late essays will be reduced by half a letter grade for each day late unless an extension is arranged with the instructor prior to the due date. Be sure to keep a copy of each assignment in the (rare) event that I lose it. If you do not have a copy, you will have to rewrite the lost assignment.

Specific requirements of individual assignments will be determined in class and may vary, but in all cases my evaluation of your essays will consider content, organization, development of ideas, expression, mechanics, and maturity of thought. If you have a question about my comments or a grade you have received, be sure to talk to me about it. For more on grading, teacher's comments, and departmental standards, see Chapter 5 ("Interpreting Written Comments and Grades") on pp. 61–91 in the Student's Guide. Note particularly the description of grades on pp. 68–69 and the grading charts on pp. 71–80. See also pp. 121–123 for information on incompletes, withdrawals, and grade appeals.

The following table lists all assignments and their point values. Required assignments which carry no point values must be completed in order for you to receive full credit for the course.

Assignment	Total Points Allowed
Diagnostic Essay (Aug. 25), Required	
Major Inquiry: Rhetorical Analysis Essay: How Arguments Work	
• First draft (due Sept. 20), Required	
• Final version (due Sept. 29)	200
Persuasive Essay: Creating An Argument	
• First draft (due Oct. 22), Required	
• Final version (due Oct. 29)	250
Reflective Analysis Essay: Inquiry Portfolio	
• First draft (due Nov. 10), Required	
• Final version (due Nov. 19)	250
Midterm exam (Oct. 6)	100
Final exam (Dec. 10)	100
Informal Writing	100
Total available points	1000

To receive an A in this course, you must accumulate at least 900 points; for a B, 800 points; for a C, 700 points; and for a D, 600 points. Remember that if you don't turn in an assignment, I must give it a 0. therefore, always turn in your assignments. Even a poorly written assignment will receive some points.

Academic Dishonesty and Plagiarism. All UA students are responsible for upholding the Code of Academic Integrity, available through the Office of the Dean of Students. For a synopsis of the code and a discussion of plagiarism and the relationships between writing and research, see pp. 119–121 in the Student's Guide. If you have any questions about whether you have plagiarized something, ask me.

Guidelines for Classroom Interaction. The University and I expect you to conduct yourself as an adult. Please familiarize yourself with the Student Code of Conduct in the Student's Guide, p. 121, and in the university catalog. Simply put, you are expected to: 1) come to class prepared for the day's activities; 2) cooperate with your classmates; 3) cooperate with me, especially when you want to come talk to me about a paper, by coming prepared to ask questions and by making sure you understand what you need to do for an assignment; and 4) use the opportunity this class affords you to grow and learn, to expand your skills and abilities. Finally, please remember that all points of view and experiences are welcome in this class, so keep an open mind and refrain from using personal attacks or insults in class or online discussions.

Writing tutors: I strongly encourage you to work with a writing tutor at one of the writing centers on campus (see Student's Guide p. 580 for locations). Writing tutors are highly skilled and give you much more personalized instruction than larger forums like this class. Generally, students who do work with a tutor conscientiously and consistently improve their final grade in this course by at least one letter grade.

CLASS SCHEDULE

SG = *A Student's Guide*
UB = *The University Book*
PSM = *A Pocket Style Manual*

Rhetorical Analysis Essay Unit

WEEK 1   M 8/23 Introductions, course overview, and brainstorming for diagnostic essay

         W 8/25
         For Class:
         1. Buy class books and materials.
         2. Get an email account.
         3. Read SG 5–18 ("Advice from the Experts"); 233–248 ("Introduction")
         4. Read LJB 3–16 ("Introduction," "Priorities ..... Reviving")
         5. Write diagnostic essay
         In Class: Diagnostic Essay due. Discuss "Priorities" and service-learning. Class phone/email list.

         F 8/27
         For Class:
         1. Read SG 249–261 ("The Rhetorical Analysis Essay")

2. Read UB 90–93 ("Inquiry") and 235–239 ("Earth Invades Mars" and "Five Letters")

3. SWl: Post a self-introduction/greeting on the class listserv

In Class: Discuss Inquiry/Research process and disciplinary assumptions. Service-learning guest speakers. Diagnostic essays returned. Organize email groups and discuss writing class summaries for extra credit.

WEEK 2   M 8/30

For Class:

1. Read UB 94-102 ("Down on their luck"); 611–625 ("The Sonoran Pimeria Alta")

2. SW2: Post a one-screen message to your assigned service-learning email discussion group on your ideas for service-learning work.

In Class: Discuss rhetorical analysis; apply to close reading of "The Sonoran Pimeria Alta."

W 9/1

For Class:

1. SW3: Respond to your group email postings from Monday, if you haven't done so already.

2. Select and contact your service-learning site.

3. Actively read and rhetorically analyze "Down on their luck" (UB 94–102).

In Class: Contrastive analysis of "Down on their luck" and "The Sonoran Pimeria Alta."

F 9/3

For Class:

1. SW4: Complete service-learning site contact information sheet.

2. Read SG 247 ("Finding Questions" and "Final Thoughts")

3. Select 2–3 possible articles to analyze for the Rhetorical Analysis Essay; and

4. SW5: Write an annotated bibliography of your selected articles (See SG 328 for an example).

In Class: Service-Learning site contact information due. Group discussions of inquiry topics and selected articles. Turn in revised annotated bibliography for the rhetorical analysis essay.

WEEK 3   M 9/6 Labor Day Holiday. Classes canceled.

W 9/8

For Class:

1. SW6: Visit your service-learning site, if you haven't already, and post a two-screen message to your email group on your first impressions of the visit and/or site.

2. Read SG 19–31 ("Writing & Revising Your Essay"); PSM 87–90 ("Supporting a thesis").

3. Please see me during office hours this week to discuss plans for your essay.

In Class: Discuss organizational patterns for the rhetorical analysis essay; SW 7: apply to your essay.

F 9/10
For Class:

1. Read SG 31–36 ("Writing & Revising Your Essay")

2. SW8: Write two different introductions for your rhetorical analysis essay (i.e. try two different ways of starting the same essay).

In Class: Group discussions of essay starts (SW8) and outlines (SW7).

WEEK 4   M 9/13
For Class:

1. SW9: Write a memo to the supervisor at your service-learning site in regards to a recent meeting, discussion, or activity you had. If this topic doesn't seem appropriate or interesting, choose one more pertinent to your current interest or situation. Post your writing to your email group.

2. Read PSM 91–101 ("Citing a source; avoiding plagiarism").

In Class: Discuss how to support claims and integrate quotes using PIE paragraphs.

W 9/15:
For Class:

1. Read PSM 103–108 ("NILA documentation style")

2. Read SG 265–272 ("Sample Assignments and Essays")

In Class: Apply MLA documentation to DWI 0 worksheet ("Summarizing, paraphrasing, and quoting"); discuss the works cited page.

F 9/17:
For Class:

1. Review PSM 109–117 ("NILA list of works cited7)

2. Read SG 286-297 ("Aryan Nation Appeals")

In Class: Discuss grading for rhetorical analysis essay and create grading rubric. Apply to "Aryan Nation Appeals."

WEEK 5   M 9/20
For Class:

1. Read "Guidelines for Writing a Draft for Peer Review" (Class handout).

2. SW 10: Write a complete draft-with a beginning, middle, and end-of your rhetorical analysis essay. Bring four copies for your classmates and one copy for me.

In Class: Discuss workshop procedures, form groups, and exchange papers.

W 9/22 & F 9/24
For Class: SW1 1: Complete peer reviews for conferences.
In Class: Class canceled to accommodate writing conferences.

WEEK 6   M 9/27
For Class:

1. SW12: Post a one-screen message to your email group discussing the connections you see between the service-learning work you're doing and the class readings, writings, and or discussions. If this topic doesn't seem appropriate or interesting, choose one more pertinent to your current interest or situation.

2.Read "Guidelines for revising your essay after peer review" (Class handout).

3. SW 13: Revise your essay per comments received in your workshop and bring one copy of the revised essay (an editing draft) to class.

In Class: Editing draft of your essay due (SW 13). Grammar workshop, editing of essays, and/or peer review and evaluation.

W 9/29
For Class:

1. Prepare a final draft of your rhetorical analysis essay and bring this along with your portfolio to class.

In Class: Rhetorical Analysis essay and portfolio due. In-class written self-evaluation of your essay and writing process. (language learning style orientation survey).

Persuasive Essay Unit Schedule

F 10/1
For Class:
(G) Read SG 29–313 ("The Persuasive Essay"); 37–58 ("Joining the Conversation").
In Class: Introduce and discuss the midterm and persuasive essay assignments.

WEEK 7   M 10/4
For Class:

1. SW14: Write a letter to your friends or family back home describing the service-learning work you're doing. If this topic doesn't seem appropriate or interesting, choose one more pertinent to your current interest or situation.

2. SW15: Complete "Choosing a topic" for your persuasive essay (class handout). In Class: Library research. Meet in the lobby of the main library (by the elevators). Please arrive on time. SW15 due.

W 10/6

For Class:

1. Read SG 46–50 ("Evaluating Sources")

2. SW16: Complete "Evaluating the articles for your paper" (class handout).

In Class: Discuss "Evaluating sources" and the use of personal experience (primary research) versus published sources (secondary/library research) in the persuasive essay assignment.

F 10/8

For Class:

1. Select one article to rhetorically analyze for your midterm. Please be sure it meets the criteria listed on the midterm assignment sheet.

2. Read SG 59–66 ("Tips for Writing the Midterm")

(H) Complete "Midterm service-learning evaluation survey" (class handout)

In Class: Discuss timed-essay writing strategies.

WEEK 8   M 10/11

For Class: Prepare for the midterm.

In Class: In-class Midterm Essay.

W 10/13

For Class: SW17: Write a self-evaluation of your midterm preparation and writing strategies.

In Class: Learning Styles survey. Service-learning and persuasive essay discussion.

F 10/15

For Class:

1. Read UB 265–275 ("Escaping," "Platinum Apples," & "Hazards").

SW 18: Post a one-screen report to your email group on the research you have done to date for your persuasive essay and the connections you see to your service-learning work.

In Class: Discuss the use of tone, diction, and evidence to appeal to an audience.

WEEK 9   M 10/18

For Class: SW19: Write an annotated bibliography of four sources you might use in your persuasive essay. At least two of these must be from sources other than the internet. Bring four copies for your classmates and one for me.

In Class: Discuss research to date in small groups. Exchange annotated bibliographies.

W 10/20

For Class:

1. SW 20: Write two short persuasive texts—one each for elementary and college students—explaining your research topic. Try to persuade your audience to see and understand the issue as you do.

2. Read SG 332–342 ("In Search of Truth")

In Class: Discuss "In Search of Truth" and grading criteria for the persuasive essay assignment.

Create grading rubric.

F 10/22

For Class: SW2 1: Write a complete rough draft of your persuasive essay. Bring four copies for your classmates and one copy for me.

In Class: Review workshop procedures, form groups, and exchange papers.

WEEK 10   M 10/25 & W 10/27

For Class: SW22: Complete peer reviews for conferences.

In Class: Class canceled to accommodate writing conferences.

F 10/29

For Class: SW23: Revise your essay per comments received in your workshop and bring one copy of the revised essay (an editing draft) to class.

In Class: Editing draft of your essay due (SW24). Grammar workshop, editing of essays, and/orpeer review and evaluation.

WEEK 11   M 11/1

For Class: Prepare a final draft of your persuasive essay and bring this along with your portfolio to class.

In Class: Persuasive essay and portfolio due. In-class written self-evaluation of your essay and writing process.

W 11/3

For Class: SW25: Write a letter to the editor of a local newspaper about an issue related to your persuasive essay topic and/or your service-learning work.

In Class: Introduction and discussion of the Reflective Essay Assignment.

Reflective Essay Unit

F 11/5

For Class:

1. Read SG 47–51

2. Read UB 3–6 ("Introduction") and 287–294 ("Remember Mohave").

Web surfers may want to check out http://www.coh.arizona.edu/planet-xeno/

In Class: Discuss "Remember Mohave" with the author.

WEEK 12   M 11/8

For Class:

SW26: Read and rhetorically analyze the preface or introduction to an anthology used in one of your classes or the one by yours truly at http://www.coh.arizona.edu/planet-xeno/awintro.html.

In Class: Discuss "What is a text?" and apply to your selection of portfolio 'texts.'

W 11/10

For Class:

1. SW27: Create a table of contents for your portfolio that includes a brief summary of the text and its purpose in your portfolio.

2. SW28: Write a brief description of the work you completed in the community, including an estimate of how much time was spent on each task.

In Class: Discuss the researcher's paradox in relation to service-learning and your portfolio work.

F 11/12

For Class: SW29: Write a rough draft of your Reflective Analysis portfolio preface (you may omit your self-evaluation and grade from this draft, if you want) and bring two copies to class, one for me and one for pair peer review.

In Class: Pair peer review of reflective essay drafts. Sign up for one-on-one conferences with me.

WEEK 13   M 11/15 - F 11/19

For Class: Prepare for your writing conference with me by writing down specific questions or concerns you have about your essay and/or inquiry portfolio.

In Class: Class canceled to accommodate writing conferences.

WEEK 14   M 11/22

For Class: Prepare a final draft of your reflective analysis and bring this along with your Inquiry Portfolio to class.

In Class: Reflective Analytical Essay and Inquiry Portfolio due. Service-Learning final evaluation survey and interview sign-ups.

W 11/24

For Class:

1. Read SG 392-397; 401–403 ("Sample Final Exam Essay Assignment" and "Sample Essay" #1 and #3).

2. Buy final exam materials at the bookstore.

3. Bring study guide questions to class.

In Class: Review midterm essay grading rubric and revise as necessary for the final exam. Organize final exam study groups. Group work in preparation for final exam essay.

F 11/26 - Thanksgiving Holiday. Classes Canceled.

WEEK 15   M 11/29

For Class: Begin outlining a response to your assigned study guide question

In Class: Continue group work in preparation for final exam

W 12/1

For Class:

1. Read SG 66–70

2. SW30: Write a detailed outline for an essay you might write in response to your assigned study guide question. Bring to class four copies for your classmates and one for me.

3. Prepare a five-minute speech explaining the essay you outlined in SW30. Be sure to note where others might want to vary from your suggested response (e.g. to include different readings, service-learning work, or past experiences).

In Class: Class presentations in small groups of your final exam study guide essay outline

F 12/3

For Class: Review SG 59–70 ("Tips for Writing the Midterm and Final Exam Essays")

In Class: Practice writing timed final exam essay (SW3 1).

WEEK 16   M 12/6

For Class: Review grading rubric for final exam

In Class: Peer review of practice in-class exam (SW3 1). Final service-learning evaluation survey.

W 12/8

For Class:

1. Prepare a brief (5 minutes) speech for the class and/or other appropriate group about your service-learning work this semester.

In Class: Final reports to class on service-learning work.

F 12/10   Final Exam 8:00a.m. – 10:00 a.m.

Note: If you would like a copy of your final class grade mailed to you, please bring a stamped, self-addressed envelope to the final with you. Otherwise, course grades should be available on Student Link about January 1, 2000.

SYLLABUS ADDENDUM: SERVICE-LEARNING ASSIGNMENT

A significant component of this class will be service-learning. Service-learning links volunteer work with classroom instruction to enhance and apply an understanding of the subject matter. In composition, service-learning offers an innovative and important way of helping students see the connection of composition, writing, and communication to "real-world" community issues. Because service-learning has students working in communities and writing for those communities, students see how writing has a real function and serves real purposes in the world, and they see the real people who are impacted by their writing. Service-learning provides an added dimension to research, understanding rhetorical situations, analyzing audiences, and creating a written product for more than just the instructor to grade. Additional benefits include:

Academic Benefits
- Deepens understanding of theoretical material

- Increases motivation to learn

- Enhances retention

Professional Benefits
- Gain practical work experience

- Enhance your resumé

- Explore possible career options

- Develop leadership skills

- Improve critical thinking skills

Personal Benefits

• Be a role model

• Make a difference in your community

• Establish rapport and trust with children and others in your community

Each of you will be asked to volunteer about fifteen hours at the non-profit agency of your choice during the semester. There are several services on campus and in the community that can help you find an agency that meets your needs and interests. These include the Center for Service-Learning (Old Main Bldg.), the Composition Program's Service-Learning database (http://w3.arizona.edu/-guide/sl/search_the_sl_dbase.htm), and the Tucson Volunteer Center (http://members.aol.com/voltucson/index.htm). Finding a suitable service-learning placement can be a challenge, so I encourage you to begin your search immediately, and see me if you have any problems or need further assistance.

3   Service-Learning Assignments

This article is reprinted permission of Newsweek.

LAST CHANCE CLASS

Newsweek, May 31, 1999 By Martha Brant

David Protess's students have freed three men from death row. They have a case now that they believe in—and haven't won.

Aaron Patterson was never one to walk away from a fight. The Illinois death-row inmate admits that back in the '80s, when he was the feared leader of Chicago's Apache Rangers, plenty of his street gang's enemies learned just how relentless he could be. Patterson's stubborn streak was still on display in 1989, when he was condemned to die for the murder of an elderly couple: he kept shouting in the courtroom that the cops had tortured a confession out of him. "You're holding me for a murder I didn't even do!" he yelled at the judge. For 10 years on death row, Patterson, 34 kept mouthing off—producing pamphlets, recording audiotapes, haranguing lawyers and writing to newspapers and anyone else who might listen to his claim that he didn't kill Rafaela and Vincent Sanchez. One of his letters reached Prof. David Protess at Northwestern University.

The journalism professor shares the prisoner's flair for getting attention. The 53-year-old teacher is something of a celebrity after helping to free three wrongly accused men from Illinois' death row. (Hollywood producer Jerry Bruckheimer is at work on a feature movie about him.) Protess can afford to be picky when it comes to capital-punishment subjects for his investigative-reporting class. Since he and his student sleuths helped spring another convict, Anthony Porter, in February, Protess estimates he's received 2,000 e-mails and letters. "My home number is scribbled on every death row in the country," he says. Something in the vehemence of Patterson's letter resonated with Protess. The story of their now-intertwined lives casts light on the role Protess and his students are playing in the enduring American debate over the death penalty. The Patterson case may be another triumph—or, just possibly, there won't be a happy ending this time. Protess and 15 of his amateur investigators have chipped away at the case against Patterson over two school years. But as this year's class has found, it's hard enough to get a case re-opened with DNA evidence; without it in this case, the task seems nearly impossible. Next month, Patterson could exhaust his state appeals. If the Illinois Supreme Court does not grant a new hearing, he'll plod through the federal courts. "If he doesn't get out of there, then there is something really wrong with the justice system," insists senior Genevieve Marshall.

Team Patterson didn't always believe so passionately that their man was innocent. Protess had told them only to "find the truth." But they did know one disturbing statistic: for every seven executions nationwide since the death penalty was reinstated in 1976, one death-row inmate has been set free. In Northwestern University's own state, Illinois, there have been just as many exonerations as executions. Last week, Ronald Jones became the 12th man to walk off the state's death row (and the 79th nationally) when DNA evidence proved he could not have committed the rape and murder he was convicted of. Even Protess's critics give him part of the credit for Illinois' streak of releases, and for raising national awareness of the argument for tightening the rules for the death penalty. Just last week, the Nebraska Legislature voted for a moratorium on executions. On the first day of class at Northwestern's Medill School of Journalism last fall, the students sat nervously as Protess straddled his chair and warned them to brace themselves for a "tough emotional ride." Most had already heard about the rigors of investigation—and the challenge of dealing with a volatile, autocratic, spotlight-loving professor. Still, they queued up to get into his class. Dave Rogers, an aspiring FBI agent from Massachusetts, wanted to scrutinize the law from the inside out; California's Bernice Yeung wanted training in "social justice" journalism. Sheri Hall, from suburban Detroit, was one of the doubters who drove two hours to visit Patterson at the maximum-security Pontiac Correctional Center. After passing through three locked gates, she finally sat across from him, separated by a thick glass divider. "He put me at ease right away," Hall says. They talked music, current events. A college and National Guard dropout, Patterson impressed her as bright. He had read everything in his file and studied the law books at the prison library. When asked straight out if he had killed the couple, he looked her in the eye and said: "Nah, I wouldn't kill no old people."

Patterson says that 12 days after the Sanchezes were stabbed to death, police rounded him up and handcuffed him to a ring in the wall of an interrogation room. For an hour, Patterson denied to detectives that he had killed the couple. Then he claims they got impatient: "The lights went out and they bum-rushed me." He says a thick plastic bag was forced tight against his face as detectives started beating his chest. They "bagged" him again, he explains, and warned him to confess or he'd "get something worse." "They are going to kill me up in here," Patterson recalls thinking. So he consented to an oral confession but refused to sign the written version. With a paper clip snatched off the desk, Patterson scratched a message onto a metal bench that was discovered several days later: "Aaron 4/30 I lie about murders/Police threaten me with violence/Slapped and suffocated me with plastic." But a physical exam at the jail revealed no signs of abuse, and the jury apparently found it hard to believe that Patterson, the son of a Chicago police lieutenant, would be mistreated. (His father, now retired and living in Virginia, believes his son.) The police version of his confession seemed more credible. According to cops, on April 18, 1986, Patterson (already wanted for two attempted murders) headed out to steal guns from the Sanchezes, who were well-known neighborhood fences. The couple resisted. According to police, this is what Patterson said about what happened next: "I came up on Sanchez like a straight-up Ninja. He got shanked... His old lady tried to run. I did her, too. I had that chick swinging everywhere." The 73-year-old Sanchez was stabbed 25 times; his wife, 62, nine times.

In the cluttered office of Patterson's pro bono lawyers, the Northwestern students began to comb through a three-foot pile of court documents. They read about nine other death-row inmates who claim they were tortured in the same police district and learned that an internal police investigation in 1990 had found "systematic" abuse, including electroshock and "ear cupping." There also was no physical evidence linking Patterson to the crime. The knife was never recovered; the fingerprints found at the scene weren't a match (and have disappeared since). Patterson's codefendant, Eric Caine, who told police Patterson did it, said he, too, had been beaten; a medical exam later revealed a shattered eardrum. "I was scared," Caine told the students. "I was making up a story."

That left the testimony of a 16-year-old named Marva Hall. She'd told the jury that Patterson, while trying to sell her a shotgun two days after the murders, had boasted about the killings. Two students, Delores Patterson (no relation) and Marc Graser, tracked her to the small Alabama town of Dothan. They used their own money for the cheapest tickets to Atlanta, then drove four hours south. As they waited in front of Hall's little house, they practiced role-playing, a technique Protess had drilled into them. He had them knock on his classroom door and try to stammer their way in, then slammed the door in their faces and made them try harder. "Do you think a mild-mannered reporter gets people out of prison?" he said. His tactics seem to work. Protess's students talked their way into Hall's tidy living room, and soon she was pouring out a tale that didn't match her courtroom testimony. Patterson had tried to sell her uncle a shotgun, but that was two weeks before the murder. As she would later swear in an affidavit, she claimed that the state's attorney, Jack Hynes, had pressured her into changing the timetable. Afraid of being jailed, she cooperated. "It was like I was reading a script," she said of her testimony. Hynes denies threatening or coaching Hall. He says she would only change her story because of threats from Patterson. But Hall says she's trying to undo a wrong. "I helped send [an] innocent man to jail," she told the students. Protess had been pacing his house for hours when he got their news. "Holy s---!" he yelled into the phone.

Many of Protess's students have come to share his bravado—and few tell their parents where they go on assignment. This term the students visited Patterson's South Side neighborhood, trying to answer the question "If Patterson didn't kill the Sanchezes, who did?" They read an affidavit obtained by Patterson's lawyers claiming that a neighborhood troublemaker, Willie Washington, had proposed robbing the Sanchezes before their murder—and discovered that Washington had been convicted in 1994 of stabbing a woman two dozen times during a burglary similar to the Sanchez case. Further digging revealed that a neighborhood man, Charlie Tillery, said he had seen Washington with a stash of guns soon after the murders. The students, working in groups of two or three, began "to stalk Charlie," says Marshall, who drove a dozen times to the neighborhood. Chicago police warn that these trips are terribly dangerous, but Medill's dean says he is comfortable with Protess's precautions: he coaches kids on how to assess the risk, spot gang colors and steer clear of the toughest housing projects. In fact the students were more frustrated than frightened. For months, they camped outside Tillery's house on a street known for drive-by shootings and drug deals. On a good day they'd tail Tillery to the liquor store and grab a few minutes of conversation—once even getting him to admit on tape that he bought a gun from Washington shortly after the murders. On a bad day, Tillery's girlfriend would come out and yell: "Get out of here, white people!"

Protess tells his class to stay objective, but they all get personally involved. His desk is cluttered with photos of himself with the men he has freed. He spent this past Valentine's Day with Porter, who was having personal problems after release from prison. At one point, the professor discovered that his own preteen son was staying home on Saturday nights to take collect calls from a lonely death-row prisoner. Protess's students often repeat his seminar for no credit, work 30-hour weeks and weekends and sometimes see the class dissolve into tears of disappointment and recriminations over tactics. "Not a day goes by that I don't think about the case," Graser says. "It haunts me." After one condemned man they were trying to exonerate lost his appeal and was executed in 1995, Protess called in a grief counselor for the devastated students. Northwestern has considered pulling the plug on the course. "He has all the plusses and all the problems of a religious martyr," says the former dean, Michael Janeway. Protess, who got his start as a better-government watchdog, found that changing one life was a bigger "rush."

Team Patterson graduates in June. Willie Washington continues to insist to the students that he knows nothing about the Sanchez murders. Patterson's lawyers hope to convince the court that their client deserves another hearing because of the new evidence and shoddy representation. (Patterson cycled through eight public defenders at trial; a commercial litigator with no criminal-law background handled his appeal.) As for Protess, he'll help launch the new Center for Wrongful Convictions and the Death Penalty this fall at Northwestern, and will keep probing Patterson's case and others. In the meantime, Aaron Patterson remains on death row. "With Protess on my case, I've got some credibility," he says. He firmly believes that the next time he's shouting in a courtroom, it will be for joy.

PRINCIPLES OF GOOD PRACTICE

The student work in David Protess's Journalism class is dramatic, laudable, and truly remarkable. Yet the principles upon which the assignments are based are not remarkable, nor are they unfamiliar to faculty. Designing good, community-based assignments requires faculty to reflect purposefully upon four basic principles:

1) **Engagement**—Does the service component meet a public good? How do you know this? Has the community been consulted? How? How have campus-community boundaries been negotiated and how will they be crossed?

2) **Reflection**—Is there a mechanism that encourages students to link their service experience to course content and to reflect upon why the service is important?

3) **Reciprocity**—Is reciprocity evident in the service component? How? "Reciprocity suggests that every individual, organization, and entity involved in the service-learning functions as both a teacher and a learner. Participants are perceived as colleagues, not as servers and clients." (Jacoby, 1996 p. 36)

4) **Public Dissemination**—Is service work presented to the public or made an opportunity for the community to enter into a public dialogue? For example: Do oral histories students collect return to the community in some public form? Is the data students collect on the saturation of toxins in the local river made public? How? To whose advantage?

In the remainder of this section we present a range of service assignments we have edited and synthesized from syllabi. Although the editing process did not allow us to present the full scope of the project, we have attempted to convey assignments that represent a range of disciplines as well as those we found innovative, comprehensive, and effective.

The assignments are sorted into 9 categories: 6 models of service-learning and 4 additional categories. While some assignments fit a number of categories, we tried to place them in the categories that best described their intent. Pure Service-Learning, Discipline-Based Service-Learning, Problem-Based Service-Learning, Capstone and Portfolio Service-Learning, Service-Learning Internships, Undergraduate Community-Based Action Research, Service as optional or as extra credit, Organizational Behavior, Multidisciplinary Projects, and Reflection-Focused Service-Learning.

SAMPLE SERVICE-LEARNING ASSIGNMENTS

"Service assignments can be points of connection, as Robert Coles reminds us in his book *The Call of Service,* between self and other, moral moments in teaching and learning that yield, Coles says, 'an awareness of the moral complexity that informs the choices we consciously make, as well as those we unwittingly make…[A]ll service is directly or indirectly ethical activity, a reply to a moral call within, one that answers a moral need in the world.'" (David Cooper and Laura Julier Writing and the Arts of Public Discourse: The Service-Learning Writing Project at Michigan State University).

Pure Service-Learning

PROVIDENCE COLLEGE, KEITH MORTON
PSP 301 Community Service in American Culture

Service component: Students develop and implement a plan for rehabilitating a house. Students form part of one of the following work groups: design and construction, fundraising, communication, worker recruitment and coordination, strategy and policy, and documentary and history.

Related assignments: Students complete a final paper or project in which they explore in depth how they understand the work they've done and whether this work constitutes a service to the community or how the class can best serve the Smith Hill community.

UNIVERSITY OF MARYLAND-COLLEGE PARK, LACRETIA JOHNSON
CPSP 259, General Service-Learning in College Park Scholars

Service component: Students are required to engage in a minimum of 20 hours of documented service with a service agency or organization.

Related assignments: Journals, reading reports, and a final report synthesizing the service experience.

CALIFORNIA STATE UNIVERSITY-MONTEREY BAY, HENRIK KIBAK AND DARCIE WARDEN
ESSP/SL 200, Introduction to Service in Multicultural Communities
Section 4: Disease and the Environment

Service Component: Students will complete 30 hours of service at a community health organization working to prevent communicable diseases.

Related Assignment: Journal assignments and a final presentation.

NEW ENGLAND COLLEGE, LARRY TAYLOR AND DEBRA NITSCHKE-SHAW
HR 399 Service -Learning Honors Seminar

Service component: Students must complete a site guide for a select agency or a complete a site guide for a minimum of two service-learning projects offered or proposed at New England College. In teams, students select two schools/agencies to work closely with and identify needs that can be met by the College community.

Related assignments: Students must complete a description of the school or agency; Identify available resources; develop a plan to meet identified needs; and identify the training and supervision needs.

Discipline-Based Service-Learning

The examples in this category use a specific disciplinary construct from which students examine a community need. The assignments are generally focused on the service experience as opposed to completing a project. The best of these have an impact that extends far beyond the classroom. For example, the assignments in David Protess's Investigative Journalism and Special Topics in Journalism: The News Media and Capital Punishment, allow for the possibility of immediate and powerful social action on the part of the students.

ART, SOUTHWEST MISSOURI STATE UNIVERSITY
Debra McDowell, Draping

The service component of the course seeks to acquaint student with body measurement specifications, problem solving and the needs of disabled population

Service component: Students complete 40 hours of service assisting physically impaired individuals in a variety of tasks (reading, writing letters or other agreed upon tasks.

Related assignments: Students maintain weekly reflective journals and activity logs. Students must make a final presentation of an apparel or accessory product designed for their client. (The client will be in class to contribute to the discussion of the feasibility of the use of the product.)

COMPOSITION, SYRACUSE UNIVERSITY
Eileen Schell, Writing and Learning in the Community

Service Component: Students must complete 20 hours of service. The service placement is facilitated by the campus center for public and community service. The Center assists students in finding a suitable placement, allowing them to choose from a list of nonprofit organizations and agencies.

Related assignments:

Project Portfolio #1—Setting your Action Agenda and Learning Goals. Find out about the organization and the responsibilities of the volunteer. Establish 4 or 5 learning goals, including at least one writing goal.

Project Portfolio #2—Writing about your Service Site/Service Experiences. Write about some aspect of service site or a significant incident. Should include interviews of site coordinator(s) and/or other volunteer(s).

Project Portfolio #3—Analyzing/arguing about community issues. Address a problem and the changes—economic, structural, social attitudes—that must take place in order to solve it. Must consult other sources to gain other perspectives on the issue.

The first project portfolio is not assigned until the fifth week of class, allowing the students time to complete readings, write reader responses and visit their community site before embarking on this first project.

COMPOSITION, MILLIKIN UNIVERSITY
Nancy DeJoy, Critical Reading, Writing and Researching

This course is designed to assist students in formulating new understandings of our cultural and personal histories of literacy.

Service component: Students tutor in local GED prep class.

Related assignments: Students write a short paper modeled on one of the GED students' assignments.

COMPOSITION, CALIFORNIA STATE UNIVERSITY-MONTEREY BAY
Frances Payne Adler, Witnessing Welfare

Service component: Students partner with Monterey Peninsula College's Cooperative Agencies Resources for Education (CARE) and students enrolled in the Extended Opportunity Programs and Services (EOPS) to produce a web page and CD-ROM which builds upon the previous year's book, Education As Emancipation: Women On Welfare Speak Out.

Related assignments: One poem/story and visual about the student's community partner's experience with welfare reform; writing (facilitated by student) by the community partner; a second poem/story about the community partner or one reflection of student's experience

Other assignments: research paper that examines one aspect of welfare reform; creation of one web site for a web page with a written introduction; visuals to accompany writings; a journal, and a web page and CD-ROM.

EDUCATION, CALIFORNIA STATE UNIVERSITY-MONTEREY BAY
Terri Wheeler, Multicultural Children's Literature

Service component: Students are required to complete 25 hours of community service in an organized storytelling or reading group in a local school.

Related assignments: Students must complete a reflection paper on the role of multicultural children's literature in liberation pedagogy and its connection with the student's personal goals.

Other course assignments: Students research children's literatures from diverse cultures while reflecting upon their own literacy development, by researching and recounting "literary gems" —stories, rhymes, songs and anecdotes from their own families.

ENVIRONMENTAL SCIENCE, CALIFORNIA STATE UNIVERSITY-MONTEREY BAY
Laura Lee Lienk, Watershed Restoration in the Schools and Community

Service component and related assignments: This course asks students to share the relevance and importance of their environmental science knowledge with culturally, linguistically, technologically, and economically diverse populations. Assignments involve implementing projects or teaching course-related topics at local schools: landscaping a native plant garden, designing a nature trail, or coordinating an Earth Day event.

ENVIRONMENTAL SCIENCE, ALLEGHENY COLLEGE
Eric Pallant, ES 589 Environmental Science: Sustainable Solutions

Service component: Students work in teams as a consulting group to the Center for Economic and Environmental Development at Allegheny College (CEED). CEED's mission is to increase the understanding of community and regional leaders for economic and environmental decisions. CEED has identified nine environmental areas students can investigate to develop projects in cooperation with community stakeholders.

HISTORY, SACRED HEART COLLEGE
John Roney, Medieval Europe

The course examines the medieval world focusing on the notion that each person had a fixed place in society and entered that role through birth. This "calling" assumed that each had a duty to live in society in a certain way.

Service component: Students may choose a service learning option in lieu of paper. The service places students as tutors to sixth grade children in nearby schools. Students present units on the medieval world and assist children with reading skills.

Related assignments: Students must produce a 15-page paper detailing their service learning activities and experiences.

JOURNALISM, NORTHWESTERN UNIVERSITY
David Protess, Investigative Journalism and Special Topics in Journalism: The News Media and Capital Punishment

Service component and related assignments: Students create a historical profile of someone who appears to be wrongly convicted and condemned to die. Students create a case analysis of a prisoner, assessing his guilt or innocence and describing the reporting necessary to publish or broadcast a story about the case.

LINGUISTICS, UNIVERSITY OF PENNSYLVANIA
William Labov, Linguistics 470/English 260 Advanced Topics in Narrative

Service component and related assignments: After examining literary narratives, including Scandinavian, Greek and Hebrew epics, medieval romances, and modern novels, with attention to differences between vernacular, literary and academic style, students will write a narrative for the teaching of reading to African American children in 2nd to 4th grades. The narratives should motivate children to read, and are to be developed in four cultural frameworks: hip-hop, traditional Southern, African-centered and Inspirational Gospel.

LIBERAL ARTS ELECTIVE, BROWN UNIVERSITY
Ellen Messer, World Hunger, Human Rights to Food and Freedom from Hunger

Service component: the course asks students to choose "a public service activity that will bring her/him personally in contact with the hungry."

Related assignments: The course objectives ask students to analyze the political and economical concerns of producing and distributing food, the sociocultural issues of defining who has membership in the community and what constitutes food, and how that complicates the questions of basic rights. Students are asked to reflect on their service as they construct three papers that address policies in the US and other countries regarding access to food.

MUSIC, UNIVERSITY OF UTAH
Bonnie Gritton, The Pianist in the Community: Career Development and Volunteerism

This class seeks to explore career development in music and the role of the arts (and the artist) in community and public service. The course focuses on professional skill preparation e.g., researching and describing all available job markets, preparing a professional vita, developing press kits, and exploring fund-raising techniques.

Service component: Students work at local schools teaching weekly music lessons to children, preparing children for recitals, and coordinating monthly recitals.

Related assignments: Students keep a weekly journal describing musical goals achieved at lessons and the influence of music on child's self discipline, sociality and self-esteem.

SOCIOLOGY, GEORGETOWN UNIVERSITY
Sam Marullo, Social Movements

The course seeks to assist students in becoming knowledgeable of a particular social movement and a particular social movement organization (SMO).

Service component: Students volunteer 3–5 hours a week at an SMO.

Related assignments: Students write a fundraising letter to raise money for their SMO and an advocacy piece, (a letter to the editor, congressional representative, or other institutional elite) designed to educate that person or the public on a particular issue about their movement.

Other course assignments: Students complete a monograph or an extensive report on a particular social movement; write a comparative paper that addresses a question about one aspect of all of the movements and present that paper; and write a final paper describing their SMO.

Problem-Based Service-Learning

Problem-based service courses presume that students bring specific disciplinary knowledge to bear on a problem, thereby increasing the potential value of the service to the community. The advantage of the problem-based approach to service-learning is that it provides highly structured learning opportunities for students, often in a series of steps that move students toward developing a specific set of skills. Johanna Poethig and Ryan Sloan's Large-Scale Digital Mural Art course for instance, asks that students complete a number of individual web assignments before embarking on the community-based group project. Likewise, D. Bloswick's Ergonomics course asks that students complete a number of assignments that are progressively more involved, each building on the skills mastered in the previous assignments. The advantage to the community is the opportunity to access sophisticated student work that is of potentially great value.

ARCHITECTURE, UNIVERSITY OF MICHIGAN
Margaret DeWar, Integrative Field Experience

Service component: This course asks students to work on community planning teams on one of three projects, with three community partners: the Gratiot Woods Neighborhood, Southwest Detroit Business Association, or Eastside Industrial Council. For example students may chose to work with housing initiatives in Gratiot Woods to address identified community needs in the areas of traffic control, assessing commercial development opportunities or developing a plan for the passing of infill housing development and housing rehabilitation.

Related assignments: Students are required to make presentations to the community partners and participate in class "rehearsals" prior to the meeting and "debriefings" after the meetings.

ARCHITECTURE, UNIVERSITY OF UTAH
Kazuo Matsubayashi and Roger Borgenicht, Architecture 602

Service component: Students work with ASSIST, an independent, nonprofit Community Design Center that provides services to nonprofit and community groups as well as low income households or persons with disabilities. Students may participate in one of the following projects: Emergency Home Repair, Architectural and Accessibility Design Assistance, Community Planning and Development Assistance, Community Education and Advocacy.

Related assignments: Weekly reviews of phases of the service project, two preliminary design reviews and a final presentation/report.

ART, CALIFORNIA STATE UNIVERSITY, MONTEREY BAY
Johanna Poethig and Ryan Sloan, VPA 306S Large-Scale Digital MURAL

In this course student's research public art, collect images, relevant readings and materials pertaining to public art in the community to assist them as they develop a digital mural/public art project.

Service component: After completing several digital images students create one large final, digital work that seeks to inform the public about a relevant issue or community concern.

Related assignments: Students must visit community sites and interview appropriate community members. Students must work together to organize their collected resources.

CHEMISTRY, TRINITY COLLEGE
David Henderson, Environmental Chemistry

Service component: Students serve throughout the semester in a local business, agency or organization on a project related to a relevant environmental topic.

Related Assignments: Students also participate in a media project working in select teams on specific environmental topics. Students research the manner in which the topic is presented in the media, and the gravity of the environmental issue to local communities.

COMMUNICATION, UNIVERSITY OF UTAH
Michael Holmes, Communication in Organizations

Service component: All students complete a communication needs assessment for a local organization involved in disaster response and emergency management.

Related assignments: Field Progress reports, and exams.

COMMUNICATION, ROCKFORD COLLEGE
Rufus Cadigan, Communication 210: Basic Forms of Oral Communication

This course is designed to assist students in developing effective communication skills fundamental to small group discussion, interviewing, oral interpretation, story telling and public speaking.

Service component: Students will research initiatives for graffiti abatement and present their findings to representatives from the city of Rockford Illinois.

Related assignments: A logbook accounting for time spent on specific activities, a reflection journal and a reflection paper.

COMMUNICATION, NEW YORK UNIVERSITY
Lynne McVeigh, Children's Television Production Workshop

Service component: Students work with a youth group to produce media for young people.

Related assignments: Students will develop public service announcements for the Fearless Theater Company, a community children's theatre. The PSA's will be part of "Count Me In!" a national advertising campaign designed to raise consciousness about access – the needs of people with disabilities to be provided with all the services and benefits of community life.

HEALTH SCIENCES, BROWN UNIVERSITY
Sally Zieler, Health of Women

This class uses a "service-based" curriculum, with an objective of involving students in public health activism.

Service component: Working in small groups, students identify, evaluate and summarize scientific research on a specific topic pertaining to the health of women with a goal of moving this knowledge to forms useful for private and pubic action.

Related assignments: Students will write about what is known and not known about a particular health or disease experience for a readership that includes social and political advocates for health of women, local and federal politicians, and women wanting information for themselves. In partnership with the National Women's Health Network (NWHN), the class will produce reports on up to 8 specific topics.

4 projects: 1) Domestic violence prevention, working with Dorcas Place and the Women's Center of RI, 2) Accessing alternative childbirth resources, 3) HIV and women, 4) incarcerated women, providing services in the women's prison at the ACI.

Questions to address in research: (syllabus includes a paragraph of questions/guidelines in each area) I. Epidemiology, II. Diagnosis, III. Treatment, IV gendered experiences, V. Policy recommendations.

Two 1-2 page written responses to readings.

Group statement—A statement of the group project, including names, phone numbers and email addresses of group members, name of group organizer, name of project, schedule of submission of written drafts for each section, statement of how the group will meet these goals. All projects are submitted to the National Women's Health Network.

COMPUTER SCIENCE, SYRACUSE UNIVERSITY
Ruth Small, IST 662, Instructional Strategies and Techniques for Information Professionals

Service component: Students identify a community organization and develop a training session related to information or technology that can benefit the organization or community constituents.

Related assignments: Four assignments in different areas of instructional strategies and techniques, e.g., a distance learning mini-lesson using the web.

EDUCATION, LASELL COLLEGE
Kerri Heffernan, SOC 304 Sociology of Education

Course examines the sociological factors that are related to education, schooling and school reform.

Service Component: Students are paired with low-income parents enrolled in ABE, GED or ESL course at an urban Head Start facility. The pair work together for 10 weeks designing a series of weekly, family-based literacy activities that seek to reinforce particular, age appropriate literacy concepts for the parents child (children). The parent-student teams utilize different children's book each week to guide the activity. In the first five weeks the student and parent present the material together to small groups of children (including the parents child or children). After 5 weeks the student must gradually remove herself from the reading activity group, transferring leadership for the group to the parent. Students and parents are required to organize and coordinate a large family literacy celebration at the end of the 10 weeks to showcase and celebrate the children's and parents work.

Related assignments: Students must complete three papers that tie the course reading into the service experience (the first paper and the third are read and evaluated by the community partner and the instructor). Students must also complete a group "resource project" for the agency – a collection of the best projects from the 10 weeks of books (projects are voted on by the parents and the students).

ENGINEERING, UNIVERSITY OF UTAH
D. Bloswick, Mechanical Engineering, Ergonomics

Service Component: Students work on nine diverse ergonomic projects designed to assist an elderly population in the local community. Projects include designing: a folding/portable ramp or system to allow a person in a wheelchair to access a van, a device to help a person in a wheelchair to move from the wheelchair to a standing or semi-standing position, a device to hold a book or a newspaper for an individual with poor hand function, a stair climb assist device and a device or system to allow a user with weak hands to insert and remove plugs from the wall and/or connect a plug to an extension cord. Other projects include analyses of: patient handling in burn unit at University of Utah hospital, lifting hazards in the sterilization unit at hospital, and lifting hazards for nursing personnel in local nursing home.

Related assignments: Five quizzes, one exam and project report and a project presentation.

ENVIRONMENTAL SCIENCE, CONNECTICUT COLLEGE
Douglas Thompson, Environmental Studies/Geophysics, River Hydrology and Hydraulics

Service component: Students develop a restoration design for a channel on the Connecticut College campus in hopes of addressing a community erosion problem.

Related assignments: Students will present their findings to local community representatives from the local wetlands commission, a fisheries biologist, a civil engineering consultant, and college representatives.

HEALTH SCIENCES, UNIVERSITY OF MONTANA
Cindy Garthwait, Explorations in Gerontology

Service component: All students design a research instrument for nursing home residents. This instrument will be administered to the residents and the results will be compiled into a written product that can be used by anyone wishing to learn to be supportive of older persons as they face the challenges of nursing home placement.

Related assignments: Reflective journals, two papers that compare the service experience to course readings.

HEALTH SCIENCES, CALIFORNIA STATE UNIVERSITY, NORTHRIDGE
Vicki Ebin, Community Health Education

Service component: Students work in small groups designing a health education program for a specified target group to address a specific health concern.

Related assignments: The course requires students to complete two papers one on Community analysis, diagnosis, program focus, and a Health Education Action Plan.

PHYSICAL EDUCATION, SPRINGFIELD COLLEGE
Anne Rothschadl, RLSR 335, Recreation Programming

Service component: All students plan, implement and evaluate a recreational program with a community agency.

Related assignments: Students present an in-service to the class, complete an assessment of the community agency in which they worked.

PHYSICAL EDUCATION, CLEMSON UNIVERSITY
Claussen Swynn Powell, PRTM 305, Safety/Risk Management/Sport Law

Service component: Students work with an agency to complete a risk management assessment and develop a risk management handbook. Students work in small groups of 3–4, and various groups work within the same agency. Each group will be responsible for a different segment of the risk management process.

Related assignments: Projects may include designing a detailed map and site assessment, creating a staff training presentation video, writing a human resources policy and procedures manual, creating appropriate accident/incident reports, designing a relevant programming plan and a useable transportation plan, and writing press releases, public service announcements or newsletter articles about the agency.

URBAN STUDIES, COLORADO UNIVERSITY
Phil Emmi, Planning for Metropolitan Regions

Service component: Students design a multimedia map of the urban wilderness in conjunction with Future Moves, a local civic organization advocating balanced approaches to transportation and land use.

Related assignments: Students develop community design concepts to improve relationships within the urban fabric, including transit-oriented developments, pedestrian pockets, traffic-reduced commercial zones and mixed-use urban activity centers.

Capstone and Portfolio Service-Learning

These assignments ask students to create materials that demonstrate the analysis, synthesis, and intersection of course work and service. Portfolios can work particularly well in problem-based service-learning courses, as the students are often asked to document a series of steps in solving a problem or in completing a project. Because students are focusing on a single project throughout the semester, all assignments in the portfolio are related, and the faculty member can chart students' learning progression. Portfolios can also be particularly useful when the service assignment is completed in groups or teams. The portfolio allows each student to demonstrate how s/he has individually contributed to the project and how the contribution fits into the group effort as a whole.

Likewise, portfolios used in capstone courses allow students to synthesize career goals and academics. As many of the assignments in capstone courses take place outside the classroom, the portfolio is an effective way for students to document their learning and to integrate class/group discussions with their service experiences.

Capstone

ENVIRONMENTAL SCIENCE
Eric Pallant, ES 588 Junior Seminar in Environmental Solutions

Service component: Students design a feasibility study for bringing an aquaponics facility to Meadville, PA.

Related assignments: Weekly report on research and comp proposal.

SERVICE LEARNING
Rick Battistoni and John Saltmarsh
PSP 450 Capstone Seminar in Public and Community Service: Developing Lives of Commitment, Forming a Community Service Identity (Two semester course)

Service component: Students work with a community partner or agency to design a project that meets an identifiable community need. At the end of the year, students make a presentation on the process of the collaboration and outcomes of the project.

Students also evaluate applications from local high school service learning programs seeking modest service grants given by the college. Students serve as consultants to those schools that are funded.

Related assignments: Students are responsible for identifying topics in conjunction with their service project and facilitating readings and discussions on the topic(s).

WOMEN'S STUDIES, PORTLAND STATE UNIVERSITY
Melissa Kesler Gilbert, Capstone Course: Women's Community Education Project

Students work with a community partner (a local nonprofit feminist bookstore). Students coordinate a series of rap sessions with local teen girls about current issues in their lives and encourage the girls to participate in the ZINE project—where girls write, edit and publish a grassroots, mini-magazine.

Service component: Students are assigned "primary and secondary community tasks." The primary task is coordinating the rap sessions and publishing of the Teen Zine. The secondary task is negotiated with the community partner and should reflect a specific interest the student has related to teen girls or the feminist bookstore.

Portfolio assignment: Students must complete a portfolio.

Related assignments: Reflective journals.

Portfolio

COMPUTER SCIENCE, SAN FRANCISCO STATE UNIVERSITY
Kristen Gates, Web Site Design and Management

Service component: Students design and build fully functioning websites for a Bay Area non-profit organizations.

Portfolio assignment: Students complete a Project Book which includes notes, flowcharts, storyboards, design docs, etc. for Individual and Team projects. These Individual and Team projects include individual web design assignments and a Team Project Report on producing the website.

HOTEL AND TRAVEL, OHIO UNIVERSITY
Christina Beck, Meeting and Conference Planning

Service component: Students organize a workshop on small group communication for 5th and 6th grade students at local schools and related curricular materials for teachers.

Portfolio assignment: Students must submit a portfolio with a preliminary and revised timeline, agendas, minutes, 2 progress reports, their midterm reflection paper, the final group report, the resource packet they prepare for their small group's workshop, and their final reflection paper. The portfolio requirements include supporting material and documentation—email interactions, internal memos; resources form other teams, reference and contact lists, etc. Students are also graded on the organization and professionalism of the portfolio.

RELIGION, EMORY UNIVERSITY
Bobbi Patterson, Violence Studies Internship Transformation and Agents of Change

Service component: Students work in local agencies or organizations committed to investigating or addressing violence (e.g., juvenile courts, battered women's shelters, the Georgia Bureau of Investigation, homeless resource center, the Atlanta Food Bank, the Southern Center for Human Rights). Students serve two hours in the community for one hour of course credit with a maximum of 12 hours of course credit.

Portfolio assignment: Student portfolios are divided into a working portfolio and a presentation portfolio. While the working portfolio contains ongoing reflective work, the presenting portfolio represents a culmination of all work and should be organized in a rational analytical or reflective scheme.

Service-Learning Internships

SERVICE-LEARNING, PROVIDENCE COLLEGE
Rick Battistoni and Dana Farrell Feinstein, PSP 401 and 402 Public Service Practicum

Service component: A large portion of the academic component of the Practicum consists of the knowledge student's gain through their role as Community Assistants working in specific community agencies and organizations. Throughout the year, students will use their role to learn as much as they can about the community organization, both for their own development as public and community service studies students and to enhance resources for their classmates (Providence College/Feinstein Center students who work at their community sites).

Related assignments: Students participate in action research, examining the mission statement, goals, objectives and history of the agency; its "organizational chart," staff structure, and budget; and an organization stakeholder and issue analysis. Students must also complete a grant application for the agency, applying for funds through the Feinstein Institute Community Grant to initiate a program or activity at the site, which will be implemented and evaluated later in the semester. Students may also participate in the COOL Conference. Those interested in pursuing this option must submit a workshop proposal to the annual Campus Outreach Opportunity League National Conference on Student Service.

Undergraduate Community-Based Action Research

ANTHROPOLOGY, CALVIN COLLEGE
Bert de Vries, IDIS 240 Introduction to Archaeology

This course introduces students to the Calvin Garbage Project. The primary assignment requires students to work in teams of two assigned a specific task contributing to a large, class field report assessing garbage produced by the Calvin College community.

Service component: Students are asked to research and assess the waste produced by the college community and to provide data for improving disposal, recycling and composting procedures. Students work with the Calvin Environmental Awareness Program.

Related assignments: Team reports, two exams, field work report and class presentation.

ECONOMICS, LEHIGH UNIVERSITY
Thomas Hyclak and Todd Watkins, Regional Economic Development Practicum

Service component: Students choose one of 7 community projects within a particular agency, e.g., identifying transportation barriers to successful welfare to work transitions. Students work with the Council on Hispanic Organizations to improve the public transportation options for inner-city residents.

Related assignments: Student responsibilities include documenting the extent to which women living in the inner city of Allentown are limited in their search for employment by the current configuration of bus routes. The study team meets with LANTA planners to identify ways in which routes could be changed or new services developed to enhance the possibility of successful transitions from welfare to work.

ENGINEERING, UNIVERSITY OF UTAH
Peter Martin, Civil Engineering, Traffic Flow Theory

Service component: Students complete an extensive analysis of speed limit violations in a local neighborhood and design traffic solutions to address the problem. Students present their work to the community and the County in public meetings, and get feedback on improving their projects.

LINGUISTICS, UNIVERSITY OF PENNSYLVANIA
William Labov, Linguistics 160/African American 160

Students investigate the use and structure of African American Vernacular English and apply this linguistic knowledge to the task of teaching African American children to read at the Wilson School.

Service component: Students develop methods for teaching reading building on home language and interests of African-American children. Students gather information by either observing children on the playground or tutoring small groups of children in the classroom.

Related assignments: The class will also produce a "Dictionary of Every-Day Words," which will define words found in daily speech and in hip-hop lyrics that the children believe the teacher does not know.

Service as optional or as an additional course credit

A number of courses allow students to choose a service option. These options are usually presented in one of the following formats:

- *A fourth credit option:* Students receive an additional (fourth) credit for participating in a service experience and completing additional assignments related to that experience.

- *Enrolling in a related "internship" or "service" track:* This option is similar to the fourth credit option. However, students participate in additional class time, and may be required to work with multiple instructors.

- *A different set of assignments:* Students do not receive any additional credits for participating in service-learning; rather, their service experience and related assignments are in lieu of another assignment(s).

A fourth credit option

THEATRE, GEORGETOWN UNIVERSITY
Carol Day, AMTH 073 Improvisation for Social Change

Students are encouraged to add a one-credit service component for the class. The service option places students in an agency or organization working directly with individuals in the community affected by many of the issues and topics discussed in class (HIV, alcoholism, domestic violence, poverty and/or disease). Assignments include preparing and performing an activating improv around a social problem, empty chair monologues, and a final exam.

WOMEN'S STUDIES, GEORGETOWN UNIVERSITY
C. Margaret Hall, Seminar: Internship, Women and Politics

In this fourth-credit option students can opt to spend an additional three hours a week at their internship site 12 hours a week as opposed to nine hours a week) and complete an additional short writing assignment.

Enrolling in a related "internship" or "service" track

COMPUTER SCIENCE, SAN FRANCISCO STATE UNIVERSITY
Gerald Eisman, CSC 301 Fundamentals of Computer Science

Students may chose multiple service options in this course. Students who participate in 8 tutoring sessions with elementary school children may drop their lowest midterm score; students who tutor may substitute a one short reflection paper for a larger ethics assignment; or students who participate in 12 tutoring sessions and complete the larger reflection assignment may obtain one credit enrolling in AU 280, Community Service Learning.

COMPUTER SCIENCE, SOUTHWEST MISSOURI STATE UNIVERSITY
Richard Martin, CSC 450 Computer Programming and Peter Sanderson, CSC 300

Students in CSC 450 may avail themselves of a service option by enrolling in CSC 300. In CSC 300, students volunteer 40 hours of their time working individually and in groups to develop software or computer system consulting services for a nonprofit or social service organization. Students apply the knowledge gained in CSC 450 to the community project in CSC 300, while the courses are linked students receive separate grades for each course.

WRITING, ARIZONA STATE UNIVERSITY
Jan Kelly, Eng 217 Personal and Exploratory Writing

Every student participates in service-learning in this course, but students may elect to earn an additional three credits by enrolling in a Service-Learning Internship, English 484. The internship option requires students to spend 6 hours a week in a tutoring program, (this is in addition to the required 10 hours a week of tutoring required for English 217.

A different set of assignments

In many courses where service-learning is optional, students may choose between assignments that require service-learning and assignments that do not. Most of the assignments on these syllabi reflect the attempt to balance learning objectives and the effort required from students to do an adequate job in the placement.

ANTHROPOLOGY, DUKE UNIVERSITY
Katherine Ewing, Cultural Anthropology 141/Psychology 113A.

The optional service-learning component of the course refers students in Duke's LEAPS program. (The LEAPS Program is described as a student organization founded to "empower students to be leaders, responsible citizens and agents of positive social change." One of LEAPS functions is to work closely with the coordinator for Service-Learning to assist students in placement sites.) Students may chose from a range of direct service opportunities (working in a halfway house for AIDS patients, working at an inpatient unit of a psychiatric hospital, tutoring children, or working in an organization that serves migrant farm workers. Students must serve 20 hours in the community during the semester and attend approximately 5 reflection sessions (one every other week). Students may use their field notes or a report of their service experience in lieu of a paper.

COMMUNICATION
Craig Denton, Photojournalism

Students explore and narrate one story with social action at its core, with street corner photos, a street corner journal, news photos with captions, a mounted photo story or essay with captions, and a slide story or essay with script. Service Component: Students who participate in the service learning option may work for a social service agency and develop a library of images that the agency can use to tell its story in a variety of print media.

COMPUTER SCIENCE, SOUTHWEST MISSOURI STATE UNIVERSITY
Peter Sanderson, CSC 300

Service Component: The course offers an optional credit in which students provide software development or computer system consulting service for a nonprofit or social service organization.

EDUCATION, UNIVERSITY OF PENNSYLVANIA
Paul Skilton-Sylvester, Ed./Urban Studies 240, Education in the Culture of the United States

Students have the option of doing fieldwork with one of three specific educational programs. Students who chose the "fieldwork" option must complete a journal, and can either complete a final exam or give a final presentation. Those choosing this option are not required to complete 4 reaction papers, or a "deeper look" (longer) paper, and may chose a presentation in lieu of the final exam.

MATHEMATICS, CALVIN COLLEGE
Gary Talsma, Math 222

Students are placed in tutoring programs through the Service-Learning Center. Students may substitute a service-learning option (including a "volunteer log") for 2 of the last 3 projects required in the course. The service options require students to spend at least 10 yours tutoring. (Student tutors become eligible to participate in a Math-in Action conference at no charge).

WOMEN'S STUDIES/PUBLIC POLICY, DUKE UNIVERSITY
Kathy Rudy, WST/PPS 108, AIDS Ethics and Policy

Students have the option of completing 20 hours of service through the LEAPS program and attend four, one-hour reflection sessions. Students who successfully complete the service option will receive an A for this work and be excused form completing one position paper.\

POLITICAL SCIENCE, SAN FRANCISCO STATE UNIVERSITY
Brigitte Davila, La Raza Studies 276 US Government and Constitution

Students have the option of participating in the Internship and Fieldnotes option instead of the Written project, (a 20–25 page research paper). Students in the Internship work 35 hours with an organization that advocates on behalf of issues that affect Latinos as a political constituency. Students choosing the service internship must complete a journal.

PSYCHOLOGY, INDIANA UNIVERSITY-EAST
Randall Osborne, P 425, Emotional and Behavioral Disorders of Childhood and Adolescence

Students may chose a 10-hour service option working in an assigned agency throughout the semester on suggested projects. Students must also do a research project in conjunction with the service placement, focusing on a specific problem or population that the agency serves. (The papers must be turned into the agency as well as Dr. Osborne)

Students who do not chose the service option face a rigorous series of exams, papers and quizzes.

RELIGION, WHEATON COLLEGE
Barbara Darling-Smith, REL 242 Religion and Ecology

Students may chose a service-learning option, volunteering 3 hours a week for 10 weeks at the Crystal Spring Center for Ecology. Students must write a weekly report on their service assignment and a reflection paper analyzing the service experience. The service option accounts for 30% of the students course grade.

SOCIOLOGY, MESSIAH COLLEGE
John Eby, SOC 101, Principles of Sociology

Students may chose a service-learning option in lieu of writing two, 5-page policy position papers. The service option requires students to complete 21 hours of service (coordinated through the Campus Volunteer Service Center and a course assistant). In addition students must maintain service journals, participate in reflective discussions and complete a summary reflection paper.

REFLECTION FOCUSED SERVICE-LEARNING

Journaling is perhaps the most common method for reflection, although there are many kinds of assignments that require students to reflect on their service experience and its relationship to course content. Perhaps the most effective journal assignments are those that ask students to address specific questions related to the service experience and the course material.

CHEMISTRY, TRINITY COLLEGE
David Henderson, Environmental Chemistry

Service component: Student volunteers 25–40 hours during the semester at a local business, government agency, or other appropriate organization on a project related to some environmental issue.

Reflection assignments: The reflection assignments in this course require students to approach their "double entry" journals, one that addresses the Community Service Project, and one that responds to the Environmental Chemistry in the Media Project, in which teams of students select an environmental topic and research the way this topic is presented in the media. The left side of the journal is a log of time spent and details student work and specific activities, while the right side is used to record observations, reflect on activities and readings, and record questions for class discussion. In addition to these two journals, however, the students must also prepare Review and Reflection papers, summaries of articles related to a particular week's topic or problem, as well as final reports for both the Service Project and the Media Project.

Additional assignments: Students are also evaluated in traditional methods of exams, quizzes, lab practicals and homework.

ENGLISH, CONNECTICUT COLLEGE
Claire Gaudiani, Literature, Service and Social Reflection

This course seeks to connect reading and analysis of literature to the experiences of the author and subjects of the literature. Through service students are asked to reflect on the connection between the life of the mind and the daily experiences of people. In addition to reading the prescribed literary texts students are asked to read a daily major newspaper and a monthly newsmagazine.

Service component: Students work 3–4 hours a week in a community agency.

Reflection assignments: Students complete one journal entry each week reflecting on both their service experience and assigned course readings. Students are required to complete 3 papers discussing the text and/or the intersection of service with texts.

ENVIRONMENTAL SCIENCE, CALIFORNIA STATE UNIVERSITY-MONTEREY BAY
Hester Parker, Environmental Justice and Environmental Policy

The course asks students to develop a theory of environmental justice.

Service component: Students complete 30 hours of service at one of eleven possible community agencies. At the Citizen for Alternative Water Solutions, for example, students would help plan and publicize community meetings, provide computer assistance, or prepare research on decommissioned dams.

Reflection assignments: Students complete a "Solutions For Environmental Injustice" essay and nine thought pieces—one page personal reflections or responses to readings or speakers in which students analyze and reflect upon their service work to theorize what they're doing.

HEALTH SCIENCES, UNIVERSITY OF MONTANTA
Cindy Garthwait, Explorations in Gerontology

This course seeks to increase students' knowledge and understanding of developmental theories and processes of older adulthood.

Service component: Students volunteer at the Village Health Care Center.

Reflection assignments: Students design a research instrument that will explore the tenets of positive aging in a nursing home environment. The results will be compiled into a useable and attractive written document that can be utilized by anyone wishing to learn how to be supportive of older persons as they face the challenges of nursing home placement. In addition, students complete a reflective journal, in which they address concepts learned/ read/ discussed regarding aging, and reactions to material covered and experiences with their assigned nursing home resident.

Other assignments: Two reaction papers (one to each of the texts)—Tuesdays with Morrie and Living and Dying at Murray Manor.

LAW, IONA COLLEGE
J.L. Yranski Nasuti, Current Issues in Immigration Law

The reflection assignments for this course are grounded in clearly stated course objectives and a detailed description of the major units of instruction. The course asks students to acquire knowledge of the history of US immigration laws, the legal basis and administrative structure of immigration laws, visa requirements, no-entry and deportation processes, refugee and asylum status, and citizenship and naturalization.

Service component: Students participate in a week-long experiential learning trip to Arizona and Mexico. Working with Borderlinks house in Tucson, Arizona, a nonprofit organization concerned with educating people about the problems of life along the US-Mexico border. Students travel to Nogales, Mexico and are hosted by families living in "squatter's villages." Students meet with a range of community residents as well as US and Mexican officials. The course allows students to observe the conditions that illustrate the complexity of immigration and the viability of immigration policy. Upon returning to campus students will do field work with a nonprofit organization concerned with immigrant issues.

Reflection assignments: Students are required to keep two journals, one commenting on their experiences on a class trip to Mexico, focusing on the integration of course readings and specific immigration laws, while the second journal focuses on the service learning project in the US.

LAW, CALIFORNIA POLYTECHNIC
Bernida Reagan Community Law Practice

Service component: Students work at the East Bay Community Law Center, providing legal service to low-income clients.

Reflection assignments: Students respond to course readings and service experience in five short reflection papers. In addition, they must also complete a final paper on one of three topics: (1) analysis of a specific clinical case, (2) analysis of the law practice more generally at EBCLC, or (3) personal and professional development at EBCLC.

ENGLISH, CARNEGIE MELLON UNIVERSITY
Professor(s) Linda Flower, Jennifer Flach and Wayne Peck, Community Literacy and Intercultural Interpretation

Service component: Students mentor at the Community Literacy Center, working with teen writers.

Reflection assignments: Reflection assignments include postings to the electronic bulletin board (B-board portfolio) and a project proposal. Each b-board posting asks students to responds to a different question listed in the syllabus and seeks to connect class readings to student's experiences as a mentor.

PHARMACY, UNIVERSITY OF UTAH
Laura Shange McWhorter, Community Practice

Service component: Students participate in 2 or 3 service activities in different settings, including directing focus groups for the elderly providing specific disease or medication information; participating in flu vaccine clinics providing vaccine and post-care information; distributing food boxes through the Food Bank and conducting nutrition assessments.

Reflection assignments: Students document their service experiences weekly, responding to guidelines or questions in the syllabus and discussing how their service experience will affect their professional practice and what changes could be made to provide a more optimal experience. Students also complete summary reports which synthesize this weekly documentation and discuss outcomes for each setting and activity and their new professional goals. In the final reflection paper students must describe and critique the organizations with which they have worked and discuss how participating in the service affected their learning outcomes.

PSYCHOLOGY, INDIANA UNIVERSITY
Randall Osborne, Emotional and Behavioral Disorders of Childhood and Adolescence

The assignments in this course require students to consistently reflect on the course content and its relationship to their service experience.

Service component: Students work in groups with agencies that work with children and adolescents at the Mental Health Association or the Townsend Community Center. Students are responsible for gathering information, volunteering in the agency and working to solve an identified problem facing the agency and the population it serves.

Reflection assignments: Students must complete exit cards at the end of every class, reflecting on how that class period relates to their service project. In their "thought papers," students choose one interesting aspect of the course and/or service project and discuss how it has challenged or changed their way of thinking. In the 3-minute updates each group updates the class on their progress, goals, obstacles, etc. once a month. The group also completes a project course paper on the population they are working with and the specific problem they are addressing for their service agency.

SOCIAL SERVICES, UNIVERSITY OF UTAH
Jeff Jenson, Violence and Youth Gangs

The course involves students in a series of readings and discussions that explore the causes and consequences of youth violence and gang behavior.

Service component: Students mentor troubled youth.

Reflection assignments: Students keep a field journal chronicling their experiences as a mentor. Some entries ask students to respond to specific questions from the readings. In addition, students are required to complete an individual case study and paper, in which they integrate class readings and field experiences in a discussion of why the student s/he is working with has been in trouble and how the youth might be assisted.

ORGANIZATIONAL BEHAVIOR
The syllabi listed below are from courses in which students work as part of a team analyzing the organizational behavior of an agency with which they are working. As students are often asked to reflect on the experience of being part of a team, peer evaluations are a common method of evaluation.

HEALTH SCIENCES, PORTLAND STATE UNIVERSITY
Sherril Gelmon, Strategic Planning in Health Services

The learning objectives include understanding basic concepts, models and theories of strategic planning and applying them to health services delivery, and developing skills in working with a community partner (an organization) to define and meet their needs.

Service component: Students work in one of three groups assessing the effectiveness of one component of Legacy Health System's partnership with one of its 25 community-based agencies, e.g., one student team works directly with a specific community based organization.

Related assignments: A group presentation and group paper, short assignments that address the course readings and lectures, and reflective journals.

LEADERSHIP, UNIVERSITY OR RICHMOND
Richard Couto, Leadership in Community Organization

The purpose of this course is to impart to students: a general understanding of the nonprofit sector; the contextual variables in that sector that impact on leadership; and specific competencies related to the nonprofit sector. In addition, many leadership competencies apparent and dominant in the voluntary sector are increasingly advocated for or practiced in formal organization in other sectors.

Service component: To work with and provide one community organization or agency in the Richmond area with resources and materials that will be useful to them for leadership development.

Related assignments: The three written assignments ask students to examine thoroughly how their service organization functions.

Written Assignment #1— select a nonprofit, examine human and social problems the organization address, the manner in which it address the problem-advocacy, service, community development, funding sources, and its historical origins and current relations, if any, to organizations in the sectors of government, business, and social movements

Written Assignment #2—select an organizational leader. Take into account development of the organization to determine the leadership challenges entailed at present and over time, when and how it got started, its evolution in size, funding ebbs and flows, organization development problems and the manner in which it addressed them. Comment on background of the leaders and why they involve themselves in the work and issue of the organization.

Written Assignment #3—Provide a list of resources applicable to the organization that you are working with, keeping in mind resource needs, including leadership development needs.

POLITICAL SCIENCE, MOUNT HOLYOKE COLLEGE
Preston Smith, Politics 348, Colloquium on Community Development

The purpose of the course is to engage students in the various ideas, debates, and strategies regarding the development of inner city communities.

Service component: Students may choose one of four community development projects:

- Mobility Study: Using site visits and interviews, students evaluate the housing satisfaction of low-income residents of Springfield for the Hampden-Hampshire Housing Partnership (HAP, Inc.). Creating a database of households and who have received section 8 certificates from the Hampden-Hampshire Housing Partnership, students evaluate how often residents move, and the housing type and neighborhood conditions of their residences

- Credit Union Feasibility Study: Students research the feasibility of a community-based credit union for South Holyoke. Students study regulations for creating a credit union and the steps needed to create a credit union. Once the research is complete, students will write a planning grant for implementation and identify potential funding sources. Students will also organize educational workshops co-led by Holyoke residents and Mt. Holyoke students on the benefits of a community-based union in South Holyoke.

- Community Gardening Output Study: Students research the agricultural production of community gardeners in Holyoke and produce a report on the benefits of community gardens that must be presented to the Mayor of Holyoke, the City Council and the Department of Community Development and Planning. Students will also survey supermarkets and bodegas that service the inner-city neighborhoods in order to assign a price value to the goods produced by the community gardens, as well as the cultural and social benefits derived by the residents from community gardens.

- Mortgage Lending Discrimination Project: This project is not fully described on the syllabus because of the sensitive nature of the data and consequences of the research.

POLITICAL SCIENCE, SYRACUSE UNIVERSITY
Michelle Walker and Frank Lazarski, Practicum in Public Policy: Government and Nonprofit Agencies

Service component: Students work in a government or non-profit organization in an effort to gain an understanding of public policy processes as they relate to the government and non-profit sector.

Related assignments: Students complete an agency mission paper in which students comment on their agency's mission and purpose, goals, activities, funding and sources and its "customers"—and a final project, in which the student identifies an area of financial need and develops a lobbying strategy to access funds from state or local government.

MULTIDISCIPLINARY PROJECTS

Unity College Lake Winnecook Water Quality Project

The Lake Winnecook Water Quality Project is a multi-disciplinary collaborative project between Unity College, the Friends of Lake Winnecook (the local lake association) and the Maine Department of Inland Fisheries and Wildlife to improve the quality of the lake water. Seventeen service-learning courses at Unity College focus on six goals:

- Monitor the water quality of the lake and the streams that feed the lake:

- Develop outreach materials to educate and mobilize the public;

- Identify the social issues that affect the water quality of the lake;

- Establish a protocol for coliform bacteria testing and conduct ongoing tests;

- Compile a "rule book" of municipal, state, and federal rule and regulations concerning the lake and its shoreland for lay readers;

- Conduct a natural resource inventory of the lake.

Individual students are likely to be engaged in the Lake Winnecook Water Quality Project through several classes during the academic year. For example, a student might be collecting and testing water samples in her Chemistry or Biology course while also analyzing data from these tests in her Statistics course. During the next semester, this same student could potentially be conducting a winter creel survey in her Ichthyology course while also conducting interviews with elderly community members to develop an oral history of Lake Winnecook. A sample of courses include:

- **Biology II**, Evolution and Diversity, David Potter. Students were responsible for Lake Winnecook Inventory. They conducted field observations including monitoring eagle nest site, collecting live samples and specimens for laboratory studies, and compiling water quality data.

- **Ichthyology**, David Potter. Students conducted winter creel survey for 1999 winter ice fishing season and participated in a continuing study of white suckers in the Lake Winnecook watershed.

- **Geology of Environmental Problems**, John Hopeck and Jerry Cinnamon. Students continued chemical testing of groundwater downstream from town dump and contributed to the mapping of ground water vulnerability and risk and the completion of a groundwater hazard inventory for the watershed.

- **Composition II**, Diana Murphy. Students wrote educational materials and reports for the Lake Winnecook Association.

- **Environmental History of the World**, Christopher Beach. Students developed an oral history of Lake Winnecook through interviews with community members.

- **Microbiology**, Emma Creaser. Students continued coliform testing of the lake water.

- **Statistics II**, Barry Woods. Students developed statistical reports for the Lake Association using data that was collected by students in Microbiology, Freshwater Ecology, and Fisheries Science and Techniques courses.

- **Practicum in Education**, Joan Martis. Students presented environmental education programs & sessions in developed in ED 3414 Environmental Education Methods and ED 2113 Instruction and Evaluation Design courses in local schools and education centers. The sessions addressed community environmental issues.

With mini-grant support from Maine Campus Compact and the presence of the Service-Learning Coordinator, faculty involved in the project met regularly to coordinate their efforts, monitor progress, and reflect upon their successes and challenges. Initially the monthly meetings were an opportunity for faculty to discuss the challenges of using a new pedagogy in the classroom and to support and learn from each other during this period. The meetings have evolved and now focus increasingly on managing the complexities of interdisciplinary projects with multiple community partners.

Community members were invited to campus at the end of each semester to hear about the progress of the Lake Winnecook Project. These community gatherings provided students with an opportunity to present information and results to the community, and to reflect on what they learned through the experience. It also provided an opportunity for students to integrate their experiences with those of students from other courses and disciplines.

As the project evolves, the focus is shifting to the development of an interactive web page. The web page will increase the regular feedback from and the interaction with the community that is so crucial to the project. The movement is from a student storyboard presentation, or an informational talk, which impacts only those in attendance, to a web based data driven community access site. The service-learning web page will archive our data, increase access to student products and make it possible for others to contribute to the databases. Incremental progress toward the goal continues to sustain project momentum.

Bentley College Course Clusters

Bentley College describes a course cluster as two linked courses that students register for simultaneously (enrolling students in both courses). The intent of clustering is to bring a level of coherence to two seemingly disparate courses and to bring the talents of students to bear on a community project from two perspectives. Course clustering attempts to keep a common group of students together in two courses centered on a common project. Faculty encourage students to stay together in subsequent semesters continuing in more and more sophisticated ways with the same community site or project. Students who opt for the clusters are given scheduling incentives and scheduling preference each semester.

CLUSTER 1: CROSSING BORDERS: IDENTITY, IMMIGRATION, AND DIVERSITY

Fall	Spring
EN 110, Expository Writing II	EN 101-C14, Expository Writing
GO 100, American Government	PS 131-C0, General Psychology

In the fall the English and Psychology courses share a focus and module on the formation of personal identity. In the spring the English and Government courses extend this theme by focusing on border communities and how America institutions structure diverse group identities with the "melting pot." Students participate in a service learning project assisting immigrants preparing for U.S. citizenship

CLUSTER 2: YOUTH AND EDUCATION IN AMERICA

Fall	Spring
EN 101-C01, Expository Writing	EN110, Expository Writing II
PS 131-C02, General Psychology	PH 101, Introduction to Philosophy

The theme for the cluster year is schooling in America and the way that schooling affects young people. The English course will focus on the social and political structures of school; the psychology course on the effects on the individual child; and the philosophy course on moral issues and moral choices in school and society. Students will participate throughout the year in a service learning project tutoring children at an inner-city school.

4 Civic Bridges

In the course description below, Ruth Mandel and Tobi Walker distinguish between conceptual frameworks for civic education and the types of knowledge and skills required of citizens in a democratic society. In doing so, the instructors construct space in the course for students to name what it is they are doing and its connection to community, citizenship, and democratic politics (Battistoni, 2000 p.5). This distinction between a conceptual vision of citizenship and specific civic skills is important as it allows students to connect concepts within a unified theme: "What does a citizen do?" Too often, service-learning courses are constructed under the assumption that there is an explicit connection between the student's service experience and democratic citizenship. We quote Tocqueville with authority as if 19th century observations of volunteerism in an emerging democracy resonate with 21st century students serving communities defined by a market economy. Faculty often operate under the assumption that there is a shared language and a collective agreement on citizenship. As there is no such agreement, most students are not apt to see any inherent connection between service and their roles as citizens (Battistoni, 2000 p. 5).

POLITICAL SCIENCE 440: BECOMING A PUBLIC CITIZEN
Connecting Community Service and Public Leadership

Rutgers University
Instructors: Ruth Mandel and Tobi Walker
Office: Eagleton Institute of Politics, Douglass Campus

In this seminar, we will explore the links between community service and public leadership, which we define as making a difference in one's community, state, and nation through government and public policymaking. Historically, community service has been the means by which women left the private realm and entered the public world. We will ask whether that connection still exists and how it can be strengthened. Students will participate in a service experience in the community and explore public policymaking and women's leadership in the classroom. Through a research paper and the development of a public advocacy campaign, students will apply academic skills and community experience to the world of public policymaking.

We will begin the course by looking at notions of participatory democracy. What does it mean to be a citizen in the American polity? What are the expectations of democracy? How have these concepts been challenged by marginalized populations? We will then look at service as a technique for educating young people for citizenship. What are the pedagogical expectations of service? What are the challenges to the concept of service?

Our focus will then shift to the role that service and voluntarism has played in women's history. Denied formal access to the public sphere, how did women exercise authority and power? How did women's service work prompt women's access to public life and how does that reflect in contemporary politics?

We will then turn to ways that students can use their service experience to engage in mainstream political activity by examining the skills necessary for political participation. Finally, we will consider political interest and motivation among the "twenty-something" generation. Studies show that young people have less interest in politics then ever before. Why? How can young people be motivated and galvanized to make a difference?

Throughout the process of gathering syllabi for this project, I found many service-learning syllabi that asked students to reflect upon the conditions of poverty and inequity. These courses often placed students with populations of people challenged by various circumstances or in communities challenged by inequity and poverty. Students were often asked to provide a service to an individual (e.g., tutor a child for 10 hours) and from that brief experience, to reflect upon very complex community issues. In this model, because social problems are defined in individual terms, service is also defined in individual terms. Need is defined in terms of individual deficiency and the ability to meet need is defined in terms of the students' individual capacity for commitment and caring. Constrained by time, resources, and institutional affiliations, many faculty opted to explore social problems by focusing on community or individual deficits—defining communities and individuals in those communities by what they lack, as opposed to community assets, social structures and public policy (Kretzman and McKnight, 1993). Additionally, a focus on individual needs and deficiencies removes the service from a political context of working with others to influence or alter social institutions. In this type of needs-based orientation to community, the syllabus often describes the students' service role as the distribution of their excess time, talent, or resources. Course goals, objectives, assignments, and reflection all flow from this perspective. Courses can exacerbate this weak civic model by encouraging or requiring students to develop personal relationships with community members, relationships based on a course requirement, that dissolve when the students' excess is doled out according to the prescribed course obligations. This perception of community as a "needy thing one attends to in prescribed blocks of time" rarely encourages students to construct an operational definition of citizenship.

While we cannot deny that communities have needs that can benefit from the distribution of our excess, one's civic identity cannot reside in the distribution of excess. Rather, curricular-based service-learning should instill in students a civic identity rooted in public purpose. For while students' political agency may find root in charity, it can only flourish when they acquire the democratic skills of dialogue and relationship building. The development of civic skills can be explicit goals of a course—the skills of critical thinking, public deliberation, collective action and community building. So, while many courses are constructed to encourage students to find political motivation in the needs of others, we were intrigued by those courses that assist students in finding political agency through community building and negotiation. Students in these courses are faced with the basic democratic tenet, that social bonds strengthen communities and institutions, and in doing so, maintain the democratic process. We have designated these courses "civic bridges" and placed them in two categories:

- Courses that have the democratic arts as a goal and use service as a way to teach students about citizenship.

- Courses that ask students to exercise civic skills as part of specific disciplinary training (e.g., courses that require students to negotiate projects with community groups and to make ongoing presentations about their work to relevant community organizations). These courses seek to cultivate specific civic skills such as—discourse and argument, the loyal opposition, and boundary crossing—all within a specific disciplinary framework.

Characteristics of civic syllabi:

- Explain the civic connection in the course description, goals, objectives, assignments, and related materials.

- Inspire students with questions of justice, equity, power, and access, and introduce students directly to the civic process. Ask students to use their emerging disciplinary expertise, not as a "helpers" but as citizens shepherding a system.

- Are intentionally political and often focus on systemic concerns in an attempt to demystify the realm of politics.

- Demonstrate the process of change as integral to democracy.

The service experiences prescribed in the following syllabi propose that specific skills (e.g., voting) are not the only ways we define and sustain our democracy; we must also have the ability to openly communicate with each other about public problems. These syllabi are testaments to the idea that while service can be a powerful pedagogical experience, constructing a fully integrated public life is difficult if students lack the ability to narrate that experience. The inability to narrate a "public life" in a service-learning course does not generally mean students lack agency, but it may be evidence of a loss of language—the inability of many Americans to narrate their journey from private life to public citizen. Many of the syllabi that follow represent courses that assist students in finding language and voice by presenting knowledge as part of public life, as integral to a broader political dialogue—one that rises above personal interest, notoriety or market value. And the syllabus must serve as a map to that experience.

These courses assist students in understanding not just the elements of a working democracy but how one exercises civic skills to address public concerns. These courses can be especially powerful as they offer students an entry into political participation that is often consistent with their ethical beliefs. Perhaps more importantly, they seek to connect students to others who model admirable traits and uphold ideals of an engaged civic life, thus affording students an opportunity to reflect upon the "equality of condition" and to construct a vision for integrating politics into their lives. Rick Battistoni suggests that "in order to be effective, we (educators) must constantly keep civic learning outcomes in mind as we design service-learning courses and programs. This raises the question of what do we mean by civic education? In answering this question we need to distinguish between substantive, conceptual frameworks for civic education, and the compliment of skills and knowledge that a person should possess to be an effective citizen." (Battistoni, 2000 p.4)

SAMPLE SYLLABI

INTD Census 2000

CALIFORNIA STATE UNIVERSITY-FRESNO

An Issue Oriented Multidisciplinary Service Learning Course

California State University-Fresno

Instructors:	Peter Tannenbaum
	Department of Mathematics
	Peters Business Bldg., Rm. 343
	Sally Tannenbaum
	Department of Communication
	Speech Arts, Rm. 36
	Spring 2000

GENERAL COURSE DESCRIPTION

INTD 192S (also listed as S SCI 192S) is a new interdisciplinary course offered for the first time during Spring 2000. INTD 192S counts towards the new upper division GE Integration requirement in area D and also satisfies the new community service designation (S) approved by the university.

The subject of INTD 192S is the U.S. Census, particularly the 2000 Census that will start in April, right about the middle of the Spring semester. In the course we will discuss the historical, social, economic and political implications of the Census, the role of Census 2000 in the life of the nation, state and our community, and we will learn about public relations, media, grass root organizing, CBO's, political campaign strategy, and most of the issues related to the organization and implementation of a public awareness campaign.

One of the unique features of INTD 192S is that it requires a substantial community service commitment. All students in the course will be expected to do community service in the form of internships with appropriate community based organizations. The goal of the community service component is that each student will be actively involved in the organization and implementation of the local effort to achieve an accurate census count for Fresno County.

WHY THIS COURSE?

As a subject of academic study, the Census is grossly neglected—probably because it is a once in a decade event. This neglect belies the fundamental role that the Census plays in our nation's life-from governmental policy (federal, state and local) to strategic planning in business; millions of decisions that significantly impact people's lives are made based on census data. Although invisible, the Census is as much a part of the nation's infrastructure as highways and telephone lines.

The most critical piece of information collected by the Census is the decennial "head count," which gives the population count for local communities, towns, cities, counties, states, and the nation as a whole. The primary uses of the population data are: (a) to apportion the 435 seats in the House of Representatives among the states, (b) to draw congressional, state and local voting districts, and (c) to allocate federal funds (approximately 180 billion dollars a year) that are formula (i.e. population) driven to state and local agencies.

In spite of the obvious political and economic impact of the Census population data, the data itself is far from accurate. Simply put, the Census faces one fundamental obstacle in obtaining accurate counts: the unwillingness of people to be counted. For the 1990 Census, the estimated "undercount" for the entire nation was 1.6%, for the state of California the estimated undercount was 2.7%, and for Fresno County, the undercount was 3.4%. This means that there are about 4 million people (850,000 in California; 25,000 in Fresno County) that the 1990 Census missed, and this undercount translated into a loss of one Congressional seat to California as well as billions of dollars in federal funds.

One of the main roles of a university is to fight ignorance. In the case of the Census, ignorance is the primary enemy to an accurate head count. By learning about the Census and the role it plays in our lives, you will be able to significantly contribute towards rooting out this ignorance, both present and future. The second half of the story is your contribution to the betterment of the community. By offering your services, skills and knowledge towards implementing a complete count, you will tangibly and materially contribute to your community.

COURSE OUTLINE

Week 1 (Jan. 25)

 Introduction to the course.

 General introduction to the Census and its role in American life.

Week 2 (Feb. 1)

 History of the U.S. Census.

 The national Complete Count effort.

 Guest speaker: Richard Flores (Community/Government Partnership Specialist, U. S. Census Bureau).

Week 3 (Feb. 8)

 Economic implications of the Census.

 The undercount and its implications.

 Guest speaker: Alan Peters (Chairman, Fresno County Complete Count Committee).

Week 4 (Feb. 15)

 Political implications of the Census.

 Redistricting and its implications.

 The apportionment of the US House of Representatives.

 Guest speakers: Tom Bohigian (Sen. Barbara Boxer's Office), Juan Arambula (Fresno County Supervisor).

Week 5 (Feb. 22)

 Local Complete Count efforts.

 Community Based Organizations (CBO's)

 Guest speakers: Alice Rocha (Catholic Charities), Eileen Jacobs (California Rural Legal Assistance)

Week 6 (Feb. 29)

 Political Campaigns: Organization and Strategy.

 Guest speaker: Carolina DeSoto (Gov. Davis's office)

Week 7 (March 7)

 Complete count implementation campaigns (national, local).

 Outreach/Training activities.

 Guest speaker: Diane Berry (U.S. Dept. of Commerce/Bureau of the Census)

Week 8 (March 14)

Targeting Specific Audiences

Advertising Themes and Modalities.

Creating Public Service Announcements

Creating Press Releases and TV Spots

Guest speaker: Eva Torres (Radio Bilingue)

Weeks 9–13

Community Service/Fieldwork

Weeks 14–15

Reflection and discussion.

Class presentations.

SELECTED READINGS

Anderson, M. J., *The American Census: A Social History.* New Haven, CT: Yale.

University Press, 1990.

Anderson, M. J., and S. E. Fienberg, *Who Counts: The Politics of Census-Taking in Contemporary America.* New York: Russell Sage Foundation, 1999.

Choldin, L. M., *Looking for the Last Percent. The Controversy over Census Undercounts.* New Brunswick, N. J.: Rutgers University Press, 1994.

Mutz, D. C., P. M. Sniderman (eds.) *Political Persuasion and Attitude Change.* Ann Arbor, MI.: University of Michigan Press, 1996.

Steffey, D. L., and N. M. Bradburn (eds.), *Counting People in the Information Age.* Washington D.C.: National Academy Press, 1994.

GRADING

Attendance and class participation: 10%

Four Quizzes: 20%

Implementation Plan: 20%

Final report: 20%

Community Service Evaluation: 30%

The Citizen in the Community: Participation and Leadership

CONNECTICUT COLLEGE

Spring 1999
Community Challenges 201
Jefferson A. Singer
MaryAnne Borrelli

Please note that this is a Writing Enhanced course.

COURSE OVERVIEW

This course is an exploration of the meaning of active citizenship in a democracy, with a particular emphasis on urban settings. As the gateway course for the Program in Community Action, it asks the following questions:

- Who and what are the constituent parts of a community in our current society?

- What are the dynamic relationships and tensions that exist among the various components of an identified community?

- What are some of the major economic and social difficulties confronting various communities at this time in our history?

- What are the obstacles and forces that block progress in ameliorating social and economic disparities in a give community?

- What innovations and new strategies are emerging to aid citizens and institutions in overcoming these impediments to growth and change?

In order to address these large and complex questions, we will employ a variety of learning strategies. In addition to readings, writing assignments, and seminar discussions, this course will employ a problem-based pedagogy. Students will work in small groups to solve problems and prepare presentations on their solutions, to be shared with the larger class. These problems will help student's master and apply concepts that are critical to an understanding of community and active citizenship.

Using this same problem-based approach, students will work on a semester-long final project that will involve a service-lean-Ling component. The overarching problem that students will address throughout the semester is the attempt by a nonprofit community organization to develop a walkway/bike route that would connect the campuses of Connecticut College and the U.S. Coast Guard Academy to downtown New London.

Each small group will work with an organization engaged in a different facet of the walkway project:

- the community organization advocating the walkway (TRAC);

- the architects and design consultants;

- the New London city government;

- the Connecticut College master planning committee;

- the neighborhood alliance representing homeowners along the walkway route;

- and the New London Historical Society.

Each member of the group will devote at least four (4) hours a week of service work to the particular organization. The group's cumulative efforts will be woven together into a presentation to be submitted toward the end of the semester.

Through an examination of a community challenge that involves the College's relationship to its home city, New London, students will gain practical knowledge of what constitutes a community and how the struggle for a community takes place.

REQUIREMENTS AND GRADING

Note: Percentages notwithstanding, students must complete each of the assignments in order to pass this course.

A. Five-page paper (20 percent)

Each student will prepare a five-page paper, on a topic stipulated by the instructors. Because this is a writing-enhanced course, students will also be expected to prepare and submit an extensive rewrite of this paper. Both the original and the rewrite will be graded.

B. Individual project (20 percent)

Each student will prepare a project; reflective of her/his service-learning experience and of the learning acquired through course readings and discussion. Students are strongly encouraged to consult with the professors regarding the format and content of their project. Whenever possible, the professors would appreciate being able to display student and group projects.

C. Group project (25 percent)

The group project has both an oral and a written component. These projects should build upon—and thereby go beyond—the individual projects submitted each group member.

D. Electronic journal (20 percent)

At regular intervals throughout the semester, students will be asked to comment upon the connections between their readings, discussions, group work, and service-learning. These insights will be posted via internet/ electronic mail. Students are expected to study their colleagues' comments prior to the class meeting, so that discussion can benefit from those same insights.

E. Participation (15 percent)

"Participation" includes each student's involvement in the following:

- class discussions;

- group work;

- service-learning, for details, see the contract for students and for sponsoring organizations; and

- attendance at the New London Colloquium. This lecture series, hosted in New London on Friday Common Hours, will address topics of direct relevance to the coursework. A complete listing of speakers will be provided and students are expected to attend at least three lectures.

F. Attendance in this course is absolutely mandatory.

You cannot expect to pass this course if you are absent from the class meetings. Class participation is 15 percent of the course grade, as noted above. We can certainly appreciate that some might find participation challenging—please see us if this is the case and we will try to work through any difficulties.

STUDENT RESPONSIBILITIES

Basics: attendance thorough preparation of assigned readings for class; responsible participation in class and group meetings; professional performance of service-learning responsibilities and papers and examinations submitted on time.

Extension policy: Extensions will not be granted on the assignments. Should serious problems develop, PLEASE CONTACT either Professor Singer or Professor Borrelli. We can then decide how to respond to your work responsibilities. (Please note that extensions will not be given for extracurricular obligations.) As a matter of policy, any extension should be for no more than an extra day.

Late papers: A 1/2 grade will be deducted for each day late.

BOOKS AND THE BOOKSHOP

The bookstore has ordered the following books for this course. All of the readings are available on reserve at Shain Library; you should not feel obliged to purchase any of these texts.

Herson, Lawrence J.R. and John M. Bolland, *The Urban Web, Politics, Policy, and Theory,* 2nd ed. Chicago: Nelson-Hall Publishers, 1998.

Taylor, Charles, *Multiculturalism and "The Politics of Recognition."* Princeton: Princeton University Press, 1992. Introduction and "The Politics of Recognition."

The Citizen in the Community: Participation and Leadership
SERVICE-LEARNING REQUIREMENTS: CONNECTICUT COLLEGE

SERVICE-LEARNING CONTRACT FOR THE PARTICIPATING STUDENT

1. The course instructors and the Office of Volunteers for Community Service (OVCS) will work with each student group and the community organization to set up the service-learning arrangement.

2. Each student will set aside at least four hours a week (e.g., one morning or afternoon a week) to assist the organization chosen by their group. Students from the same group can work together or separately. The service work may be conducted at the office of the organization, in the community, or using the resources of the College (e.g. library or computer research). The type of work and the schedule of work will be negotiated by group members and the sponsoring organization.

3. Some possible activities may include:

   - attendance at organizational and community meetings;

   - library and internet research;

   - interviews, preparation and compilations of oral histories

   - writing press releases, policy statements, or position papers;

   - assistance with archival or document research;

   - outreach to individuals to expand awareness of and involvement with the walkway;

   - general assistance to the organization, as needed.

4. All students are required to comport themselves professionally with regard to appropriate dress, punctuality, reliable attendance, and respect for organizational standards of language, confidentiality, and non-discrimination.

   We will distribute a copy of these guidelines to your supervisor at the community organization with which you will be working. We will also ask that you sign the following statement:

   I have read the above listed service-learning requirements for Community Challenges 201: The Citizen in Community, taught at Connecticut College, Spring Semester 1999. I agree to these service-learning requirements and will comply with them as partial fulfillment of my course responsibilities for Community Challenges 201.

SERVICE-LEARNING CONTRACT FOR THE PARTICIPATING ORGANIZATION

1. For the Spring Semester 1999, beginning in February and ending in the second week of May, we have agreed to oversee a four hours-a-week service-learning placement of approximately six students with our organization. This placement is part of the Connecticut College course, Community Challenges 201: The Citizen in Community, sponsored by the Connecticut College Holleran Center for Community Challenges and taught by Professors Jefferson A. Singer and MaryAnne Borrelli.

2. We will engage this group of students in activities of our organization that will both provide assistance to our goals and, at the same time, will provide, meaningful education experience for the students. Such activities might include, but need not be limited, to the following:

   • attendance at organizational and community meetings;

   • library and internet research;

   • interviews; preparation and compilations of oral histories

   • writing press releases, policy statements, or position papers;

   • assistance with archival or document research;

   • outreach to individuals to expand awareness of and involvement with the walkway;

   • general assistance to the organization, as needed.

3. Though at times students may be asked to perform basic office tasks (e.g. Copying, word processing, filing, answering telephones), these duties will constitute only a minor and occasional part of their service-learning experience.

4. We will identify an individual at our organization as a supervisor or the students and that individual will have weekly contact with the members of the student community.

5. We understand that this service-learning placement is only one of several responsibilities these students have for this course, and we will avoid exerting pressure on them to provide additional hours of service.

6. We have read the students' contract for their service-learning placement and understand their obligations with regard to professional comportment and responsibility. If students do not abide by their contract, we will notify Professors Jefferson A. Singer and MaryAnne Borrelli immediately.

7. Our signing of this contract is not binding and we may end the service-learning arrangement at our discretion for any reason we deem necessary.

If you have any questions regarding the terms of this arrangement, please contact Jefferson A. Singer, Director, Holleran Center for Community Challenges or Professor MaryAnne Borrelli, Department of Government.

I. Defining Problem and Process

> *Earth has not anything to show more fair;*
> *Dull would he be of soul who could pass by*
> *A sight so touching in its majesty:*
> *This City now doth, like a garment wear*
> *The beauty of the morning; silent, bare,*
> *Ships, towers, domes, theatres, and temples lie*
> *Open unto the fields, and to the sky;*
> *All bright and glittering in the smokeless air.*
> *Never did sun more beautifully steep*
> *In his first splendour, valley, rock, or hill;*
> *Ne'er say 1, never felt, a calm so deep!*
> *The river glideth at his own sweet will:*
> *Dear God! the very houses seem asleep;*
> *And all that mighty heart is lying still!*

WILLIAM WORDSWORTH, "COMPOSED UPON WESTMINSTER BRIDGE."

Organizational Meeting, January 25.

Introduction, January 27.

Donald J. Olsen, *The City as a Work of Art: London, Paris, Vienna.* New Haven: Yale University Press, 1986. Chapters 1 (Urban Virtue and Urban Beauty) and 17 excerpted (pp. 281–287; Architecture as Language: Representation and Instruction).

Robert Fishman, *Urban Utopias in the Twentieth Century: Ebenezer Howard, Frank Lloyd Wright, and Le Corbusier.* New York: Basic Books, 1977. Chapter 13 (Broadacre City).

James Howard Kunstler, *Home From Nowhere, Remaking Our Everyday World for the 21st Century.* New York: Simon a "My Kind of Town," *Northeast, The Hartford Courant Sunday Magazine* (2 August 1998): 9–17+.

The Walkway, The Problem, and The Course, January 30.

Saturday meeting, 10am – 2pm, with lunch included.

John R. Stilgoe, *Outside Lies Magic, Regaining History and Awareness in Everyday Places.* New York: Walker and Company, 1998. Chapter 1 (Beginnings).

Charles E. Little, *Greenways for America*. Baltimore: Johns Hopkins University Press, 1990.

Chapters 5 (The Paths and Trails) and 9, excerpted (Coney Island to Fort Totten, New York: The Brooklyn - Queens Gateway, pp. 166 – 172).

Grant Proposal: The Surdna Foundation.

Grant Proposal: United States Department of Transportation.

Fieldwork: Preparation of "policy map." Students should walk the trail, creating a map of policy challenges along the way.

Qualitative Research Design in an-Urban Setting, February 1.

Louise G. White, *Political Analysis: Technique and Practice,* 2 nd ed.. Pacific Grove, California: Brooks/Cole Publishing Company, 1990. Chapters 2 (Building Propositions) and 5 (Designing Research to Show a Causal Relationship).

S. Taylor and A. Bogdon, *Qualitative Research Methods: The Search for Meanings.* New York:, 1984. Chapter 4 (In-Depth Interviewing).

William H. Whyte, *City, Rediscovering the Center.* New York: Doubleday, 1988. Chapters 1 (Introduction) and 7 (The Design of Spaces).

New London: An Introduction to Urban Challenges, February 3.

Charles 0. Jones, *An Introduction to the Study of Public Policy,* 3rd ed. Monterey, California: Brooks/Cole Publishing Company, 1984. Chapter 3 (The Nature of Public Problems).

Carmelina Como Kanzler (ed.), *New London, A History of Its People.* City of New London 350 Anniversary, 1996. Chapters to be announced.

Clay McShane, *Down the Asphalt Path, The Automobile and the American City.* New York: Columbia University Press, 1994. Chapter 10 (The Motor Boys Rebuild Cities).

Michael J. Dear and Jennifer R. Wolch, *Landscapes of Despair, From Deinstitutionalization to Homelessness. Pr*inceton: Princeton University Press, 1987. Chapter 2 (The Social Construction of the Service-Dependent Ghetto).

II. Who defines the community?

Agents in the Community, February 8.

> William Finnegan, *Cold New World, Growing Up in a Harder Country.* New York: Random House, 1998. Chapter 1 (New Haven: Work Boy).
>
> Robert N. Bellah et al., *Habits of the Heart, Individualism and Commitment in American Life,* updated edition. Berkeley: University of California Press, 1996. Chapter 1, excerpted (section entitled "Joe Gorman"). pp. 8–13, 165–187.
>
> Esmeralda Santiago, *When I was Puerto Rican.* New York: Vintage Books, 1993. pp. 213-237.
>
> Tom Wolfe, *Bonfire of the Vanities.* New York: Farrar, Straus, and Giroux, 1987. Chapter 3 (From the Fiftieth Floor).

Problems of Inequality, February 10.

> Video resources: *Roger and Me.*
>
> Robert N. Bellah et al., *The Good Society,* updated edition. New York: Vintage Books, 1991.
>
> Chapter 3 (The Political Economy: Market and Work).
>
> Peggy McIntosh, "White Privilege and Male Privilege: A Personal Account of Coming to See Correspondences Through Work in Women's Studies," Wellesley College Center for Research on Women.
>
> Lawrence J.R. Herson and John M. Bolland, *The Urban Web, Politics, Policy, and Theory,* 2nd ed. Chicago: Nelson-Hall Publishers, 1998. Chapter 16, excerpted (Urban Services, Market Considerations, and the Underclass, pp. 411–434).
>
> *1993-1994 Assessment of Community Needs,* United Way of Southeastern Connecticut. GalesFerry, Connecticut.

Responsibility and the Community, February 15.

> Michael J. Sandel, "America's Search for New Public Philosophy," *The Atlantic Monthly* 277.3 (March 1996): 57–74.
>
> Charles Taylor, Multiculturalism and "The Politics of Recognition." Princeton: Princeton University Press, 1992. Introduction and "The Politics of Recognition."

Martin Luther King, Jr. "Letter from Birmingham Jail," in *A Testament of Hope, The Essential Writings of Martin Luther King, Jr.*, ed. by James Melvin Washington. San Francisco: Harper San Francisco, 1986. pp. 289-302.

Individuals and Institutions February 17.

Jonathan Kozol, *Savage Inequalities, Children in America's Schools.* New York: Crown Publishers, Inc., 1991. Chapter 2 (Other People's Children).

Bel Kaufman, *Up The Down Staircase.* Englewood Cliffs, New Jersey: Prentice Hall, Inc., 1964. pp. 3–25, 166–171, 311–314, 323–326, 339–340.

John Powers, "Tough Love at Latin," The Boston Globe Magazine (7 November 1993): 10–11+.

Institutions: A Formal Definition and Introduction, February 22.

Robert N. Belch et al., *The Good Society.* New York: Vintage Books, 1991. Introduction (We Live Through Institutions).

Derek Bok, *Beyond the Ivory Tower, Social Responsibilities of the Modern University.* Cambridge: Harvard University Press, 1982. Chapters 3 (The Purposes of the University and Its Responsibilities to Society) and 9 (The University and the Local Community).

The College as an Institution in Society, February 24.

Robert N. Bellah et al., *The Good Society.* New York: Vintage Books, 1991. Chapter 5 (Education: Technical and Moral).

Writings by Claire L. Gaudiani; see: www.conncoH.edu, Headers: "Community -> President Claire L. Gaudiani. Titles: "Respectfully Submitted." (1994), "Needed: A Language of Aspiration." (1994), "Grassroots Democracies." (1995), "We Are the People of the Hyphen." (1996), "Social Stewardship and the American College Presidency," *The Presidency 2* (Winter 1999): 20–25. (This article on reserve; not available on the 'net.)

The Mass Media as an Institution: Seeking to Control the Press, March 1.

Doris A. Graber, *Mass Media and American Politics,* 51h ed. Washington, D.C.: CQ Press, 1997. Chapter 4 (News Making and News Reporting Routines).

Howard Kurtz, *Spin Cycle, Inside the Clinton Propaganda Machine*. New York: The Free Press, 1998. Introduction, Chapters 2 (The Master of Spin) and 3 (In the Dungeon).

Andi Rierden, "New London's Feisty Newspaper, The Day, *New York Times* (20 December 1998): 14:1+.

Packet of Articles: The New London Development Corporation, *The Day* and *The Freedom of Information Act*.

Mass Media, Part II: Courting the Press March 3.

Stuart Ewen, *PR! A Social History of Spin*. New York: Basic Books, 1996. Chapters 1 (Visiting Edward Bernays), 2 (Dealing in Reality: Protocols of Persuasion), and Coda.

Carolyn Tribble '98, "How-To Booklet on Public Relations." Unpublished manuscript, 1998.

Karen K. Gaughan, *Community Relations Guide, For Volunteer Literacy Programs*. Literacy Volunteers of America, Inc., 1985. Chapter 3, excerpted (pp. 22–37, Publicity).

Packet of Articles: The Vista Walkway.

A Case Study for the Definition of community and the Role of Its Institutions: The Civil Rights Movement: Ideals, Meologies, and Political Strategies, March 8.

A Testament of Hope, The Essential Writings of Martin Luther King, Jr., ed. by James Melvin Washington. San Francisco: Harper San Francisco, 1986. "11. Nonviolence: The Only Road to Freedom," and "12. A Gift of Love."

Jan Howard, "The Provocation of Violence: A Civil Rights Tactic?" in *We Shall Overcome, The Civil Rights Movement in the United States in the 1950s* and the 1960s, Volume II, ed. David J. Garrow. Brooklyn: Carlson Publishing, Inc., 1989.

Henry Hampton and Steve Fayer (ed), *Voices of Freedom, An Oral History of the Civil Rights Movement from the 1950s through the 1980s*. New York: Bantam Books, 1990. Chapter 14 (Malcolm X: Our Own Black Shining Prince!).

By Any Means Necessary; Speeches, Interviews, and a Letter by Malcolm X. New York: Pathfinder, 1970. Chapter 3 (The Founding Rally of the OAAU).

A Case Study for the Definition of Community and the Role of Its Institutions: The Civil Rights Movement: Selma March 10.

>   Robert Weisbrot, *Freedom Bound; A History of America's Civil Rights Movement.* New York: W.W. Norton and Company, 1990. Chapter 5, excerpted (pp. 128–143; The Voting Rights Campaign).

>   Warren Hinckle and David Welch, "Five Battles of Selma," in We Shall Overcome, The Civil Rights Movement in the United States in the 1950s and the 1960s, Volume II, ed. David J. Garrow. Brooklyn: Carlson Publishing, Inc., 1989.

>   Henry Hampton and Steve Fayer (ed), *Voices of Freedom, An Oral History of the Civil Rights Movement from the 1950s through the 1980s.* New York: Bantam Books, 1990. Chapter 13, excerpted (pp. 212–236; Selma, 1965: "Troopers, Advance.").

SPRING BREAK.

Review Session, March 29.

III. Who wins?

>   *Down all the avenues of time architecture was an enclosure by nature, and the simplest form of enclosure was the box. The box was orna-mented, they put columns in front of it, plasters and cornices on it, but they always considered an enclosure in terms of the box. Now when Democracy became an establishment, as it is in America, that box-idea began to be irksome. As a young architect, I began to feel annoyed, held back, imposed upon by this sense of enclosure, which you went into and there you were—boxed, crated. I tried to find out what was happening to me: I was the free son of a free people and I wanted to be free. I had to find out what was the cause of this impris-onment. So I began to investigate.*
>
>   FRANK LLOYD WRIGHT

Theories of Urban Government and Urban Politics, March 31.

>   Steven Kelman, *Making Public Policy, A Hopeful View of American Government.* New York: Basic Books, Inc., Publishers, 1987. Chapter 9 (How Should We Evaluate the PolicyMaking Process?).

>   Lawrence J.R. Herson and John M. Bolland, *The Urban Web, Politics, Policy, and Theory,* 2nd ed. Chicago: Nelson-Hall Publishers, 1998. Chapters 3 (Theories of Urban Politics) and 5 (Political Rules and Political Realities in the City).

William L. Riordan, *Plunkitt of Tammany Hall*. New York: E.P. Dutton and Co., Inc., 1963. Introduction, "Honest Graft and Dishonest Graft," Reformers Only Mornin' Glories," "Dangers of the Dress Suit in Politics."

Citizen Participation and Mobilization, April 5.

Saul D. Alinsky, *Rules for Radicals, A Practical Primer for Realistic Radicals*. New York: Random House,1971. "The Education of an Organizer." Also recommended: "Tactics."

Lawrence J.R. Herson and John M. Bolland, *The Urban Web, Politics, Policy, and Theory*, 2nd ed. Chicago: Nelson-Hall Publishers, 1998. Chapter 7 (Informal Citizen Participation in Local Politics).

Diane Dujon and Ann Withorn (ed.) *For Crying Out Loud, Women's Poverty in the United States*. Boston: South End Press, 1996. "Speaking for Ourselves, A Lifetime of Welfare Rights Organizing," Marian Kramer; "Apologies Don't Help," Milwaukee Welfare Warriors.

State and National Urban Policy April 7.

Lawrence J.R. Herson and John M. Bolland, *The Urban Web, Politics, Policy, and Theory*, 2nd ed. Chicago: Nelson-Hall Publishers, 1998. Chapters 11 (Beyond the Central City: Cities, Their Suburbs, and Their States) and 12 (Cities and the National Government).

United States Department of Housing and Urban Development, Empowerment, A New Covenant with America's Communities: President Clinton's National Urban Policy Report. 1995. Chapters 1 (The Community Empowerment Agenda) and 2 (Metropolitan America in the 1990s).

Speeches and press releases by Governor John Rowland; see: www.state.ct-us/governor/ Speech: State of the State Address, 1999. Press releases: 19 March 1998, "Governor Rowland Offers Plan to Promote the Redevelopment of Downtown Hartford."

29 January 1998, "Governor John Rowland Proposes New Plan to Preserve Connecticut's Open Space"

25 June 1997, "Governor Announces State Support for $12.7 Million in Bridgeport Development Projects."

Urban Development Programs, April 12.

Lawrence J.R. Herson and John M. Bolland, *The Urban Web, Politics, Policy, and Theory*, 2nd ed. Chicago: Nelson-Hall Publishers, 1998. Chapter 5 (Political Rules and Political Realities in the City).

Robert Halpern, *Rebuilding the Inner City, A History of Neighborhood Initiatives to Address Poverty in the United States*. New York: Columbia University Press, 1995. Chapter 7 (Emerging Neighborhood-based Initiatives) and Conclusions.

Charles E. Little, *Greenways for America*. Baltimore: Johns Hopkins University Press, 1990. Chapter 10 (The Practical Matters).

Policy Entrepreneurs. April 14.

Lawrence J.R. Herson and John M. Bolland, *The Urban Web, Politics, Policy, and Theory*, 2nd ed. Chicago: Nelson-Hall Publishers, 1998. Chapter 10 (Policy Entrepreneurs and Agendas).

Randy Kennedy, "When Scraping the Sky Makes a City Bleed," *New York Times*, 23 October 1998, p. A20.

Bernard J. Frieden and Lynne B. Sagalyn, Downtown, Inc., How America Rebuilds Cities. Cambridge, Massachusetts: The MIT Press, 1989. Chapter 6 (Entrepreneurial Cities and Maverick Developers).

Steven Kelman, *Making Public Policy, A Hopeful View of American Government*. New York: Basic Books, Inc., Publishers, 1987. Chapter 11 (Evaluating the Political Process).

Implementation and Evaluation April 19.

Jeffrey L. Pressman and Aaron Wildavsky, Implementation, 3rd ed. expanded. Berkeley: University of California Press, 1984. Chapter 9 (What Should Evaluation Mean to Implementation.

Richard Moe and Carter Wilkie, *Changing Places: Rebuilding Community in the Age of Sprawl*. New York: Henry Holt and Company, 1997. Chapter 5 (The Revival of Main Street).

Packet of Articles: Captain's Walk: Implementation Failure in New London.

Defining the Future April 21.

Witold Rybczynski, *City Life, Urban Expectations in a New World*. New York: Scribner, 1995.

Chapter 10 (The Best of Both Worlds).

Bernard J. Frieden and Lynne B. Sagalyn, Downtown, Inc., *How America Rebuilds Cities.* Cambridge, Massachusetts: The MIT Press, 1989. Chapter 14 (An Unfinished Renaissance).

Lawrence J.R. Herson and John M. Bolland, *The Urban Web, Politics, Policy, and Theory,* 2nd ed. Chicago: Nelson-Hall Publishers, 1998. Chapters 17 (Reinventing the City: Policy and Reform as the Century Turns) and 18 (The Shape of Things to Come).

April 26.   *Group presentation.*

April 28– May 10.

        Group presentations.

May 12 Conclusion.

Political Theory and Citizen Education
UNIVERSITY OF MINNESOTA

James Farr, Pol 5610: Abbreviated Syllabus

COURSE DESCRIPTION

This course—Pol 5610—will investigate critically some major texts and arguments in the history of political thought that address the question of political education, broadly speaking. It will be concerned to trace changing conceptions of "politics" and "education," as well as to articulate the various relationships between the discursive activity of theorizing about politics and the practice of educating citizens. It is driven by the renewed contemporary interest in questions of civic education; but it will address that interest in terms of some very important texts and arguments in the tradition of political theory. principal authors include Plato, Niccolo Machiavelli, John Locke, and Jean Jacques Rousseau from the premodern era; and John Dewey, Myles Horton, Paulo Freire, and a series of recent writers from the contemporary period. The texts and arguments of these important authors should be understood as being about political education, as well as actually attempting to politically educate their audiences.

The course also has a required attendant course—Pol 3090: Practicum (as described in the attached sheet). It will also address questions of democracy and education practically, in the form of an educational practicum. Students will put their education and democratic citizenship into practice by serving as "coaches" in our Public Achievement Project for middle-school students (at

St. Bernard's Middle School or J. J. Hill Middle School, both in St. Paul). The younger students at these schools will be investigating and debating their own questions about politics, public problems, and social issues, in and around their school. The fundamental premise of the course is that we learn theoretically about citizenship and education in large part by being engaged practically as citizens and educators. Or to put it differently: to learn what must be learned about democratic education just is to be engaged in the practice of educating democrats. Overall, in short, we are interested in the theory and practice of political education.

Note well that the 5610 course has 4 credits, and the 3090 practicum has an additional total 4 credits, 2 credits in each of Fall and Winter quarters. That is, the practicum will continue into winter quarter (in order to complete our work). Further credit will be available for spring, should students wish to continue.

COURSE REQUIREMENTS

Requirements for 5610 and 3090 reflect their diverse goals. It will entail lectures, but also frequent class discussions. Thus it will be essential that class attendance be preceded by close reading(s) of the text(s).

Besides close reading and class discussion, the requirements of the course will consist in [1] a take-home midterm examination and [2] a take-home final examination. Both exams will be essay format.

The additional requirements for Pol 3090—especially regarding coaching and keeping a notebook—are on the attached sheet.

REQUIRED BOOKS

Plato, *The Republic*

Niccolo Machiavelli, *The Prince and the Discourses*

John Locke, *Some Thoughts Concerning Education*

Jean Jacques Rousseau, *Emile*

John Dewey, *Democracy and Education*

M. Horton and P. Freire, *We Make the Road by Walking*

D. Matthews, ed., *Higher Education and the Practice of Democratic Politics*

WEEKLY READINGS

1 Introduction: Political Theory and Citizen Education

2 Guardians, Forms, and Myths: the Engineered Republic

  Read: Plato, *Republic*

3 Humanists, Realists, and Republicans: Educating the Prince

Read: Machiavelli, *The Prince*

Machiavelli, *The Discourses,* selections

4 Civil Society and Liberal Education: the Englightened Gent

Read: Locke, *Some Thoughts Concerning Education*

Locke, selections from *Two Treatises*

5 Nature, Culture, and Gender: Tutoring Man and Citizen

Read: Rousseau, *Emile*

6 Progress, Development, and Truth: the Self-Educated Liberal

Read: Mill, *Autobiography*

Mill, Inaugural Address to St. Andrews

7 Pragmatism, Progress, and the Public: Educating Democrats

Read: Dewey, *Democracy and Education*

8 Radical Action and Social Change: Educating Adults Politically

Read: Horton and Freire, *We Make the Road by Walking*

9 Citizenship and Liberal Education: Educating Students

Read: Matthews, ed., *Higher Education;* selected essays

PRACTICUM

The 5610 topics course on Political Education has attached to it an additional 4-credit course—or Practicum—that involves students working as Public Achievement "coaches" at St. Bernard's Middle School or at J. J. Hill Middle-School, both in St. Paul. The middle school students are involved in year-long projects in which small working groups have identified issues and problems in and around their school that they are trying to address and solve.

The experience is intended to provide students with an exciting opportunity to integrate theoretical reflection on political education with some practical work in helping formative young citizens to educate themselves about the public world.

The practicum will begin this quarter, and continue into winter quarter. Students are expected to commit themselves to the two-quarter project, in order to begin and hopefully bring to some conclusion the practical civic projects of the younger students at the respective schools.

Besides the theoretical readings for PS 5610: Political Education, the Practicum has one text designed to help you as a coach: Making the Rules. This text has been designed by the Public Achievement staff of Project Public Life, which represents the ongoing civic outreach component of the Center for Democracy and Citizenship at the University.

There are prerequisites for involvement in the practicum, or in PS 5610 more generally. Certainly students need not be majors in Political Science or the School of Education, or even intend to become professional teachers. A willing experimental attitude is all that is needed.

The 3090 practicum will entail weekly hour-long coaching sessions at the respective schools, as well as weekly hour-long follow-up evaluation sessions with all other coaches. Thus, besides travel to and from the respective schools, the coaching experience will be a two-hour weekly involvement.

Students will also keep a notebook that records weekly reflections on the practium experience and that attempts to integrate the theoretical readings with that experience.

There will also be a final (4-page) evaluation of the practicum due at the end of the course.

Finally, there is a mandatory training session on Public Achievement coaching to be held on the first Saturday of the quarter.

The Individual and Community in Democratic America
NORTHEASTERN UNIVERSITY

Instructor: John Saltmarsh
Course Listing: CHST 1805, Sec. 1, Seq. 9: Approaches to History
Spring 1995: Tuesday, Friday: 10:30 AM; Wednesday: 4:05 PM.

> *"I believe once more that history is of educative value in so far as it presents phases of social life and growth. It must be controlled by reference to social life. When taken simply as history it is thrown into the distant past and becomes dead and inert. Taken as the record of man's social life and progress it becomes full of meaning."*
>
> JOHN DEWEY, "MY PEDAGOGIC CREED" (1897)

COURSE DESCRIPTION: This course will explore the historical meanings of individualism and community in American culture, focusing on the relationship of the self to the larger community of others and institutions, examining the historical dimensions of the tensions between the individual and society in light of the consequences for a democratic political culture.

In analyzing various approaches to historical study, the course has three components:

1) analysis of primary and secondary source material to explore the traditions that define the tensions between individual aspirations and community values and assess how these have changed over time and in different cultural settings;

2) analysis of readings to focus discussion on questions of method, theory, and evidence and the interpretation/analysis/writing of history in the exploration of the theme of the course; and

3) service activity and reflection that will focus our discussion on approaching the contemporary context of our historical understanding, making connections between ideas and experience to integrate others' observations and interpretations with our own, to bring a certain immediacy to the readings.

TEACHING METHODOLOGY: Seminar. Discussion/dialogue will 1) focus on common readings to explore the traditions surrounding the theme of the course and to provide the social context for the students' community service activity, and 2) consist of reflection on experience of involvement in the community and the relationship between their experience and the readings/ideas of the course.

SERVICE EXPERIENCE: A requirement of this course is that students will engage in community service activity for at least two hours each week (20 hours over the course of the quarter). Service assignments can be arranged by the instructor in collaboration with 1) the Tobin School in the Mission Hill Neighborhood next to Northeastern University or 2) with the John Shelburne Community Center in Roxbury. The Tobin School in situated in one of Boston's poorest neighborhoods and is part of the Boston Public School System. It is the only kindergarten through eighth grade school in the Boston Public School System and serves a predominantly Latino and African American student body. The Shelburne Community Center is the only community center in Roxbury and for twenty-five years has focused its services to the ethnic and economic diversity of the residents of the area neighborhoods who utilize the Shelburne as a safe haven for their children.

REQUIRED READINGS

Jane Addams, *Twenty Years at Hull House* (19 10)
Robert Bellah, et al, *Habits of the Heart: Individualism and Commitment in American Life* (1985)
Thomas Bender, *Community and Social Change in America* (1978)
Christopher Lasch, *The Culture of Narcissism* (1978)
Robert and Helen Lynd, *Middletown: A Study of Contemporary American Culture* (1929)
David Reisman, *The Lonely Crowd* (196 1)
Tocqueville, *Democracy in America* (1835/1840)
Also: Classpack at Gnomon Copy

COURSE SCHEDULE

Week 1: April 5, 7 and Week 2: April 11, 12, 14

Traditions and Definitions, Approaches to History: Method, Theory, and Evidence.
Bellah and Bender
Christianity and Republicanism, Bellah and Bender

Week 4: April 25, 26, 28

> *Democracy and America in the early 19th Century,* Tocqueville

Week 5: May 2, 3, 5

> *Industrial Capitalism: Challenges to Individualism and Democracy,* Addams

Week 6: May 9,10,12

> *The Self and Community in a Consumer Culture,* Lynds

Week 7: May 16, 17, 19

> *Post- War America: The Quest for Individuality in a Mass Society,* Reisman

Week 8: May 23, 25, 28

> *The Personal and the Political: Community Lost and Found: Approaching the Past and the Future,* Lasch

Week 9: May 30, 3 1, June 2

> (last week for Seniors)
>
> Presentations of Final Papers

Week 10: June 6, 7, 9

> Presentations of Final papers

Week 11: June 12-16: Exam Week

"Democracy must begin at home, and its home is the neighborly community. " (1927)

"Regarded as an idea, democracy is not an alternative to other principles of associated life. It is the ideal of the community itself." (1927)

"Individuality cannot be opposed to association. It is through association that man has acquired his individuality and it is through association that he exercises it. [Individuality means] performance of a special service without which the social whole is defective" (1891)

"Information is an undigested burden unless it is understood. It is knowledge only as its material is comprehended. And understanding, comprehension, means that the various parts of the information acquired are grasped in their relation to one another—a result that is attained only when acquisition is accompanied by constant reflection upon the meaning of what is studied." (1933)

JOHN DEWEY

Table of Contents
CHST 1805

REQUIRED WRITTEN WORK AND PRESENTATIONS

1) *A Reflective Journal:* The journal will focus on the community service activity and reflections on the experience and the connections between that experience and the literature of the course. You will be asked to keep a journal during the quarter. The journals are a reflection tool that will be shared periodically. There is the minimum expectation of weekly entries. Journals will be turned in for review the last day of class (and will be returned).

2) A review of *Habits of the Heart.* The review/analysis should focus on the approach the authors took to creating historical understanding. What methodology (ies) do they employ? What theory guides their interpretation? What evidence do they turn to? Who are the authors (provide a cultural profile of the authors)? Be sure to incorporate at least two published reviews of the book in your essay and cite them properly. 3–5 pages minimum, typed, double-spaced. Due May 2.

3) A small group presentation and short paper of one of the assigned books in the class. The small group will present together and may collaborate on the written work, but each student will turn in a paper. The presentation and the paper will focus on:

- the way in which the author(s) addressed the issues of individualism, community, and democracy in the particular book

- the author(s) approach (methods, theory, evidence) to the subject

3–5 pages, typed, double-spaced. Papers are due two weeks after presentation.
Presentation: (%) Paper: (%)

4) A final paper due at the end of the course will consist of an analysis of the service experience in the community, placing that analysis in a larger context drawn from the readings from the course and seminar discussions, integrating the students' own interpretations with those from the literature of the course. Your paper should integrate your experience in the community with the readings from the class to answer the question, "what is the relationship between my approach to the present and my approach to the past." 8–12 pages, typed, double-spaced. Papers are due for presentation during the last two weeks of the course, to be turned in on the last day of class. Presentation: (%) Paper: (%)

5) Class Participation.

6) Class Attendance.

7) Community Service.

Community Service in American Culture
PROVIDENCE COLLEGE

Faculty: John Saltmarsh and Jim Tull
Public and Community Service Studies: PSP 301
Class Meetings: Monday and Thursday 2:30-3:45 PM, Room FC 218

PUBLIC AND COMMUNITY SERVICE STUDIES AT PROVIDENCE COLLEGE
Furthering the mission of Providence College, Public and Community Service Studies involves a systematic and rigorous study of the major conceptual themes of community, service, compassion, public ethics, social justice and social change, and leadership. The goals of the major include providing students with the civic skills of critical thinking, public deliberation and communication, public problem solving, collective action and community building.

THE COURSE
Within the context of the public and community service studies curriculum, this course provides the historical context for understanding community service in American culture. Contemporary understandings of community and service along with current experience in community and with service provision have been socially constructed in the United States over the past two hundred

years. Meanings assigned to community and service have also been highly contested, in large part because they are concepts that embody values, beliefs, attitudes, and ideas that are central to definitions of democracy, social justice, civic resiliency and public life.

This is an interdisciplinary, experientially based course designed to provide community and classroom-based opportunities to examine this historical context. The method of study relies upon your service experience, allowing you to apply and examine concepts addressed in class to your own practical experience in service others.

COMMUNITY SITE

Amos House
415 Friendship Street
Adrienne Marchetti (Assistant Director and Maggie Meany (Volunteer Coordinator)
Community Assistant: Sarah Long

Amos House is a comprehensive social service organization that provides support to homeless and transitional men and woman in South Providence. Amos House operates a men's and women's shelter as well as a meal site, which provides free breakfast and lunch Monday-Saturday. Founded and developed in the Catholic Worker tradition, Amos House has since undergone major changes, as it has become one of the largest social service organizations/shelters in the state. Last year, an on-site medical clinic was established.

GOALS AND OBJECTIVES

The goals and objectives of this course are:

- *Goal:* Draw upon your introduction to community service and service learning from PSP 101.

    Objective: Demonstrate an understanding of the history of participatory democracy in the United States

- *Goal:* Deepen your thinking and practice of community partnerships and relationships in community.

    Objective: Demonstrate an understanding of the history of community organizing and its relevance to service provision.

    Objective: Describe a historical framework with which to analyze structures of service provision.

    Objective: Describe a context for examining the organization of knowledge and institutions of higher education in relation to community-based public problem solving.

- *Goal:* Provide a framework and grounding for community service that makes connection between service and political engagement.

Objective: Demonstrate an ability to analyze and critique the dominant charity model of service and its institutional context.

This third goal reflects a particular critique of the dominant "charity" model of community service and service learning that encourages students to think that individual actions are a substitute for focusing on larger structural issues. The approach to social problems as individual concerns positions service as distinct from political activity, which involves working with others to influence (or alter) societal institutions. Part of our readings and community-based activity will be focused on exploring alternatives to the charity model.

READINGS
Assorted handouts, including:

Jane Addams, "The Subtle Problems of Charity" (1899)

Wendell Berry, "Does Community have a Value?" and "Conserving Communities"

Nina Eliasoph, Avoiding Politics: How Americans Produce Apathy in Everyday Life (1998) (selected chapters).

John McKnight, "Professionalizing Service and Disabling Help"

Keith Morton and John Saltmarsh, "Addams, Day, and Dewey: The Emergence of Community Service in American Culture" (1997)

Sara Mosle, "The Vanity of Volunteerism" (2000); "Community Profiles"

BOOKS
Robert Coles, Dorothy Day: *A Radical Devotion* (1987)

Robert Fischer, *Let the People Decide: Neighborhood Organizing in America,* Updated Edition (1994)

Jedidiah Purdy, *For Common Things* (1999)

Howard Zinn, *A People's History of the United States*

REQUIREMENTS
• Community Service/Expectations and Obligations   _____%

Complete an average of 3-5 hours of community service per week.

The intellectual and practical foundation of this course is the relationship with the community partner. Service sites invest resources to accommodate you and willingly make themselves dependent on you. Clients at the sites value the consistency and reliability of your presence. Your reliability and commitment are non-negotiable. If you need to reschedule or alter your commitment in any way, you are expected to arrange this as much in advance as possible, call in if circumstances warrant, and/or to arrange back-up as necessary. If problems arise, contact the instructors or TA as soon as possible.

- Weekly Journal Entries including Reflections on Readings   _____%
- Attendance and Participation   _____%
- Seminar Facilitation   _____%
- Final Paper   _____%

SCHEDULE

Week 1:   Thursday, September 7:
Introductions

Week 2:   Monday, September 11 and Thursday, September 14
Community, Charity, and Politics.
- Eliasoph
- Mosle

Students are required to attend the Institute Student Orientation, FAC 4th Floor, September 14, 4–5 PM.

Week 3:   Monday, September 18 and Thursday, September 22
Community, Charity, and Politics. (cont.)
- Berry
- McKnight
- Community Profiles

Week 4:   Monday, September 25 and Thursday, September 29
The Catholic Worker Tradition and Amos House
- Coles

Week 5:   Monday, October 2 and Thursday, October 5; Facilitator   1._____
A Context for Service: I. The Crisis of Community (1880–1920)
- Zinn, 11–14.
- Fischer, 1
- Addams

Week 6:   Monday, October (9) 10 and Thursday, October 12
A Context for Service: 2. *The Origins of Amos House*
- Morton and Saltmarsh

• Coles

Week 7:   Monday, October 16 and Thursday, October 19; Facilitator 2._____
           A Context for Service: 3. *Radical Organizing* (1920–1945)
           • Zinn, 15-16
           • Fischer, 2

Week 8:   Monday, October 23 and Thursday, October 27; Facilitator 3._____
           [MID SEMESTER]
           A Context for Service: 4. *Community in the Affluent Society* (1945–1960)
           • Zinn, 17
           • Fischer, 3

Week 9:   Monday, October 30 and Thursday, November 2; Facilitator 4._____
           A Context for Service: 5. Community Building in the 60s and 70s (1960–1970)
           • Zinn, 18–20
           • Fischer, 3

Week 10:   Monday, November 6 and Thursday, November 9; Facilitator 5._____
           A Context for Service: *The Crisis of Civic Renewa*l (1980–2000)
           2) Zinn, 21-23
           3) Fischer, 6

Week 11:   Monday, November 13 and Thursday, Nov. 16;   Facilitator 6._____
           Higher Education, Community Building, and the Lessons of Service.
           • (selected handouts)

Week 12:   Monday, November 20   Facilitator 7._____
           Politics and Service in Contemporary Times
           • Purdy

Week 13: Monday, November 27 and Thursday, November 30
           Politics and Service in Contemporary Times (Cont.)
           • Purdy

Week 14:   Monday, December 4 and Thursday, December 7

Week 15:   Reading and Exam Week

Sociology 380: Workshop in Sociology
RHODE ISLAND COLLEGE

Professor Sandra Enos
Wednesday 4:00 – 6:50

This service learning course will provide students with an opportunity to apply social research skills in the context of performing community service. We will explore issues related to homelessness, family violence and criminal justice combining field experience and scholarly work in these areas. Objectives here are to gain familiarity with social problems and social responses, to learn about their communities as social scientists and to examine relationships among individuals, families, organizations and the state.

REQUIREMENTS AND GRADING

Final Paper 30%

Special reports 30%

Civic arts 15%

Community study 15%

Journaling/field notes 20%

Class presentations 10%

Class participation 10%

Students are required in this course to be involved in field work, preferably work that involves service to the community. Community here is broadly defined. Students enrolled in this course to complete an internship requirement must work in the field ten hours per week. The final paper will provide the student with an opportunity to examine and present what has been learned in the field. This final project will link field knowledge to an appropriate literature in sociology. There are no examinations in this class. You will be demonstrating "learning" by virtue of your written work and class presentations.

Materials—Purchase a three-ring binder to hold articles and other handouts. You will need to purchase a separate notebook or create a system to take field notes. These will be collected and responded to three times over the semester. Also, at the end of the semester, you will submit all the work you have done over the semester as a collection.

Articles on reserve—Articles will be on reserve at the library. Please obtain a picture ID so you may take these out.

Email and the Internet—I will be providing a list of helpful and interesting internet resources so you can learn what other students are doing in these sorts of courses nationwide.

Class participation is required. We have limited enrollment to 20 in this class so that we can employ a seminar design. This means that success of the learning opportunity depends on you and your fellow students. This course has been designed to surface some important and controversial topics. I do not expect or desire universal agreement by all students. I do expect respect of each other's opinions, positions and rights to learn and grow. You should come to class having read all the assigned material.

REQUIRED TEXTS

Michigan Journal of Community Service Learning Volume 4

On Reserve

Putnam, Robert. "Bowling Alone: America's Declining Social Capital." *Journal of Democracy* Volume 6, No. 1 January 1995.

Bunis, William K., Angela Yancik, and David A. Snow. 1996. "The Cultural Patterning of Sympathy Toward the Homeless and Other Victims of Misfortune." *Social Problems,* 43(4): 387-402.

Anspach, Renee R. 1991. "Everyday Methods for Assessing Organizational Effectiveness." *Social Problems* 38(l): 1–19.

Walker, Alice. 1997. *Anything We Love Can Be Saved: A Writer's Activism.* New York: Ballantine Books. Introduction, xxi–xxv.

Coles, Robert. 1993. *The Call of Service: A Witness to Idealism.* Boston, MA: Houghton Mifflin. Chapter 2 "Kinds of Service" & Chapter 5 "Doing and Learning" & "Epilogue"

Roby, Pamela Ann. 1998. "Creating a just World: Leadership for the Twenty-First Century." Social Problems 45:1–20.

Lofland, John and Lynn H. Lofland. 1995. *Analyzing Social Settings: A Guide to Qualitative Observation and Analysis* 3d Ed. Belmont, CA: Wadsworth Publishing. Chapter 5

ASSIGNMENTS

Materials with asterisk (*)are on reserve

Class 1   Overview of course

Introduction to service-learning

Models and opportunities

Reflection guides: Introduction to fieldwork

Starting field notes and journaling

Coles Handout; Boyer Handout

Class 2   Morton and Saltmarsh (MJCSL)
           Qualitative research
           Walker Introduction
           McKnight in class

Class 3   Finding literature about the setting
           Two page report due 10 points
           Lofland and Lofland*

Class 4   The helping relationship
           Coles Ch. 2*

Class 5   Community and gender
           Hatcher (MJCSL)

Class 6   Coles Ch. 5*

Class 7   Bunis*
           Community study due (15 points)

Class 8   Anspach*
           Field notes (Part 1) (10 points)

Class 9   Bullard and Malloney (MJCSL)

Class 10   Field trips and discussion questions
           No class

Class 11   Putnam*
           Civic Arts project due (15 points)

Class 12   Nonprofits: Community foundations
           Coles Epilogue*

Class 13   Hayes and Cuban (MJCSL)
           Field notes (Part 11) (10 points)
           Class presentations from the field

Class 14   Class presentations
           Roby*
           Final Paper due (20 points)

Additional readings may be assigned. Because we are covering topics that are newsworthy and the subject of considerable debate, I may add items to our readings that are found in the popular media and academic press.

SPECIAL REPORTS

Civic arts: Responsibilities of citizenship; what does this mean? what are the links between the social and the political? what are obligations as members of the civil society?

Assignment: *15 points; Due date: November 18*
One of the obligations of citizenship is keeping informed about issues or letting elected representatives know about our opinions about public policy. The assignment here is to prepare a letter to the editor, to an elected official, to a director of a nonprofit organization to inform them about an issue important to you. You also have the option of attending a public meeting and sending a follow-up letter to the organizers. These letters win be discussed in class.

Community study: *3–4 typewritten pages; 15 points; Due date: October 14*
In most communities; individuals and organizations are working to solve problems. These efforts may be taken up by individuals, nonprofit organizations, churches and publicly funded organizations. Select one of the following issues (homelessness, hunger, youth violence, teen pregnancy) and find out what your community is doing to help address the problem. You will need to contact individuals in your community to research this issue gathering at least 3 sources of information on this. It is important to remember here that addressing a problem includes direct service, advocacy, lobbying and so on and that social problems are complex and involve great many efforts. Your paper should begin with a national perspective on the issue, explain why the topic is of interest to you and then focus on community based efforts.

Field notes: *20 points Due dates: October 21 and December 2*
Field notes are the basis of qualitative research. In some instances, these can be taken right on the scene where the observer is unobtrusive and not part of the action. In other instances, the observer must make mental notes and then get these on paper, as soon as possible. There are a number of guides for taking field notes and we will use a combination of approaches. Later in the semester I will distribute some field notes from my research in a women's prison.

Finding a placement: During the first class, we will be discussing possible placements for service. We will brainstorm as many as we can. Three factors should go into your selection of a service site. 1) Practical: Can you get there and back? do their needs mesh with your availability? 2) Personal: Do you have a particular interest in this issue? the population? 3) Course related concerns: Is the placement one that conforms to the aims of the course? Check these with the instructor. Last summer, you completed a survey to identify your interests and talents so that we can make a good match between community needs and what you have to offer. There are many organizations that can help you find a volunteer/ service activity. You are expected to do community an average of 10 hours per week over the course of the semester. I will be checking in with agency staff to follow your progress in these assignments. There are many organizations that can help you locate service/ volunteer placements. One of the major one is Volunteers in Action (VIA). Contact them at 421-6547. Also refer to the class handout on local opportunities for service. Speakers will be addressing the class over the course of the semester and this will provide some ideas as well.

Class presentations: *10 points*
Students will be responsible for presenting the assigned readings in class. These, along with original research, performed by students, will provide the basis for the final report. The schedule for class presentations will be determined in week two of class.

Final paper: *30 points Due date: December 9*
Details for the final paper will be distributed in week three of class. This 10–12 page paper will provide a synthesis of what you have learned over the course of the semester. What follows are questions and quotations that win serve as a framework for your thinking and reflection in the final paper and for the field notes, as well.

QUOTATIONS FOR REFLECTION

> *"Time and again I have been persuaded that a huge potential of good will is slumbering within our society. It's just that it's incoherent, suppressed, confused, crippled and perplexed—as though it does not know what to rely on, where to begin, where or how to find a meaningful outlet."*
>
> VACLAV HAVEL

Some of the following will become the basis of questions that should be addressed in field notes. We will also address some of these in class.

What are some of the responsibilities of citizens? When you think of citizenship what comes to mind? Where do social problems come from? What are the reasons for poverty, homelessness, violence, etc.? When you consider these problems, do you usually examine the individuals involved and try to figure out how specific behaviors and attitudes have contributed to the problem or do you usually examine larger factors? What are the pros and cons of each approach?

Why is poverty defined as a social problem? Playing a thought experiment, imagine what our society would be like if excess wealth were a social problem. What values would underlie the definition of 'too much money' as a social problem? What sorts of programs might be in place to solve this problem?

Who is responsible for solving social problems? Should families be the primary providers of care? If families fail, should extended families be the next layer of care? When should we rely on formal organizations? When should the state step in?

Think of one social problem and pose one question you would like to know more about in order to begin solving it. This does not have to be a problem that is widely recognized or that affects a majority of the population. First, describe the problem; then suggest some questions; finally, suggest some ways to learn more about this in an effort to do something about it.

JOURNAL ESSAYS

1. What are the possible connections between service and learning? Or experience and learning? As sociologists, how do we connect what we learn from texts and professors to what we see in the 'real world'? What is closer to the truth?

2. Identify two sociological lessons you have learned and review what is that you found so true or compelling? What did these theories or concepts tell you or explain?

3. Have you ever volunteered in the past? Do you remember how that experience was?

4. If you are thinking about volunteering or doing service in this course, what do you think you would anticipate your experience being if you were to go to a different setting from one you are accustomed to? For example, if you had the opportunity to work as a tutor in a school different from that you attended, let's say a school for the physically handicapped or a school with students who are primarily another race or ethnic group, how would you prepare yourself for these experiences?

5. After your first visit to the field site, what questions have come up? We will be discussing these visits in class. What is the most significant thing you noticed about the site? Did it meet your expectations? What questions are in the back of your mind? What do you want to observe closely the next time?

6. How does your organization work with others in the community? Does it have a particular niche? How does it get clients? How do clients get better? What is provided to them? What does the agency need to support itself?

7. The helping relationship is generally thought of as positive. What are some of the negative aspects? Some argue for a dismantling of social programs because they disable people and communities. Present this position. Others argue that professionals are able to diagnose and treat problems. Argue this position as well. Chose one social problem and discuss how each position might treat the issue, identify clients, suggest blame and propose fixing the problem.

8. Write an essay that incorporates different perspectives on a social situation. For example, in an intake situation, write from the different perspectives of the client giving information, the person taking the information and the entity requesting such data. What are some of the rules governing interaction here? What could be better? What is at stake?

The Civic Community: Theory and Practice

RUTGERS UNIVERSITY

Political Science 220–01
Instructor: Dr. Rick Battistoni
Department of Political Science

COURSE DESCRIPTION AND REQUIREMENTS: This course is part of a pilot program, now in its third year, which seeks to bring together an academic, classroom-based curriculum and community service to create a holistic learning experience for the student. Although this class has been taught before, we are stiff trying out concepts, reading materials, and methods, and the course will still be somewhat experimental. We appreciate your willingness to be "pioneers" in this exciting exploration of a new frontier in civic learning. I will be describing more fully the content and aims of this course in class during our orientation, but a beginning statement of our ends is in order. This course will focus on what "community" means in contemporary democratic culture and will explore the role of each individual, both as individual and "citizen" in the democratic culture of the United States. We will look honestly and critically at both the promises and challenges of civic life in the U.S. context. In particular, we will examine questions of diversity and inequality in American life, especially those based on race, gender, class, religion, and sexual orientation, and the challenges these pose to contemporary understandings of democratic community.

Seminar Format: The class will be conducted as a seminar, even though our numbers will make this difficult. Therefore, it is imperative that students come to class prepared to discuss class themes and reading assignments. I will provide some context-setting and may present additional material in some instances, but for the most part the class will be an opportunity for us to reflect upon and analyze together critical questions about citizenship, democracy and community. Students will be encouraged to bring into class discussions their community service experiences as they relate to topic themes. To facilitate this discussion and your structured journal entries, you will be provided with regular handouts setting the context of particular authors/readings and asking a series of questions for reflection and for writing about it in your journals.

Readings: We will be spanning a wide range of reading materials, all meant to serve as resources to you as you think about what it means to be a democratic citizen and a member of the communities in which you find yourself. I have chosen the selections to give you as broad a range of ideas, topics, and disciplinary perspectives as possible. You may not find all of the readings inspiring, and you may not agree with the perspective of some of the authors. But I hope they will provoke thought and discussion of the relevant matters of the course. Your responsibility is to read each work by the time it is listed in the course outline, as well as respond to journal questions about the reading in question.

CIVIC COMMUNITY

Community Service: Because democracy is not a spectator sport, and because democratic citizens are active participants in their communities, in addition to the regular class meetings you and other students in the class will participate in approximately 4–5 hours of community service a week. Community service allows you the unique opportunity to apply theories and concepts discussed in class to your own practical experiences in serving others in the community. The additional hour of academic credit you signed up for under Political Science 399 takes account of this service work. You will have a choice among possible community service projects, and will be able to schedule your service around your other classes, work, or extracurricular activities. These projects will include (among others): Tutoring, coaching, and working with children in one of three after-school programs in New Brunswick elementary schools; Working as coaches/resources to high school students as they mentor younger New Brunswick children in a project designed to curb violence and victimization; Serving as a Literacy Tutor, ESL Instructor, or Teaching Assistant in the Adult Learning Center in New Brunswick; Working as a child care of social work assistant at Amandla Crossing, a transitional housing program for homeless families. All placement possibilities will be described and arranged in the first week of the semester.

Structured "Experiential Journal": You will document your thoughts and experiences working in the community, reflecting critically on the assigned readings and class discussions, and responding to specific questions presented for writing. You should aim for a minimum of five pages per week of freely written material; the writing will not be scrutinized for "quality" along typical academic lines—it can be loose, informal, associative, and in alternative forms to straight prose. I will provide questions to guide you in your weekly journal writing, but there will be ample opportunity for you to write freely of your various experiences. Entries will be evaluated in light of the overall quantity of entries and the general quality of your intellectual explorations, responses to specific questions, musings, speculations, and the like. I'll be responding to the journals along the way so that all will get feedback. Journals will count for 40% of your final grade in the three-hour portion of the class.

Group projects: We will talk much more about these in class, but they should concern issues that are related to your community service experience. You will be broken up into groups based on your choice of community service, and will have as a resource and "team leader" an advanced undergraduate student whom you can consult as you work on your project. You will work on your projects collaboratively throughout the semester, culminating in some form of written (probably) and oral presentation of your group's findings. Group projects will be worth 30% of the final grade.

It is imperative that you do the readings, come prepared to discuss their relevance and implications each class, and faithfully participate in community service as per your agreement with your particular community service agency. Active attendance and participation in class sessions will make up the rest of your grade, so if you miss classes or don't contribute to our seminar sessions, your grade will suffer relative to the severity of the problem.

Over the course of the semester, we hope that students and faculty will form a democratic community as we discuss and reflect upon the nature of democratic community. Please feel free to raise concerns, questions, criticisms, and suggestions as we go along, either publicly or in private consultation with me, or if you are more comfortable, with one of the student team leaders. The course outline is tentative, and should be seen as a general guide, not a box.

COURSE OUTLINE

Date	Topic Under Discussion
	Reading Assignment
Jan. 20	Orientation; Introduction to Class; None; begin reading for next time
	Community Service Placements
Jan. 25, 27	Democracy and Community
Feb. 1, 3, 8	Civic Values: The Morals, Psychology, and Problems of Belonging to Communities
Feb. 10, 15, 17	The Meaning of Democratic Citizenship: Historical and Contemporary
Feb. 22, 24 Mar. 1, 3	The Responsibilities of Citizenship: Philanthropy, Service, "Civic Duty"

Civic Community
Katherine Mansfield, The Garden Party; John Dewey, "The Search for the Great Community," The Public and Its Problems (1927)

Robert Bellah, et al., *Habits of the Heart* (1985), selections; Scott Peck, "Me True Meaning of Community," from *A Different Drum: Community Making and Peace;* Simone Weil, *The Need for Roots* (1949), selections; Shirley Jackson, *The Lottery;* Ursula Le Guin, "The Ones Who Walk Away from Omelas"

Thomas Jefferson, *Selected Writings;* Benjamin Barber, "Neither Leaders Nor Followers" (1985); Harry Boyte, "Practical Politics," The Atlantic (1993)

Martin Luther King, "On Being a Good Neighbor," from Strength to Love (1963) 16–24; Mother Teresa, *Words to Love By,* selected quotations; George Santayana, "The Philanthropist," Dialogues in Limbo (1925); Allan Luks & Peggy Payne, *The Healing Power of Doing Good,* selections; Edward Bloustein, "Community Service: A New Requirement for the Educated Person" (1988)

Challenges to Democratic Community: Inequality & Diversity in American Life

Mar. 8, 10   Class and Poverty

Mar. 22, 24, 29 Race and Democratic Community
         Jonathon Kozol, Savage Inequalities (1991), selections
         Ralph Ellison, The Invisible Man, prologue (1947);
         Shelby Steele, *The Content of Our Character* (1990), selections;
         Gloria Anzaldua, *Borderlands: La Frontera,* selections

Civic Community

Date	Topic Under Discussion
	Reading Assignment

Mar. 31,   Gender and Democratic
Apr. 5   Community

Apr. 7   Religion, Sexual Orientation, and the Nature of Prejudice

Apr. 12   Suburbanization and the Decline of Democratic Community

Apr. 14   The Challenge of "Multiculturalism"

Levels of Citizenship: School, Neighborhood, Nation
Apr. 19   The University as a Civic Community

Apr. 21   The Local Community & Public Space

Apr. 26   Nationalism & Democratic Community

Apr. 28 & May 1   Group Project Presentations

     S. Okin, "Justice and Gender"; E. Fox-Genovese, "Women and Community," from Feminism Without Illusions (1991)

     "Minersville School District v. Gobitis," in The Courage of Their Convictions; "The Gay Cadet," The Village Voice (1990)

     Kenneth Jackson, "The Loss of Community in Metropolitan America" (1986)

Catharine Stimpson, "Meno's Boy: Hearing His Story - & His Sister's"; Michael Morris, "Educating Citizens for a Multicultural Society" (1990); Dinesh D'Souza, "Illiberal Education" (1991)

Michael Moffatt, "What College is Really Like," from Coming of Age in New Jersey (1989), 25-53,71-73; Benjamin Barber, "The Civic Mission of the University" (1989)

Evans & Boyte, "The People Shall Rule," from Free Spaces (1992); Alexis de Tocqueville, "The Local Spirit of Liberty," from *Democracy in America*

John Schaar, "The Case for Patriotism," *Legitimacy in the Modern State* (1981)

Note: Dr. Rick Battistoni is currently the Director of the Feinstein Institute for Public Service at Providence College in Providence, Rhode Island.

Becoming a Public Citizen: Connecting Community Service and Public Leadership
RUTGERS UNIVERSITY, FALL 1996

Political Science 440
Instructors: Ruth Mandel and Tobi Walker
Office: Eagelton Institute of Politics, Douglass Campus

COURSE DESCRIPTION

In this seminar, we will explore the links between community service and public leadership, which we define as making a difference in one's community, state, and nation through government and public policymaking. Historically, community service has been the means by which women left the private realm and entered the public world. We will ask whether that connection still exists and how it can be strengthened. Students will participate in a service experience in the community and explore public policymaking and women's leadership in the classroom. Through a research paper and the development of a public advocacy campaign, students will apply academic skills and community experience to the world of public policymaking.

We will begin the course by looking at notions of participatory democracy. What does it mean to be a citizen in the American Polity? What are the expectations of democracy? How have these concepts been challenged by marginalized populations? We will then look at service as a technique for educating young people for citizenship. What are the pedagogical expectations of service? What are the challenges to the concept of service?

Our focus will then shift to the role that service and voluntarism has played in women's history. Denied formal access to the public sphere, how did women exercise authority and power?

How did women's service work prompt women's access to public life and how does that reflect in contemporary politics?

We will then turn to ways that students can use their service experience to engage in mainstream political activity by examining the skills necessary for political participation. Finally, we will consider political interest and motivation among the "twenty-something" generation. Studies show that young people have less interest in politics then ever before. Why? How can young people be motivated and galvanized to make a difference?

This course has five objectives:

1) to make a connection between academic and extra-curricular interests and the public arena;

2) to understand the theoretical expectations of democratic citizenship and challenge those concepts;

3) to carefully consider the dynamics of service learning and its consequences;

4) to discover the ways that service has moved women into the public arena;

5) to explore the various roles one can play in the political process and to expand opportunities for connecting to that process.

COURSE REQUIREMENTS

This will be an intense and highly participatory class that will require everyone's involvement. Students will be expected to read each week's selections completely and critically and to be active participants in class discussions.

Community Service: This course has a community service requirement. You will volunteer 4 hours per week for 10 weeks in a community service placement in an issue area of interest to you. The placements will be organized by the CASE program. You will receive one additional credit, but you must register for both this class (790:440:03) and for the community service placement (790:400) and attend all scheduled trainings conducted by the CASE program.

Community service credit will be graded separately from classroom activities. You will be expected to keep a simple log of your activities during your volunteer hours and submit the log to the instructors on December 2nd. Community service hours must be completed by November 25.

Paper: One major paper is required for this class. Students will select a public policy question of concern to them and related to their community service placement. Each student will identify and interview at least two leaders who share an interest in the policy question. One of the leaders must hold a formal leadership position and one must be a community advocate.

The paper should describe the policy question and identify the key advocacy organizations, elected officials, bureaucracies, and boards or commissions, which address the issue. The paper should present the varying approaches to addressing the issue. However, in the end the author should take a stand on the issue and advocate for a preferred approach to solving the problem, whether that is through improved implementation of current policies, support for proposed legislation, or a different policy approach. The author's proposed solution will then be the basis of her/his action plan.

To facilitate the writing and research process, the papers will be graded in a "rolling fashion," with bibliographies, interview questions, and a rough draft due during the semester. By October 7th, students will submit in writing their paper topics and arrange a meeting with Ms. Walker to discuss the topic and their preliminary ideas. No later than October 21 at, students will submit a bibliography. No later than October 28, students will submit the names of the two people they wish to interview and a list of interview questions; these must be approved before interviewing can proceed. A rough draft of the paper is due November 18th.

To provide students with more feedback on their papers, as well as provide experience in constructive feedback, students will participate in a group review process. Students will be assigned to groups of three and rough drafts will be exchanged among group members. Reviewers have one week to read the paper and make comments. Reviewers will be provided with a series of questions, which will guide their feedback. One copy of the review will be given to the paper writer and a copy should be submitted to the instructors.

All component parts must be submitted on time; lateness will affect the grade. The papers are due December 9th. There are no exceptions to this deadline, for every day the paper is late, the grade will be reduced by one letter.

ACTION PLAN

In order to explore how to relate academic study and research with political practice, students will also develop an action plan for an advocacy campaign around the issue each has researched. Each student will present her/his action plan in class during the last two weeks of class. We will discuss these action plans in more detail later in the semester.

READINGS

Readings are available for purchase from Joanne on the second floor of the Eagletan Institute of Politics.

INSTRUCTORS' EXPECTATIONS

1. Utilize the assigned readings, lectures, and discussions for the research papers, action plans, and community service experiences.

2. Bring the community service experiences into the classroom as a basis for questions and discussion.

3. Submit all written assignments on time, typed, and proofread. The instructors will expect students' writing to conform to the rules of grammar, punctuation, and spelling of standard written English.

BREAKDOWN OF SEMINAR GRADE

15% . . . . Attendance and Participation

15% . . . . Bibliography, Interview Questions, & Rough Draft

5% . . . . Reviews

40% . . . . Paper

25% . . . . Action Plan

DATES TO REMEMBER

Sept. 9:   Course overview, discussion of community service placements, and Introduction of basic concepts

Sept. 14:   CASE orientation (mandatory)

Oct. 7:   Paper topic due

Oct. 2l: Bibliography due October 28

Nov. 18:   Interview names and questions due

Nov. 25:   Rough draft due (3 copies)

Nov. 25:   Reviews due

Dec. 2:   Community service hours completed

Dec. 9:   Placement logs due. Paper due/Action plan presentations

Dec. 18:   Action plan presentations

CLASS SCHEDULE

Sept. 15:   **A Basis for Discussion**

Harry C. Boyte and Kathryn Stoff Hogg, *Doing Politics: An Owners Manual for Public Life,* Minnesota: Hubert H. Humphrey Institute of Public Affairs, 1992.

Sara M. Evans, "Women's History and Political Theory: Toward a Feminist Approach to Public Life," in Nancy A. Hewitt and Suzanne Lebsock (eds.), *Visible Women,* Urbana: University of Illinois Press, 1993, pp. 119–140.

Oliver Sacks, "The Revolution of the Deaf," in Benjamin R. Barber and Richard M. Battistoni (eds.). *Education for Democracy,* Iowa: Kendall/Hunt Publishing Company, 1993.

Sept. 23: **Citizens, Community, Democracy**

John Dewey, "Search for the Great Community," excerpted in Benjamin R. Barber and Richard M. Battlstoni (eds.), *Education tbr Democracy*, Iowa: Kendall/Hunt Publishing Company, 1993.

Thomas Jefferson, "Letter to Samuel Kerchoval," in Benjamin R. Barber and Richard M. Battistoni (eds.). *Education for Democracy.* Iowa: Kendall/Hunt Publishing Company, 1993.

Alexis do Tocqueville, "That the Americans Combat the Effects of Individualism by Free Institutions," and "Of the Use which the Americans Make of Public Associations in Civil Life," in Richard D. Heffner (ed.) *Democracy in America,* New York: Penguin Group, 1956.

Sept. 30: **Citizens, Community, Democracy**

Martin Luther King, Jr. "Give Us the Ballot—We Will Transform the South," in James M. Washington (ed.) *A Testament Of Hope,* San Francisco: Harper, 1986.

Carol Pateman, "Feminism and Democracy," in Benjamin, R Barber and Richard M. Battistoni (eds.), *Education for Democracy,* Kendall/Hunt Publishing Company. 1993.

Richard Reeves, "Canandaigua," *American Journey,* New York Simon and Schuster, 1982.

Roger M. Smith, "Beyond Tocqueville, Myrdal and Hartz: The Multiple Traditions in America," in *American Political Science Review.* Vol. 87, no. 3, September 1993, pp. 549–566.

Cornel West, "Introduction," *Race Matters,* New York: Vintage Books, 1994, pp. 3–13.

October 7: **Community Service: Educating Future Citizens;** *Paper Topics Due*

Bryan Barnett and Grace Losso. "For Self and Others: Some Reflections on the Value of Community Service" *Getting the Most from Community,* New Jersey: The Civic Education and Community Service Program, 1991, pp. 19–24.

Brad Belbas, Kathi Gorak. and Rob Shumer, "Commonly Used Definitions of Service Learning: A Discussion Piece," October, 1993.

William James, "The Moral Equivalent of War," in John J. McDermott (ed.). New York: Random House, 1967. 660–671.

Matthew Moseley, "The Youth Service Movement America's Trump Card In Revitalizing Democracy," *National Civic Review,* Summer/Fall, 1995.

Oct. 14: **Library Session: Meet in Douglass Library**

Oct. 21: **Critiques of Service and "Charity;"** *Bibliography Due*

Theresa Funiciello, "Filling the Gap: A Charitable Deduction" and "City Silos and the Pop-Tart Connection," *Tyranny of Kindness,* New York: The Atlantic Monthly Press, 1993.

Eric B. Gorham. "National Service, Political Socialization, and Citizenship," *National Service, Citizenship, and Political Education.* Albany: State University of Now York Press, 1992, pp. 5–30.

Paul Rogat Loeb, "Tangible Fruits: The Community Service Movement," in Generation at the Crossroads: Apathy and Action on the American Campus. New Brunswick: Rutgers University Press, 1994, pp. 231–247.

Carrie Spector, "Empty the Shelters: Anatomy of a Struggle," *WhoCares,* Winter, 1995, pp. 40–43.

Oct. 28: **Woman's Voluntarism and Moral Authority;** *Interview Names and Questions Due*

Catharine Beecher. "The Peculiar Responsibilities of American Women," in Nancy F. Cott (ed.) Roots of Bitterness, New York: E. P. Dutton & Co., 1972.

Karen J. Blair, "Sorois and the New England Woman's Club," *The Clubwoman as a Feminist,* New York: Holmes & Meier Publishers. Inc., 1980.

Paula Giddings. "To Be a Woman, Sublime: The Ideas of to National Black Women's Club Movement (to 1917)," *When and Where I Enter. The Impact of Black Women on Race and Sex in America,* New York: William Marrow and Company, 1984, pp. 95–118.

Barbara Welter, "The Cult of True Womanhood, 1820–1860." *American Quarterly* 18:151–74.

Nov. 4: **From Service to Reform: Women Entering the Public Sphere**

Paula Baker, "The Domestication of Politics Women and American Political Society, 1780–1920," *American Historical Review* 89 (1984) pp. 820–647.

Mary Pardo, "Mexican American Women Grassroots Community Activists: 'Mothers of East Los Angeles,'" *Frontiers,* vol. xi, no. 1, 1990, pp. 1–7.

Ann Firor Scott. "Women's Voluntary Associations: From Charity to Reform" in Kathleen D. McCarthy (ed.) *Lady Bountiful Revisited,* New Brunswick: Rutgers University Press, 1990.

Nov. 11:   **Women In Contemporary Politics**

Susan J. Carroll, "Me Politics of Difference: Woman Public Officials as Agents of Change," *Stanford Law & Policy Review,* 5 (Spring. 1994), pp. 11–20.

Tamara Jones, "A Candidate's Uneasy Station in Life," *The Washington Post.*

Celinda C. Lake and Vincent J. Bregilo, "Different Voices, Different Views: The Politics of Gender," *The American Woman 1992–1993,* New York: W.W. Norton, 1992, pp. 178–201.

Joseph P. Shapiro, "The Mothers of Invention," *U.S. News,* January 10, 1994.

Nov. 18:   **Political Advocacy;** *Rough Drafts Due*

Guest Speaker Christy Davis, state director, U.S. Senator Frank Lautenberg.

Nancy Amidei, *So You Want to Make a Difference: Advocacy is the Key,* Washington DC: OMB Watch, no date.

Kim Bobo, Jackie Kendall, Steve Max, "Direct Action Organizing," in *Organizing for Social Change,* Washington: Seven Locks Press, 1991, pp. 2–48.

Nov. 25:   **A Life in Politics; Reviews Due;** *Community Service Hours Completed*

Madeleine Kunin, *Living a Political Life,* New York: Alfred A. Knopf, 1994, Chapters 2, 3. 4, 7, and 11.

Dec.2:   **Apathy and Activism in the 20-Something Generation;** *Placement Logs Due*

Susan B. Glasser, "Do 20somethings Hate Politics?" WhoCares, Fall, 1994, pp. 20–28.

Harwood Group, *College Students Talk Politics,* Ohio: Kettering Foundation, pp. 1–30.

Paul Rogat Loeb, "The World of Activists: Communities of Concern" in *Generation at the Crossroads: Apathy and Action on the American Campus,* New Brunswick: Rutger's University Press, 1994, pp, 207–230.

Dec. 9:   **Oral Presentation of Action Plans;** *Papers Due*

Dec. 18:   **Final Exam period/ Oral presentation of Action Plans**

The Democracy Seminar: The Politics of Community Action
SWARTHMORE COLLEGE

Professor Meta Mendel-Reyes
Spring 1995, T 6–9 pm

The "Democracy Seminar," one of the core courses of the Political Science Department's Democracy Project, is a community-based exploration of democratic political practice. In the United States, such problems as poverty, racism, homelessness, inadequate education, lack of access to health care, unemployment, environmental pollution, etc., have become daily realities for many people. The pervasiveness of injustice and inequality call into question the meaning of American democracy. More and more people have given up on political participation, even as politics becomes more urgent. The recent elections make it even less likely that the national government will act on behalf of local, especially urban, communities. Yet, at the grassroots, in many American neighborhoods, people are organizing and trying to resolve the tremendous problems, which confront them. How do communities empower themselves to take action? How can individual activists, from inside and outside the community, help to achieve democratic political and social change?

In trying to answer these basic questions of the course, we will encounter many others. Is it possible to achieve significant political change at the local level, when critical decisions are made at the national, and even international levels? How can communities have an impact on large, bureaucratic nation-states, and on multinational corporations? What role, if any, should outsiders play in community politics? How should an activist work with people who are different in terms of education, race, income, gender, etc.? Can people from one group understand, judge, or work politically with other groups? What is the relationship between community service and community action? What type of knowledge and education is appropriate to community politics? Does providing direct service to people undercut their political empowerment? Should community organizations be democratic in structure? Are there times when too much internal democracy makes it harder to achieve democratic political change? What is democratic leadership? How do activists sustain their work without burning out? How do community organizations sustain themselves?

In this course, each of you will explore the politics of community action in American democracy, through community-based learning. You will have many opportunities to integrate reflection and experience, primarily through public service internships, but also through dialogue with local activists, community-building within the class, reading and writing assignments, and group exercises, which connect theory and practice. (Note: this version of the Democracy Seminar has been designed to complement PS-10. "Democratic Theory and Practice" also offered this semester)

COURSE FORMAT AND ASSIGNMENTS
The main focus of the Democracy Seminar will be our public service internships; the course is designed to facilitate learning from our own experiences and from each other. Each of you will

complete a minimum of 60 volunteer hours by the end of the semester (approximately five hours a week through the middle of April). The internship will give you the opportunity to explore in a sustained way a particular approach to community action. The internship experience is structured by the role and the responsibilities the host organization agrees to provide you, your own interests and learning objectives, and my course design. These three components will be formalized in a Learning agreement, to be signed by the student, a representative of the host organization, and myself, as the professor of the course. It is important that the relationship between the intern and the host be as reciprocal as possible; the community organizations and activists who share with us this semester should be respected, not simply treated as "labs" or "data," for our purposes only.

Our weekly meetings will be conducted seminar-style, beginning with a shared meal. During our time together, we will share and reflect on our internship experiences, discuss democracy and the politics of community action, in light of our experiences, readings, and other class activities. In our discussions, we will integrate scholarly and other kinds of discourse and activities, with an emphasis on community "voices" which are not often heard in academic or public policy debates. Our sessions will also include individual presentations on internships, and dialogue with community activists. I have invited the first several community presenters; the rest will be people you invite from your host organizations.

The primary written work of the course will be a journal, intended to give you the opportunity to integrate reflection and experience on a frequent, regular basis. Plan to write at least three times a week, and to address the following topics at least once a week each: an issue or theme from the class readings, in light of your internship; the seminar discussions and activities, in light of your internship; a critical incident from or reflection prompted by your internship, which may not be directly connected to either the readings or the activities for that week. Feel free to add other topics, to include newspaper articles, photographs, flyers, or other material relevant to your topic, and to be creative. Remember that, although this journal is not expected to be a polished essay, it should not be purely stream of consciousness, either. Writing in your journal will be most valuable if you use it consistently to reflect, intellectually and emotionally, on specific issues and experiences. The journal must be typed or word-processed, double-spaced. You will hand in your journal every other week during the semester; the final entry will be a summary analysis of your internship experience. There will also be a community service writing assignments.

There will also be several activities scheduled to take place outside of class, including videos, and a class community work project. Additional information about assignments will be given in class. The assignments are indicated in the course outline below. It is likely like that the syllabus will change, in response to your interests as well as my perceptions of what the group needs to work on. Be sure to check email regularly. There will also be a folder for this class on the classes server, which includes a folder for you to talk with each other, and another internal folder containing this syllabus and other assignments, and all changes and updates, etc. (This is an experiment; I want to be able to communicate with you more efficiently, and conserve paper. You may also submit written work to me electronically). The video classroom has been reserved for Wednesdays 4–11 (to make it easier for everyone to see the films, we will schedule two showings);

a schedule will be posted in the class folder. So, you will also need to get in the habit of checking the classes server from time to time.

Because of the nature of this course, your participation is essential. You must attend all class meetings, having done the readings, and completed any other assignment for that session. I expect you to be equally responsible about your internship.

During our meetings, we will work together to create a class environment, in which we all try to express our views AND to listen to the views of others. This requires a degree of courage and trust; it is sometimes very hard to take a different stand on a controversial or sensitive issue, or to open ourselves to a very different viewpoint. But if we can't do it in the class, how will we ever be able to do so in our internships, or in public life?

Your final grade will combine your grades for the internship, based on the internship evaluation meeting, the internship presentations, and the community service writing assignment (33% of the grade, taken together), and for class participation (33% of the grade), based on your participation in discussions and other class activities (33% of the grade), and the journal (33% of the grade).

READINGS

The following required books are available for purchase in the bookstore; they are also on reserve in McCabe library. "Reader" refers to *Writing for Change: A Community Reader*. Readings marked with an asterisk will be distributed.

Melissa F. Greene, *Praying for Sheetrock*

Peter Medoff and H. Sklar, *Streets of Hope: The Fall and Rise of an Urban Neighborhood*

Ann Watters and M. Ford, *Writing for Change: A Community Reader*

COURSE OUTLINE AND SCHEDULE OF ASSIGNMENTS

T 1/17   Introduction: What is community action?
           Dialogue with Zulene Mayfield, Chester Residents Concerned for Quality Living (neighborhood organizing against the incinerator) Learning agreements distributed Praying for Sheetrock

T 1/24   Community service and community action
           Dialogue with Lisa Gaffney, Chester Community Improvement Project (housing) Handouts on service learning, housing* Internship presentation Learning agreement due.

Sat. 1/28 Community work project with CCIP

T 1/31   Family and community

Internship presentation
Reader, pp. 1-39
Roots assignment
Learning agreement due
Journal due

T2n   **Multicultural politics**
Dialogue with Fernando Chang-Muy (local activism)
Internship presentation
Reader, 40-81.

T 2/14   **The individual and community action**
Internship presentation
Reader, 86–135
Journal due

T 2/21   **Knowledge, education, theory, and practice**
Internship presentation
Reader, 139–199
Handouts on different ways of knowing*

T 2/28   **Health and community action**
Midsemester internship self-evaluations
Reader, 303–72
Journal due

Spring Break

T 3/14   **Outsiders and community action**
Internship presentation
Reader, Community service writing student projects at the end of each chapter
Handouts on community service writing*
Community service writing proposals due

T 3/21   **Power and empowerment**
Internship presentation
Reader, 206–50
Journal due

T 3/28	Participatory democracy and leadership
	Internship presentation
	Reader, 251–299

T 4/4	The environment and community action
	Internship presentation
	Reader, 379-446
	Journal due

T 4/11	The politics of community action: case study
	Internship presentation
	Streets of Hope, Chs. 1–5

T 4/18	The politics of community action: case study, cont.
	Final internship presentations and self-evaluations
	Streets of Hope, Chs. 6–9

| May 13 | Complete journal and summary essay due |

Political Science 19: Democratic Theory and Practice

SWARTHMORE COLLEGE

Professor Meta Mendel-Reyes
Spring 1995, Th 11:20 am – 12:35 pm, Trotter 128.

> *"In the case of a word like democracy, not only is there no agreed definition, but the attempt to make one is resisted from all sides. It is almost universally felt that when we call a country democratic we are praising it; consequently the defenders of every kind of regime claim that it is a democracy, and fear that they might have to stop using the word if it were tied down to one meaning."*
>
> GEORGE ORWELL
> "POLITICS AND THE ENGLISH LANGUAGE"

> *"What we call today democracy is a form of government where the few rule, at least supposedly in the interests of the many."*
>
> HANNAH ARENDT, ON REVOLUTION

The root meaning of the word democracy is "rule of the people." This seems like a simple, straightforward idea. Today, nearly everyone agrees that political power belongs in the hands of the people. But the appearance is deceptive: democracy in the United States raises a host of complex questions, both practical and theoretical. What explains the gap between the nearly universal commitment to democracy, and the fact that most people barely participate in ruling themselves? Can people wield power effectively in a large, bureaucratic, nation-state? Is democracy simply about the institutions of government? Power is surely also exercised, for example, in the economy, families and educational institutions. What does democracy entail in these contexts? Can political democracy occur in a country in which there are tremendous economic and social equalities? Does democracy require absolute equality? And what does it mean for "the people" to "have" power, anyway? Must political decisions be made by consensus to be considered truly democratic? When and how do political movements arise, in which people attempt to empower themselves and to reclaim democracy?

In this class we will explore these and other questions by comparing a wide range of democratic political theory to the practice of American politics. Because the questions are big and difficult, we can pursue them only in a preliminary way. The aim of our work together is not to reach definitive conclusions, but to challenge your preconceptions, raise some basic problems, introduce you to some of the most important attempts at answers, and to give you opportunities to engage in the activity of theorizing about democracy, which is, in my experience, essential yet often missing from democratic practice.

COURSE FORMAT AND ASSIGNMENTS

This class emphasizes discussion and brief lectures, but there will also be classroom exercises, videos, one or more outside speakers and a theory in practice experience, which will take place in the community. Your participation is indispensable, because the most important political thinking occurs in public discourse about common problems or divisive differences. Although a classroom has different purposes and standards from those of a town meeting or a campaign debate, this course should still be a forum for genuinely political conversation.

Together, we will try to create a class environment in which we all try to express our views AND to listen to the views of others. This requires a degree of courage and trust; it is sometimes very hard to take a different stand on a controversial or sensitive issue, or to open ourselves to a very different viewpoint. But if we can't do it in the class, how will we ever be able to do so in public life?

Class participation is a large percentage of the final grade: 25%. You will be graded on your daily participation in class discussion, and in other class activities, including helping to lead discussion, a debate, and a town meeting. On the first day, I will collect information about the kind of class participation that helps each of you learn the best (small group discussion, large group discussion, debate, lecture), and I will try to accommodate you as much as possible. There is no midterm or final, so your participation in class will be the only way to demonstrate your overall knowledge of the subject matter of this course. So, I expect you to come to class each day, having read the materials and thought carefully about them. I will let you know what your class participation grade is at mid-semester.

There will be several, very short writing assignments (25% of the grade), which will ask you to do different kinds of written work appropriate to democratic theory or practice, including a theory in practice report. There will be an essay grade (50%), based on one 5 – 7 page essay and one 10 – 12 page essay. Writing about and doing political theory will likely be new to many of you, and challenging to all of us. In the first paper, you will critically analyze political theories about an issue raised in the first part of the course. The second paper will give you an opportunity to theorize politically yourself about a problem in democratic theory and practice, in light of texts from the last part of the course. NOTE that no late papers will be accepted, and all assignments must be completed to pass the course.

Additional information about assignments will be given in class. The assignments are indicated in the course outline below (subject to change). There will be a folder for this class on the classes server, which includes a folder for you to talk with each other about democratic theory and practice, and the class. Another internal folder will contain this syllabus and all assignments, reading and discussion guides, the video dates, and all changes and updates, etc. (this is an experiment—I want to be able to communicate with you more efficiently, and conserve paper—You may also submit written work to me electronically). The video classroom has been reserved for Wednesdays 4-1 1 (to make it easier for everyone to see the films, we will schedule two showings); a schedule will be posted in the class folder. IMPORTANT: please get in the habit of checking the classes server the day after each class, and checking email from time to time.

READINGS

The following required books are available for purchase in the bookstore; they are also on reserve in McCabe library. Readings marked with an asterisk are in Green, ed., *Democracy*; readings marked with a @ will be distributed.

John Gaventa, *Power and Powerlessness: Quiescence and Rebellion in an Appalachian Vale*

Phillip Green, ed., *Democracy: Key Concepts in Critical Theory*

Melissa F. Greene, *Praying for Sheetrock*

Daniel C. Kemmis, *Community and The Politics of Place*

Abraham Lincoln, ed. and introduced by Cuomo and Holzer, *Lincoln on Democracy*

James Miller, "Democracy is in the Streets " From *Port Huron to the Siege of Chicago*

COURSE OUTLINE AND SCHEDULE OF ASSIGNMENTS

T 1/17   Introduction

            A. What is democracy?

Th l/19   Green, Williams (intro &selection I)* Personal experience in democracy due (1/2 page)

B.   Democratic theory and practice 1: the civil rights movement

T 1/24   Greene, *Praying for Sheetrock,* Parts One and Two

Th 1/26   Greene, Part Three

C.   The classical theory of democracy

T 1/31   Rousseau, Mill, Tocqueville (sels. 2- 4b abstract due (I page)

D.   Representative democracy

Th 2/2   Madison, Mill, Dahl (5-7)*

E.   Democratic theory and practice III: Lincoln, slavery, the Civil War

T 2/7   Lincoln, tba

Th 2/9   Lincoln, tba

            Class debate: Lincoln-Douglass

            Debate statement due (I page)

T 2/14   Lincoln, tba Happy Valentine's Day!

Th 2/16   King, "Letter From a Birmingham Jail- Theory in practice proposal due

F.   Inequality and democracy

T 2/21   Freidman, Macpherson, Parenti, Green (17-20)*

Th 2/23   Bowles & Gintis, Elkin, Parenti, Phillips (21-24)*

G.   Democratic theory and practice IV: Appalachian miners

T 2/28   Gaventa, Power and Powerlessness, Part I (I. 1- 1.3), Part I I (all)

Th 3/2   Gaventa, 5, 6 (intro, 6.3), 7 (intro, 7.4, 7.5), Part IV (all), 10

BREAK   Be sure to theorize and practice democracy regularly!

H. Democratic elitism

T 3/14   Michels, Weber, Schumpeter, Berelson, Crozieet al, Dahl (8-13)*

Th 3/16   Dewey, Bachrach, Prewitt & Stone (14-16)*

I.   Democratic theory and practice V: SDS during the Sixties

T 3/21   Miller "Democracy is in the Streets" tba

Th 3/21   Miller, tba
            First essay due
            J. Action

T 3/28   Luxembourg, Arendt, Carter, Walzer (25-28)*
            K. Participation and Representation

Th 3/30   Gould, Green, Barber (29-30)*
            Theory in practice report due
            L. Community and Democracy

T 4/4   Kemmis, Community and the Politics of Place, Chs. One-Five

Th 4/6   Kemmis, Chs. Six-Eight
            M. Town meeting
T   4/11 no readings Citizen statement due (I page) Th 4/13 no readings

            N. Democratic rights
4/18   Rousseau, Mill, Bay, Kateb, Young (intro, 32-36)
            O. Democratic theory and practice VI: Contemporary rights issues

Th 4/20   Immigration: guest speaker readings to be assigned

T 4/25   Issue of class's choice readings to be assigned

Th 4/27   Conclusion
May 3   Final essay due

Multiculturalism and Ethnicity in Education:
Transforming the Trinity Community and Curriculum for the Millennium
TRINITY COLLEGE, HARTFORD

Interdisciplinary: Educ 236, Amst 236, Anth 234, CDES 236
Professor: Janet Bauer
Spring, 1999 TR 2:40 – 3:55, McCook 307

COURSE DESCRIPTION

What are the prospects for achieving social integration and equal opportunity in a diverse society through education and what is the importance of multiculturalism or diversity in a cultural democracy? This course explores the cultural and social bases of learning, achievement, and interactions among linguistic, cultural, class, and 'racial' groups primarily in the United States, using case studies, research findings, and personal experiences. We will explore the role of schooling and the classroom in both creating and challenging inequalities on the basis of ethnicity/race and cultural expectations. We will also consider the importance of learning about our own and others' cultures and how this can be achieved. Finally we will debate bilingualism (and ebonics), multiculturalism, cultural pluralism, ethnic or diversity studies, magnet schools, and other programs and approaches or policies which address the needs, concerns, and interests of African American, Hispanic American, Asian American, Native American, Immigrant American, and White ethnic American learners as well as American society generally. Our research focus this semester will be Trinity College.

COURSE GOALS

1) to achieve a basic conceptual, theoretical and emotional understanding of race/ethnic/minority status and multiculturalism/diversity agendas as these operate in American culture and education;

2) to understand the relationships and experiences of various minorities and cultures in American schools and to understand the way in which educational processes both sustain and challenge inequalities and different opportunities by race, ethnicity and culture (racial formations)

3) to begin thinking about different pedagogies and methods for teaching about and to different groups

4) to learn the methods of cultural research (interviews, for example) and observation

5) to develop different skills of oral presentation, especially in teaching activities for enhancing diversity

6) to apply this knowledge to thinking about the programs or policies a plural, diverse society might use to achieve real equality of opportunity through education and social participation

through a class research project at Trinity College that will result in a report on diversity at Trinity to be submitted to the President of the College.

REQUIRED READING

These required texts are available at the Trinity Bookstore.

G. Williams, *Life on the Color Line*

Tatum, *Why Are All the Black Kids Sitting Together in the Cafeteria?*

Delpit, *Other People's Children. Cultural Conflict in the Classroom*

Seller and Weis, *Beyond Black and White. New Faces and Voices in US Schools*

Nussbaum, *Cultivating Humanity*

The Multicultural/Diversity Reader

COURSE REQUIREMENTS

You are responsible for understanding the contents of this syllabus and what is announced, presented or assigned in class. The course readings have been selected to provide you with interesting and timely material with which to ponder the questions we will address. However are also responsible for assigned events, assigned films, class lectures and whatever supplemental material is necessary for you to complete your assignments. You are expected to ask questions about what you don't understand because I will evaluate your written work in terms of how well you integrate and consider class concepts and readings.

In order to get a passing grade, you must complete all assignments, including (1) Participation (15%)--instructor, peer, and self evaluations; attendance (2) Journal (15%)—1 will look for these specific entries for the collaborative Trinity for the Trinity Race Experience Component with cultural group on campus and for The Trinity Transformation Component "interviews and "observations "self commentary/reflect on the group project process or collaborative learning" comments on pedagogical issues like the effectiveness of films as medium for (3) Trinity Diversity Project (with both individual and group components (70%) "The Race Experience Component (25%) involves (1) 5-7 page group paper and presentation from collecting race and ethnic experiences at Trinity, based on participation and discussion with individuals in different cultural groups on campus; the paper will be judged partly on your integrating class concepts/readings into the paper (10%); (2) a text for your five minute "guerrilla theater" or skit presentations of your findings on campus and the actual presentation (10%) and your journal reflections (2-3 pgs) on what you have learned about race/ethnicity from this project and the process of collaborative learning submitted separately (5%). "The Trinity Transformations Component (45%) which involves (1) two (4-5 page) individual papers (20%)--on aspects of diversity education using our class readings as they apply to Trinity as background for doing (2) campus research on the aspect of the campus diversity project assigned to your group and the preparation of a final 7-8 page written report (with assessment of situation and recommendations) that will be presented in class with recommendations (20%) and (3) your journal reflections what specifically you have learned about diversity and education at Trinity and the processes of collaborative learning involved, submitted as separate 2-3 page paper (5%) and "The Report to the President-- involves an class endeavor to integrate the various aspects of the report to send or present in person to President Dobelle (part of your participation grade).

ASSIGNMENT FORMAT

Paper assignments should be typed, with pages numbered and stabled before they are handed in. You should always keep a copy for yourself and when working on the computer you must save more than one copy of your documents in the event of disk errors. In fact it's best to have a second backup disk, not just a second backup file. Paper assignments will be graded on how well they fulfill the assignment as well as the extent to which they integrate class terms, concepts, and examples in supporting observations and points. Journals can be in binders or kept on computer disk (*note I will then review printouts when journals are checked.)

CLASS FORMAT

Lecture/discussion sections. Themes and questions are provided for each class period and you should read the assigned materials with these in mind. You should read assigned material by the class period for which it is assigned so that you can enrich class discussion, understand lectures better, and contribute to the work of your assigned project groups. You will also be meeting outside of class in assigned groups. You are responsible for critically assessing films, lecture materials, and the assigned reading, whether those reading materials are fully covered in class or not.

PLAGIARISM AND LATE POLICY

Absences will affect your participation grade. You will be absent if you are not present when role is taken. Use your three absences well so that if you have an emergency or illness you will have these "sick days" available to you. After its due date, your papers will be penalized one grade level for every week they are late. Plagiarism is unacceptable and results in academic disciplinary action. If you are unsure about what plagiarism is, review the student handbook for this information. Be extremely careful when paraphrasing or quoting the material of others; always provide citations for the material you use.

COURSE OUTLINE

Part I.   **Introduction to Concepts of Race, Culture, and Multiculturalism in Learning**

1/19   Introduction, I-Am assignment; read over "Journal Learning" exercise
            What is Whiteness?

1/21   in-class exercise and discussion

Reading: Williams, ch. 1-4, Macintosh; recommended: Roman

The significance of race, ethnicity, class and identity in schooling

1/26   Reading: Williams, ch. 5-10; Tatum ch. 1-2; recommended: Omi and Winant

1/28   Reading, Williams, 11-17; Tatum, ch. 3-5; recommended: Hatcher and Troyna
        check journals; group progress reports and group meetings on plans/questions
        above continued, with Pedagogical Focus

2/2   Reading: Cohen, ch. 2; workbook exercises ("Critical Incident Review")
        *in class viewing of the following films on reserve: "The Colors Between Black and
        White" and "Race: The World's Most Dangerous Myth"
        From Difference to Cultural Democracy and Multiculturalism

2/4   Reading: Williams, 18-21; Greener; Cushner; recommended: Pinar*
        *class discussion and checking journals for film commentary and progress on inter-
        views and outline of important questions

2/9   Reading: Nussbaum, ch 3-4; Feinberg, ch. 8; recommended: Feinberg, ch. 5*;
        McLaren
        *Discussion groups
        *recommended Feb. 6 Gomez Pena performance, Borderscape 2000; 8 p.m. Austin
        Arts

Part II.   **Between Culture, Family and School: the different experiences and needs of
            diverse students**

2/11   Reading: Seller and Wise, Ch. 4, 7; Recommended: Claude Steele
        group paper due on experiences of others; groups discussion: check journals and con-
        sider performance texts

        Language, Bilingualism and Identity
2/16   Reading: Seller and Wise, ch. 1,3; Tatum: ch. 8
        Films "How We Feel: Hispanic Students Speak Out"; and "Cultural Bias in
        Education"
        *individual assessments of the collaborative process due

2/18   Immigrants and Biracial families: strategies in schooling
        Readings: Seller and Wise, 5-6; Tatum ch. 9; recommended: Morales, Swenson
        *theater text due--set performances work on over reading week

Reading Week meetings to practice and/or give performances

3/2   Asian and American Indian experiences
     Reading: Seller and Wise 8-10, 2;
     Film: "Asianization of America"

3/4   White diversity: class, sexuality and gender
     Reading: Seller and Wise 11-13, Tatum, ch. 6; Recommended: Feinberg, ch. 6*

     *group meetings to discuss plans for continuing Trinity Project, topics, interviews and information. Pinpoint and evaluate multiculturalism in several areas: (1) social /interactional atmosphere—dorms, extracurricular programs, political representation, and activities; (2) curriculum and academic programs (courses, in class interation etc.); (3) the Trinity neighborhood and learning corridor involvement—tutoring, program planning, museums (4) demographics: student population and retention—diversity of students, faculty and staff—hiring, admissions and testing and retention policies, and (5) faculty and administration policies, mission statements and philosophy about diversity. Some groups may be duplicated if the class is too large.

Part III. **Inside the Schools: Classrooms Culture and Multicultural (to/for) teaching-Culture and Teachers: pedagogical strategies**

3/9   Reading: Delpit, Parts I and 11; recommended: Sleeter
     The cultures of knowledge: Curriculum Content and Special Studies

3/11   Reading: reading: Nussbaum Ch. 1-2, Kohl; Recommended, Banks, Ch. 7-8
     *First background paper due on some aspect of curriculum or content; group discussions

3/16   Continued, Reading: Valdes; Laframboise. Film: "Bilingualism a True Advantage"

3/18   continued, Reading: Nussbaum ch. 5-8

     *Preliminary reports due on Trinity Projects; checking journals

3/23   continued, review evaluations of previous films; reading: Wallace; McCarthy

     Film: "Where the Spirit Lives",
     Racial Dialog and Interaction

3/25   Reading: Tatum, ch. 10; Perez
     Film: Dealing with Diversity in the Classroom

     *second background paper due on aspects of pedagogy, interaction and learning; checking journals and detailed outline of group projects due; discussion

Spring Break

Part IV.   The cultural democracy and Policy debates: one culture or many?

4/6   Reading: Nussbaum, conclusion; Delpit Part 111; recommended: Feinberg, ch. 1-2*

4/8   Continued, reading: Tatum, ch. 7; Iris Young, Cohen, ch. 7, AAU&C Diversity
             Report
             *Discussion of group progress; checking journals

4/1   Structural approaches: single sex schools and charter schools versus magnet schools,
             school choice and desegregation
             Reading: Riordan; Murdock; Wells & Crain; Feinberg, ch. 9

4/15   continued discussion and Begin Group presentations
             *Beginning the dialog: Draft of all Group Projects due, bring to class

4/20   Group Presentations

4/22   Group presentations

4/27   Final Group Reports Due—begin working on integration of separate reports, includ-
             ing first group reports on experience

4/29   continued, personal evaluation and journals due

RESERVE READING BIBLIOGRAPHY (IN ORDER OF READING)

Macintosh, Peggy, 1997 White Privilege and Male Privilege. In *Critical White Studies*. Delgado and Stefancic, eds. Pp. 291–9. Temple University Press.

Beverly Daniel Tatum, 1997 *Why are all the Black Kids Sitting together in the Cafeteria*. New York: Basic Books.

Roman, L. 1993 White is a Color Too. In *Race, Identity and Representation in Education*. McCarthy and Crichlow, eds. Pp. 71-88. New York: Routledge.

Omi and Winant, 1993 On the Theoretical Concept of Race. In *Race, Identity and Representation in Education*. McCarthy and Crichlow, eds. Pp. 3 10. New York: Routledge.

Hatcher and Troyna, 1993 Racialization and Children. *In Race, Identity and Representation in Education*. McCarthy and Crichlow, eds Pp. 109-125 New York: Routledge.

Cohen, M. 1998 The Innocent Scapegoat: Human Biological Variation and Race. Culture of Intolerance. New Haven: Yale University Press.

Greener, 1993 The White Problem. In *Blacks at Harvard*. Sollers et al., eds. New York University Press.

Pinar, 1993 Notes on Understanding Curriculum as a Racial Text. *In Race, Identity and Representation in Education*. McCarthy and Crichlow, eds. Pp. 60-70. New York: Routledge.

Feinberg, Walter, 1998 *Common Schools. Uncommon Identities. National Unity and Cultural Difference.* New Haven: Yale University Press.

McLaren, Peter, 1994 White Terror and Oppositional Agency: Towards a Critical Multiculturalism. In *Multiculturalism.* Goldberg, ed. Basil Blackwell.

Cushner and Trifonovitch, 1989 "Understanding Barriers to Dealing with Diversity" in *Social Education* (Sept.)

Steele, Claude, 1992 Race and the Schooling of Black Americans. *The Atlantic Monthly,* pp. 68-78 (April).

Morales, J. 1996 Unpacking the White Privilege Diaperbag. In *Everyday Acts Against Racism.* Reddy, eds. pp. 40-49. Seal Press.

Swenson, S. 1996 "That Wouldn't Be Fair." In *Everyday Acts Against Racism.* Reddy, eds. pp. 40-61. Seal Press

Sleeter, C. 1993 How White Teachers Construct Race. In *Race, Identity and Representation in Education.* McCarthy and Crichlow, eds Pp. 157-171. New York: Routledge.

Kohl, R. 1995 Should We Burn Babar. *In Should We Burn Babar.* The New York Press.

Banks, James, 1991 *Teaching Strategies for Ethnic Studies.* Allyn and Bacon.

Valdes, G. 1997 Dual-Language Immersion Programs: A Cautionary Note. Harvard Educational Review 67:3:392-429 (fall)

La Framboise et al. 1995 Psychological Impact of Biculturalism. In *The Culture and Psychology Reader,* Goldeberger and Veroff, edspp.489-535. New York University Press.

Wallace, Michelle 1993 Multiculturalism and Oppositionality. In *Race, Identity and Representation in Education.* McCarthy and Crichlow, eds. Pp. 251-261. New York: Routledge.

McCarthy, Cameron, 1993 After the Canon. In Race, Identity and Representation in Education. McCarthy and Crichlow, eds. Pp. 289-305. New York: Routledge.

Perez, G.

1993 Opposition and the Education of Chicana/os. In *Race, Identity and Representation in Education.* McCarthy and Crichlow, eds. Pp. 268-279. Routledge.

Feinberg, Walter 1998 *Common Schools, Common Identities.* New Haven: Yale University Press.

Young, Iris, 1995 Social Movements and the Politics of Difference. In *Campus Wars. Multiculturalism and the Politics of Difference.* Arthur and Shapiro, eds. Pp. 199-225. Westview Press.

Cohen, Mark, 1998 Affirmative Action and Curriculum Inclusion. Culture of Intolerance. New Haven: Yale University Press.

AAC and U Diversity Report Diversity Works. The Emerging Picture of How Students Benefit.

Murdock, 1998 Numbers Game. Reason (October)

Riordan, 1998 The Future of Single Sex Schools. In Separated by Sex. pp. 41–52. AAUW

Wells and Crain, 1997 Saving Face in the Suburbs. In *Stepping over the Color Line.* Yale University Press.

Workbook Exercises from: *Human Diversity in Action. Developing Multicultural*

Competencies for the Classroom (Cushner, McGraw Hill, 1999)

Suggested WebSites for Diversity Information
http://www.execpc.com/-dboals/diversit.htmI
http:Hcurry.edschool.virginia.edu/go/multicultural/home.html

Appendix

Urban Planning 634
Integrative Field Experience
University of Michigan

URBAN PLANNING 634: INTEGRATIVE FIELD EXPERIENCE

Art and Architecture Building
Professor Margaret Dewar
University of Michigan
Fall/Winter 1999
Integrative Field Experience

- Number of credits is most likely 3, but will be determined depending on the number in the class and the work plan.

- Urban planning students must take 6 credits for this course by the end of the school year.

- Other students may take the course for 3 credits for one semester with an appropriate work plan and permission of the instructor.

This class will work as a community planning team on a variety of projects with community partners in Detroit during the year. We will begin with three projects:

1) Completing four parts of a plan for strengthening housing in the Gratiot Woods neighborhood. Our partner is the Detroit Catholic Pastoral Alliance.

2) Analyzing information collected from businesses in the West Vernor area of Southwest Detroit and laying out alternative ways for community-based organizations to strengthen the commercial district. Our partner is the Southwest Detroit Business Association.

3) Analyzing and presenting information and laying out ideas for directions for action to help with the planning for an in-place industrial park in the Grinnell/City Airport area of the Eastside of Detroit. Our partner is the Eastside Industrial Council and the steering committee for the industrial park.

Students working on different teams will meet for class at different times, to be scheduled as much as possible within the block of time reserved for this course in the class schedule.

The scope-of-services statements detail the work our community partners and I expect that the projects will entail. You will revise these statements with me in the first weeks of class so that the work is consistent with our partners' needs and the background and interests that students bring to each team.

GOALS AND APPROACH

This course aims:

1. To allow you to use the range of skills gained during graduate study in helping to resolve urban problems;

2. To produce work that helps our community partners in their work to strengthen their neighborhoods;

3. To give you experience in working with clients/partners on issues that are at the heart of much urban redevelopment: finding ways to provide and reinforce affordable housing; planning ways to strengthen neighborhood-oriented retail and services in lower income areas; strengthening existing, often declining, industrial areas that can be an important source of jobs for residents of the city.

4. To help you gain experience in organizing and working in teams;

5. To give you experience in using written, graphic, and oral communication to convey information effectively.

This course differs from most other courses you have taken because of the work on a project with a community partner:

• Faculty, students, and community partners will work together in a style that enables everyone to bring his or her different skills and talents to the projects. None of us has single "right" answers, but we will collaborate to discover ways to do excellent work. Our community partners will teach us a great deal in this process.

• The course will be complete when you deliver a very good final product to the community partner. Unlike the writing of a term paper dashed off the night before, completing a high quality product will involve numerous drafts and revisions. Planning the work so that you are finished with that excellent final version at the end of the semester or the school year is one of the challenges of the course.

• We will often be working with people with quite different life experiences than some of us, and, therefore, addressing issues of multicultural communication will be a theme throughout the course.

• To the greatest extent we can, we will be doing "community-based" planning. This means that the agenda and the definition of need comes from our community partners. The scope of services statements are a result of my work to define needs with the community partners. Throughout the year, we will decide choices among alternative directions through consultation with our partners. We work with our partners as colleagues with complementary skills and resources rather than as technical experts who have the final answers.

- We will expect and adapt to considerable change in the scope and definition of our work through the semester. Our community partners' situations will change for numerous reasons—for instance, their funding will fluctuate, city policies and regulations will change, the membership of their community-based boards will turn over, staff will resign and new staff will join the organization. As a result, what they need from us will also change, and we will respond to this need as much as we can.

INITIAL SCHEDULE

Student teams will meet with our community partners during the next week:

Sept. 13:   Gratiot Woods group will meet with Cleophilus Bradley of Detroit Catholic Pastoral Alliance for a tour and background information on the neighborhood. We will leave at 1:30 p.m. from the southeast corner of the building and will return by 5:00. (The Gratiot Woods group needs to make sure that someone in the group attends the Housing Committee meeting on the fourth Monday of each month at 7 p.m.)

Sept. 15:   Vemor group will meet with Kathy Wendler of Southwest Detroit Business Association for an overview and background and discussion of the needs. We will leave at 1:30 p.m. from the southeast corner of the building, and we expect to be back by 5:00.

Sept. 17:   Grinnell/City Airport group will meet with Linda Stingl at the Eastside Industrial Council for a discussion of the in-place industrial park and the group's needs. We'll leave at 1:30, from southeast corner of the building, and return by 5 o'clock.

Sept. 20:   Chris Bray, director of housing for DCPA, will meet with the Gratiot Woods group in Ann Arbor to discuss the needed work and to offer more background.

After the orientation meetings, the first task will be to develop a work plan for the fall semester based on the scope of services, additional input from the client/partner, and the skills and interests of the students. This plan will be as detailed as we can make it, with the dates products are due and with steps in completing products.

Oct. 1:   (optional) Urban planning students are organizing a tour of Detroit, which you can join for a more general view of the city. In addition, we can organize a broader tour for the class for a Saturday, if that context would be helpful.

Beginning about a month into the project, you will have meetings and presentations with the clients/community partners. We will plan the meetings in detail and do "dry runs" or "rehearsals." We will give each other extensive feedback on the dry runs. After the presentation/working session, we will have a "debrief" session to discuss what went right and what could have gone better and how better outcomes might have been achieved. At the meetings we will likely get extensive feedback from the community partner that will lead to revisions and determine next steps.

GRADES

For written and graphic materials to be presented to the community partners, you will do drafts, often several drafts, on which I will provide feedback. Before drafts, we will work on outlines and plans for graphics. Drafts, dry runs, and interim presentations are learning experiences and will not be graded.

Grades will be determined primarily by the quality of the final products, the work you ultimately deliver after the processes of feedback and revision to respond to faculty's, other students', and community partners' input:

Final product quality (75% of grade): The written products, the oral presentations of final products, and any other forms of final products are included. I will assess this with input from our community partners. My views about the quality of the work will be heavily influenced by how well you have addressed the needs the community partners have expressed throughout the work period. Your views about the quality of products, both of your own and others' are also welcome. A major difference between this and other courses is that the coursework will only be complete when it is of quality that will meet the community partners' needs.

Team and class participation (25% of grade): This relates to the extent of your involvement with your team's work and with the class. I may ask for your views on this through a form I will distribute. I will also be interested in your assessment of your own contribution and others', if you wish to give it.

EXPENSES

Your expenses that exceed those of a normal course will be paid by funds from grants to the Urban and Regional Planning Program. (See the written policy on cost reimbursement.) The Gratiot Woods project is part of a much larger, two-year University of Michigan/Detroit Eastside Community Collaborative partnership to strengthen the capacity of nonprofits to do large-scale development of affordable housing. This is funded by a grant from the Fannie Mae Foundation.

RESOURCE MATERIALS AND READINGS

We will collect readings and reference materials as needed and will place them somewhere that the class agrees upon. These materials will often be someone's personal property and are available for you to borrow for your convenience. We will add to the reference list throughout the year. Library-owned books will be on reserve, as needed, at the Media Union.

DRAFT, URBAN PLANNING 634, SCOPE OF SERVICES

Strengthening Housing in Gratiot Woods

The Detroit Catholic Pastoral Alliance works to strengthen housing in the Gratiot Woods neighborhood. Most of the organization's work in the past has involved the rehabilitation of individual houses. DCPA has developed a plan for affordable housing development, current as of March 1999. The "target area" is the Gratiot Woods neighborhood, bounded by Gratiot, I-94, Cadillac, Rohns, and Warren (see attached map).

The plan that DCPA developed identifies five strategies: expand community involvement in affordable housing development activities; build organizational capacity by expanding and diversifying funding sources and obtaining training for staff and committee members; increase the quantity of quality, affordable housing through rehabilitation and infill construction for resale or rental; increase the quality and value of owner occupied homes by coordinating home repair; and coordinate demolition of houses that cannot be rehabilitated.

DCPA would now like to develop the plan further. The needs include looking at traffic problems and how to deal with them; examining commercial opportunities, especially on Gratiot; and analyzing how to phase development to achieve certain goals.

Students will work closely with Chris Bray, Housing Director of the Detroit Catholic Pastoral Alliance, on the following tasks:

1. *Plan ways to address traffic problem.* Residents feel that heavy traffic, moving at high speeds, is a major problem for the strengthening of the neighborhood. McClellan, which runs through the middle of the neighborhood, is a connector between Warren and I-94. Students will collect information on traffic volume and speed and other issues to analyze the traffic problems and will develop alternative ways to solve the problems, including the calming of traffic on McClellan.

2. *Assess commercial development opportunities.* Gratiot, once a thriving commercial corridor, now has much less activity, although it carries a high volume of traffic. Gratiot is not pedestrian-friendly. Students will address the question of where neighborhood-oriented commercial activity might be encouraged and why. They will consider opportunities on Gratiot as well as other neighborhood streets.

3. *Develop a plan for the phasing of infill housing development and housing rehabilitation.* The DCPA housing plan lays out several strategies for strengthening housing. The plan needs to be extended to detail the phasing of activities. The questions to address are where the efforts should focus and why and what order of activities will have the greatest impact and why.

4. *Satisfy ways to develop neighborhood identity through the nature of the physical fabric of the area and the character of the housing and other structures.* The DCPA details numerous guidelines for housing design and community design. However, these are not yet detailed enough to be implemented. The plan will be extended to illustrate concepts of architectural design and to map and illustrate alternative ways to create a neighborhood identity through physical design.

Students will work with Bray, members of the Housing Committee, and others as appropriate to lay out alternative ways to address the four topics. They will meet intermittently with Bray and others for presentations and feedback.

At the end of the students' work on this project, the students will deliver a report that details the plans they have developed with Bray and community residents.

Contact information: Chris Bray, Housing Director, Detroit Catholic Pastoral Alliance (DCPA). Cleophilus Bradley, Housing Coordinator, DCPA. Sister Cathey DeSantis, Executive Director, DCPA.

Strengthening Neighborhood-Oriented Retail and Services

The Southwest Detroit Business Association is involved in planning and encouraging the redevelopment of Southwest Detroit in ways that improve the quality of life for people who live and work there. Its major focus is on strengthening the commercial areas along West Vernor from Dearborn to the former train station near Corktown and the old Tiger Stadium.

Our work will relate to two distinct areas that SDBA serves, the Vernor/Junction area and the Vernor/Springwells area. Vernor/Junction is one of the most active commercial areas in the Detroit Empowerment Zone. It serves a residential area with a large Latino, population; its dominant physical feature is the Holy Redeemer Church and School. Vernor/Springwells is the last commercial node on Vernor before one reaches Dearborn. It is an even busier retail area than Vernor/Junction, serving a diverse residential population.

A year and a half ago, I began working with students on a community-based research and planning project to assess the effects of the Detroit Empowerment Zone on employers and to make recommendations for strengthening the Empowerment Zone efforts. Although we were working most closely with the Empowerment Zone leaders at the time, I also worked with leaders of community-based organizations to make sure the interviews with employers included questions for which they needed answers and reflected their knowledge of the commercial and industrial areas. I worked with Southwest Detroit Business Association on the plan for the work in the two West Vernor areas. The interviews are complete, and the data, combined with other information, can now be used to give SDBA considerable information on the status of the area and to build on employers' suggestions for making a range of recommendations for SDBA's action.

Students will work on three related tasks:

1. *Analyze the data from the interviews and other information to detail the characteristics of each of the two areas.* The analysis will address questions such as: What kinds of businesses operate in each area? How many people work there? Why are the businesses located there? What changes have they made in the way they operate in the last four years or so? How many offer jobs for low-skilled, inexperienced workers? What are these jobs like? What are the characteristics of the workers and where do they live?

2. *Analyze the employers' views about the changes most needed in the area.* Write out alternative ways that SDBA might address these needs, if they are not already doing so. These recommendations

should draw on information from cases of community-initiated commercial revitalization around the country, on understanding the nature of the market the commercial area serves, and on knowledge of what SDBA already does.

3. *Assemble and present all information directly related to SDBA from each site so that SDBA knows the views expressed.* Some interviews include statements about SDBA, and these need to be collected and interpreted.

The data cover interviews with 36 employers in the Vernor/Junction area and 56 employers in the Vernor/Springwells area. In addition, we have photos of the street face, aerial photos, Sanborn maps, CAD versions of the Sanborns, and data on employee zip codes to use to map the geographic distribution of workers' residences using GIS.

We will work with Kathy Wendler, the director of SDBA. The final products for Wendler will be a presentation of the findings and recommendations and a report that details these.

Planning for an in-place industrial park on Detroit's Eastside

The Eastside Industrial Council's mission is to strengthen industry on the Eastside of Detroit. The organization's major current program is the creation of in-place industrial parks. In-place industrial parks are areas of older, already existing industry within cities. The businesses in the in-place parks organize themselves to work together to improve the environment for the businesses and to address common needs.

The director of the EIC, Linda Stingl, is now working with a steering committee to do a plan for an in-place industrial park in the Grinnell/City Airport area. The City Airport part is within the Detroit Empowerment Zone; Grinnell is outside the EZ. Renaissance Zones, where businesses are exempt from state and local taxes, are nearby.

Over the last year-and-a-half, I have worked with students to interview as many of the employers in the Grinnell/City Airport area as possible. Although the main purpose of the interviews was to learn about the effects of the Detroit Empowerment Zone, I also worked closely with the leaders of community-based organizations in the areas where we interviewed so that we could incorporate questions that they needed and so that the questions reflected their knowledge of the area. Linda Stingl was one of those leaders, and the information from the interviews and other sources can now be useful to her in planning the in-place industrial park.

Students will work on three major tasks:

1. *Analyze the data from the interviews and other information to detail characteristics of the area.* Explain who the employers are, why they are in the area, what they do, whom they employ, the kinds of entry-level jobs available, and any other important findings from the interviews and other available information.

2. *Analyze the employers' views about changes most needed in the area and lay out the recommendations for EIC that come from the interviews.* Lay out the major challenges the employers face in operating in this area.

3. *Recommend ways to strengthen an industrial area through an in-place industrial park, other than the ways EIC is already using.* To do so, draw on case studies and information about ways to strengthen existing, old industrial areas and to enable them to benefit neighborhoods as they themselves become stronger.

The final products for the project will be a presentation to Linda Stingl and/or the steering committee and a report detailing the findings. We may have interim presentations with Linda as well because she may need information as soon as it is ready.

Other preparations already completed in connection with this project are: Sanborn maps and aerial photos acquired, some photos taken of the Grinnell area, zip codes entered in a file ready for ArcView, and—soon—CAD versions created of the Sanborn maps.

ON DETROIT:

Fall 1999/Winter 2000.

Joe T. Darden, Richard Child Hill, June Thomas, and Richard Thomas, *Detroit: Race and Uneven Development* (Philadelphia: Temple University Press, 1987).

Thomas J. Sugrue, *The Origins of the Urban Crisis: Race and Inequality in Postwar Detroit* (Princeton: Princeton University Press, 1996).

June Manning Thomas, *Redevelopment and Race: Planning a Finer City in Postwar Detroit* (Baltimore: Johns Hopkins University Press, 1997).

ON COMMUNITY DEVELOPMENT PLANNING:

Peter Medoff and Holly Sklar, *Streets of Hope: The Fall and Rise of an Urban Neighborhood* (Boston, MA: South End Press, 1994).

John P. Kretzmann and John L. McKnight, *Building Communities from the Inside Out* (Evanston, IL: Center for Urban Affairs and Research, 1993).

Jim Rooney, *Organizing the South Bronx* (Albany: State University of New York, 1995).

ON INDUSTRIAL AND RETAIL/SERVICE AREAS:

Bennett Harrison and Marcus Weiss, *Workforce Development Networks: Community-Based Organizations and Regional Alliances* (Thousand Oaks, CA: Sage, 1998).

William Julius Wilson, *When Work Distances: The World of the New Urban Poor* (New York: Knopf, 1996).

Harry Holzer, *What Employers Want* (New York: Russell Sage, 1996).

Katherine Newman, *No Shame in My Game: The Working Poor in the Inner City* (New York: Knopf, 1999).

For Gratiot Woods:

The DCPA neighborhood housing plan.

The City of Detroit's Community Reinvestment Strategy plan for this area.

Traffic circulation plans for the Eastside by Kami Brown.

For West Vernor:

Background on Southwest Detroit Business Association.

Livernois and Vernor commercial development plan from Auerbach class.

City of Detroit Community Reinvestment Strategy plan for this area.

For Grinnell/City Aims:

Background on the Eastside Industrial Council.

Report from an architecture/planning studio on the Grinnell area.

East Williamsburg In-Place Industrial Park.

Background on another in-place industrial park plan in the city—Islandview industrial area.

Plan for industrial redevelopment in Delray, by Jackson, Robinson, et al.

Delray industrial development plan from Laura Auerbach's class.

City of Detroit Community Reinvestment Strategy plan for this area.

Public Life in America
Michigan State University

ATL 135: Public Life in America, Section 002

The Service-Learning Writing Project
Professor David Cooper
American Thought and Language at Michigan State University
Spring, 2000

The American Thought and Language Department prepares students for effective writing in various contexts, including academic, professional, personal, and public. The department recognizes that writing is an essential component of a student's intellectual endeavor linked to other aspects of communication such as reading, evaluating, reasoning, and speaking about specific subject matters. The American Thought and Language Department therefore emphasizes development of students' discourse skills in courses with American heritage content, stressing interdisciplinary and culturally diverse themes and readings as well as introducing students to literary, historical, social, political, and moral perspectives that seek to establish a coherent overview of American society and its place in the global community.

ATL 135 COURSE DESCRIPTION

Debate and deliberation are essential ingredients of democracy. For democracy to work, ordinary citizens must take part in the process of identifying social problems and finding solutions together. Unfortunately, too many citizens are not engaged in the ongoing work of democracy. Their lack of engagement is not a sign of satisfaction with the status quo, but too often an expression of cynicism, apathy, or a sense of powerlessness.

Why have we withdrawn from public associations? Why does our democratic system—the envy of the rest of the world—seem to be failing us? Why have so many of us lost faith in our common life? This special section of ATL 135—"Writing: Public Life in America"—will examine these difficult questions.

ATL 135 is a writing intensive course that engages students in public discourse on social issues that affect local and national communities. Students will analyze, evaluate, and present arguments on topics of current concern to different audiences. Students will also learn to moderate differing points of view on an issue and to find strategies that build toward consensus. An important goal of ATL 135 is to encourage student participation in the public sphere through active participation in open public forums as well as through classroom reading and writing. A significant portion of sections 002 and 003 of ATL 135 will be organized around three National Issues Forums (NIF) held in our community and around a smaller version of these forums (Study Circles) that students will be responsible for conducting in class at the end of the semester. We will use the NIF model of deliberation and consensus building to explore several critical issues in contemporary American public life. In addition, ATL students will collaborate with Lansing Community College students in preparing for, helping to organize, and actively participating in the local NIF forums. For more information on the NIF please visit their Web site at: http://www.nifi.org/.

Our goals throughout the course will be to deepen our awareness of important public issues and concerns, to build our problem-solving capabilities, and to strengthen and improve public life in our community.

COURSE FORMAT, AIMS, AND OBJECTIVES

Since ATL 135 is a new course, students will help design, shape, and critique the class as we engage new material and never-before tested learning models and formats. We will set out to follow a seminar and workshop model emphasizing the development of independent thinking as well as collaborative learning processes. Assignments for class preparation and daily discussion, analysis, evaluation, and critique of readings, along with frequent in-class writing workshops, stress constant refinement and routine practice of varied writing activities, including outlining, paragraphing, peer-editing, essay and report writing and revision, leading class discussion, drafting discussion questions, developing group proposals and conducting group research, etc. Our overall objective is to strengthen the following critical competencies:

Critical Reading

- identifying central ideas, issues, problems of a text

- synthesizing and reconstructing an argument

- determining relevant information

Critical Thinking

- evaluating hypotheses or conclusions

- distinguishing between fact and opinion

- formulating appropriate questions

- incorporating others' opinions and perspectives

Development of Critical Writing Skills

- defining audience

- generating and organizing ideas

- drafting, revising, and editing for standard usage

- using and documenting sources

- researching library materials

PERFORMANCE EVALUATION

Students are required to participate in all class activities and complete all assigned work. Work submitted for evaluation is graded on a four-point scale in accordance with common standards adopted by the faculty of American Thought and Language consistent with the policies of Michigan State University. Each assignment has an evaluation ranking—I, II, or III—determined by the amount of time and work it takes to complete the assignment and its relative importance to other assignments. Final grades are calculated by averaging assignments at each rank and weighting them as follows:

Level I Assignments . . . . 60% of Final Grade

Level II Assignments . . . . 30% of Final Grade

Level III Assignments. . . . . 10% of Final Grade

Work submitted by Study Groups—subject to the same ranking system—receive common evaluations. Each member of a Study Group receives the same grade for an assignment submitted for evaluation on behalf of the Study Group.

Students are also required to attend the three public NIF forums held on the following dates: Feb. 10th from 6:30 to 8:30 pm; Feb. 24th from 6 to 8 pm; and March 28th from 6:30 to 8:30 pm. Two of these forums will be held off-campus, one at Lansing Community College and one at a Lansing-area school. We will arrange transportation as a class to these events.

REQUIRED BOOKS

AC: Gary Layne Hatch, *Arguing in Communities,* Second Edition. (Mayfield Publishing Co., 1999)

AP: James Crimmins, *The American Promise: Adventures in Grass-Roots Democracy* (KQED Books, 1995).

National Issues Forums Booklets (available only at the Student Book Store, Grand River Ave.):

BFS: *The Boundaries of Free Speech: How Free Is Too Free?*

SPILL: *Alcohol: Controlling the Toxic Spill*

JOBS: *Jobs: Preparing a Workforce for the 21st Century*

Other NIF Booklets as required. For Reference: Diane Hacker, *A Writer's Reference.* Fourth Edition. (St. Martin's, 1999)

Health Science 592
California State University, Northridge

HEALTH SCIENCE 592: ADVANCED BIOSTATISTICS FOR THE HEALTH SCIENCES

Vicki J. Ebin, Ph.D.
California State University, Northridge
Department of Health Science
Spring 2000, Monday 7-10 pm
KN 276
Ticket # 32050
Office: Eng 2250

COURSE DESCRIPTION

The purpose of this course is to provide health education students with the understanding and ability to use statistical methods and reasoning in their chosen discipline. This course combines data collection, design of data gathering instruments, data analysis, and report writing into a practical method of understanding the role of statistics in the field of health education. The students will design their own questionnaire, administer the instrument, enter the data, and analyze the data with a final report due as the end result. The project will focus on the Student Health Center, and health prevention issues that may impact health education policy at California State University, Northridge. This course provides students with the experience of applying the theory and methods of health education to "real world" health issues. The course uses an intensive student-instructor interaction approach in the actual preparation, implementation and analysis of the student project. The project approach encourages the exploration and analysis of the many dimensions of health education practice as it is involved in identifying and solving university health problems.

COURSE OBJECTIVES

By the end of the course the student will be able to:

1. Identify current school and community health problems and the role of health educators as they are involved in those problems.

2. Collaborate with health officials to respond to the needs of the university community.

3. Design and implement assessment instruments used in the process of community analysis and educational diagnosis.

4. Design a data entry program.

5. Code an assessment instrument in preparation for data entry and analysis.

6. Enter and clean the data into the selected program.

7. Implement individual statistical analyses of stated research project.

8. Interpret the analyses to determine the relevance of the statistical findings.

9. Prepare a report elaborating upon the significance and implications of the findings to the university community. Incorporate policy and health education suggestions.

10. Present individual work to peers.

REQUIRED TEXTS

Introduction to the Practice of Statistics, D. Moore and G. McCabe. (3rd Edition). 1998, W.H. Freeman and Company, New York (M & M)

SPSS 10.0 Guide to Data Analysis, Norusis

SPSS 10.0 for Windows. Brief Guide, Norusis

HIGHLY RECOMMENDED TEXT

SPSS 10.0 CD Rom, Student Statistical Package

COURSE OUTLINE

Jan. 31   Overview of Course Content, discuss possible topics for the research instrument. Brainstorm research instrument content areas. Prepare a literature review of possible content areas for the next class session. Begin Computer tutorials. Overview of SPSS.

Feb. 7   Read Chapter 1 (M & M), Review Basic Concepts. Discuss research issues in study design and implementation. Small group discussion of content areas.

Feb. 14   Read Sections 2.1, 2.2, 3.1, 3.2, 3.3, 3.4. Decisions of sampling.

Small group discussion of content areas. Discuss first version of research instrument. Finalize research instrument. Review basic statistical concepts.

Feb. 21   Begin data collection this week through March 6. Read Sections 2.3 through 2.7.

Feb. 28   Continue data collection. Review data editing and coding. Discuss problems and issues. Read Chapter 4.

Mar. 6   Data entry. Read Chapter 5.

Mar. 13   Continue data entry. Data cleaning techniques. Read Chapter 6.

Mar. 20   Read Chapter 7. Where do we start?

Mar. 27   Read Chapters 8 and 9. Preliminary analyses. What questions are you asking?

Apr. 3   Read Chapter 10 and 11. Linear Regression. Begin Multiple Regression. Project abstract due at the beginning of class.

Apr. 10   Read Chapter 15. Logistic Regression. Multiple Regression (con't).

Apr. 17   Spring Break, no class.

Apr. 24   Read Chapter 12. One-Way Analysis of Variance.

May 1   Read Chapter 13. Two-Way Analysis of Variance.

May 8   Nonparametric tests (Chapter 14). Preparation of policy statement for the university. Discussion of research findings and implications.

May 15   Paper due at the beginning of class. Begin Student Presentations.

May 22   Student Oral Presentations (con't), 5:30-7:30pm

STUDENT EVALUATION

Students' grades are based upon the following:

- **Project Abstract due April 3.** This abstract is a short overview of the student's class paper. The student must include a brief introduction, purpose of the paper, and hypotheses to be addressed. A conceptual framework and proposed analyses must also be included in this short paper. (100 points)

- **Project Paper due in class on May 15.** Each student is required to submit a comprehensive project paper. The student must include a thorough introduction and literature review, problem statement, methodology, result section, discussion and policy implications. Papers will be evaluated for grammar, punctuation, spelling, conceptual and intellectual design, as well as the required project elements. (200 points)

- **Oral Presentation.** Each student will present his/her research on May 15 or May 22. The presentation will address research findings, policy implications, suggestions for future research, and a tangentially related topic assigned prior to the presentation. (100 points)

A detailed description of each grading component will be distributed at a later date.

GRADE DISTRIBUTION (TOTAL POINTS POSSIBLE IS 400)

A 95%-100%

A- 90%-94%

B+ 87%-89%

B 84%-86%

B- 80%-83%

C+ 77%-79%

C . . . . < 77%

Community Organizing
Hunter College—CUNY

INTRODUCTION TO COMMUNITY ORGANIZING

Hunter College of the City University of New York
Course Coordinator: Professor Terry Mizrahi, Ph.D.
Classroom 404 West
Spring 1997

COURSE DESCRIPTION

The purpose of this course is to provide an introduction to community organizing; specifically, the knowledge, skill and value base underpinning community organizing, planning, development and change. It will emphasize the myriad roles, goals, and strategies used by community organizers in effecting social change. It will examine the history of organizing as a context of analyzing contemporary issues and organizations in the country and in New York City. Models of community organizing including mass mobilization, social action, grass roots empowerment, leadership development and advocacy, as well as newer community building approaches will be assessed for effectiveness in the current conservative climate. Special attention will be paid to issues of gender, class, race and ethnicity and sexual orientation in organizing. Field-related experience is included to expose students to an actual organizing environment.

COURSE OBJECTIVES

Knowledge

- to understand the various concepts of community and their application to community organizing;

- to understand the different types of organizing goals, roles and organizing strategies;

- to recognize the value, power and resource differences that impede community organizing and development.

Skills

- to begin to assess the assets (strengths) and deficits (problems) of geographic (neighborhood) and functional (interest) communities;

- to begin to apply models of organizing to specific social change endeavors;

- to acquire beginning skill in specific organizing tools and techniques such as running meetings and public speaking, and use of media.

- to acquire ability to critically analyze situations and problem-solve.

Values

- to appreciate the complexity of and competence needed for the organizer role.

- to value citizen, community and client/consumer participation and empowerment.

- to value the struggles and conflicts inherent in organizing for social and economic justice within an historical context and democratic framework.

COURSE FORMAT

This course is being offered as part of an interdisciplinary Hunter College faculty collaboration to explore the feasibility of establishing an undergraduate program in Community Organizing and Development (C.O.D.). Students who successfully complete the requirements will receive 3 credits through a course number in Urban Studies (URBS 403.95), Political Science (317.06), Sociology (225.35) and Community Health Education (400.50). Much of its content, structure and process were suggested through a series of meetings with faculty as well as community organizers outside of Hunter. It has been revised with input from students who took the course in Fall 1995 and 1996. Guest lecturers include members of the faculty and organizers working in NYC. Students will be encouraged to actively participate in and evaluate the course and all its features. Suggestions for improving the course will be welcome. Students will be expected to volunteer 20 hours during the semester in a community organizing setting as part of the major class assignment.

COURSE PROTOCOL

Attendance and punctuality at each class session is required. Please call in advance if an unexpected or anticipated lateness or absence occurs due to an emergency situation. Because of the participatory nature of the course, credit will be not given to a student with excessive latenesses or absences without prior permission. Extensions on course assignments and receipt of an "Incomplete" grade for the course are assigned at the discretion of the Instructor.

STUDENT EVALUATION CRITERIA

Students will be evaluated on their written work and participation in class (approximately) as follows: Logs (20%); Neighborhood analysis (15%); Meeting analysis (10%); Paper on Organizing Project and related

Paper and Presentations (40%); and Classroom participation including discussion, the group recording assignment and small group leadership (15%).

COURSE ASSIGNMENTS

I. Log of Selected Readings

Each week, select one article or chapter in a book to highlight from the readings. In no more than one page include: 1) brief summary; 2) your opinion about it; 3) the most interesting point; 4) a reason why you think it is an important article; 5) its relevance for community organizing. A total of 12 logs are required including two from outside or non-required readings. No more than 3 chapters from any one book or guide.

At the end of the semester, present in writing an outline or essay on the major themes and learning points from the readings you have done for the course. What do they have in common? Are there any differences in their perspectives? (2–3 pages).

II. Neighborhood Observation and Beginning Assessment

Take a walk around a geographic area in which you live or work. As one of the tools for community assessment, you should use your five senses (and your sixth sense!) to begin to understand that neighborhood. (Guidelines for the observation will be given out in class.) Come prepared to discuss your observations and preliminary analysis. In class, we will compare and contrast experiences. (It would be ideal if two or more students chose the same area to observe independently and then compare observations). Submit in writing a 3–4 page paper, answering the following questions: What does it look, feel, smell, sound and "taste" like? From your observations, what strengths does the area have? What problems are visible? Is this an area/neighborhood which is stable? in transition? improving? deteriorating? What additional questions are raised from your observations that need further fact-finding and assessment? Most importantly, what are the potential organizing issues that emerge from your preliminary assessment (eg. Need for programs, resources; campaigns to improve something; etc.) You can supplement with photos, drawings, maps, etc.

III. Meeting Analysis

Attend a meeting of a community organization or some local government meeting (eg. community planning board), civic body or neighborhood organization (eg. block association, tenant association, women's group) concerned with a neighborhood or issue; preferably an organization which is working to improve conditions, policies or services. Describe the meeting in detail and then analyze it according to written guidelines to be distributed in class. Preferably, the meeting you attend should be connected to your volunteer field experience.

IV. Class Recording

Once during the semester, small groups of students will be asked to take notes on a class session, compare them and together prepare and distribute to the whole class a summary and synthesis of major themes. This provides an opportunity to improve your observational and analytical skills and to understand how minute-taking is a political and professional (not a clerical) function. The combined document should be duplicated and given to fellow students to serve as a resource for them.

V. Participation in a Community Organizing Project

Select an organization, agency or group with which to volunteer during the semester for a minimum of 20 hours. A list of possible community organizations will be provided by the instructor. Alternatively, you can locate one on your own with permission of the instructor. The purpose of this assignment is to give you first hand experience observing and participating (to the extent possible) in the organizing work of the group. You will need to negotiate entry and assignment with the organization leaders and/or staff. At the very least, you should have access to meetings, minutes and other materials of the organization, and be able to interview leaders and members. In exchange, the group may ask you to participate in furthering the group's agenda, help them carry out a project or event, and/or provide feedback on your observations to them. This effort can be done individually or with other students.

Students will present their experiences orally in class at the end of the semester. Minimum written expectations are to keep a log of your observations and submit at the end of the semester a paper (4–5 pages) answering the following questions: 1) What model or approach to organizing is being used? 2) What are both the strengths and limitations of the group's effort? 3) What opposition and allies does it have? 4) What roles do the organizers and leaders play? 5) What has been accomplished? Were there any disappointments, failures or defeats? 6) What lessons did you learn? Refer to relevant course readings and class discussion.

COURSE READINGS

Students are not required to purchase any books or journals. All required readings are on reserve in the library. Also samples of past student work are on reserve to serve as models and guides.

Required Texts

Kim Bobo, Jackie Kendall, Steve Max. *Organizing for Social Change: A Manual for Activists in the 1990s.* Washington, D.C. Seven Locks Press, 1991.

Si Kahn, *Organizing: A Guide for Grassroots Leaders* Revised Edition, 1991.

G. Speeter. *Power: A Repossession Manual. Citizen Involvement and Training Project,* 1978.

Other Required Readings

City Limits Magazine and the "City" Section of the *Sunday Edition of The New York Times.*

Recommended Readings

Peter Medoff & Holly Sklar. *Streets of Hope: The Fall and Rise of an Urban Neighborhood.* Boston: South End Press, 1994 (A Case Study).

R. B. Warren and D. 1. Warren. *The Neighborhood Organizer's Handbook.* University of Notre Dame Press, 1977.

R. Shaw. *The Activist's Handbook: A Primer for the 1990s and Beyond.* Berkeley, U. of Cal. Press, 1996.

J. Rooney. *Organizing the South Bronx.* (IAF) Albany State University Press, 1995.

UNITS

1. Purposes, Goals and History of Community Organizing.

T. Mizrahi, "Community Organizers: For a Change," in *Mental Health and Social Work Career Directory.* First Edition. B.J. Morgan and J. M. Palmisano, Eds. Detroit, 1993, pgs. 131–136.

Kahn, Chapter I.

Rubin and Rubin, Chapter 2 "Goals of Community Organizing: Lessons from History," *Community Organizing and Development* Second Edition. Columbus Ohio: Merrill Publishing Co., 1992.

F. Cox, "A History of community organizing since the Civil War with Specific Reference to Oppressed Minorities." in F.M. Cox, J.L. Erlich, J. Rothman and J.E. Tropman (Eds.) 5th Edition *Strategies of Community Interventions.* Itasca IL.: F.E. Peacock, 1994.

G. Delgado, "Roots of the CO Movement." *Beyond the Politics of Place: New Directions in Community Organizing.* ARC, 1994.

II: Defining and Understanding "Community" in Community Organizing: Communities as Places, Spaces, Symbols, Shared Heritage and Sentiments

Jane Jacobs *Death and Life of Great American Cities,* Chapter I and 2

Warren and Warren, Chapter 2: What's in a Neighborhood? Chapter 5: Which Neighborhood Are You Talking About? *The Neighborhood Organizer's Handbook*

R. T. Hester, Jr. "The Sacred Structure in a Small Town: A Return to Manteo, N.C." *Small Town* Jan/Feb. 1990 pp 5–21.

W. Tolliver. "Community Building: A Black Church Response. *Hunter CSSW Alumni Update,* Spring, 1995.

III: Defining "Organizing" in Community Organizing: Analyzing Models, Types, Auspice and Levels

* Geographic/Neighborhood   * Functional/Issue-based   * Ideological/Value based
* Constituency/Identity-based

A. Overview and Alternatives

G. Speeter, *Power: A Repossession Manual: Organizing Strategies for Citizens.* Introduction and Chapter 1: Approaches to Organizing: Which one best suits my style?"

Barry Checkoway, "Six strategies of Community Change." *Developmental Journal* 30 (1) January 1995 pp 2–20.

Bobo, Kendall and Max. Chapter 6: Organizing Models.

B. Case Examples

N. Freudenberg and Uta Urayoana-Trinidad. "The Role of Community Organizations in AIDS Prevention in Two Latino Communities. (Washington Hts and the South Bronx). *Health Education Quarterly* 19, 1992 pp. 219–232.

J.C. Pozzo. "Street corner labor." (on the immigrant workers assn.) *City Limits.* Jan. 1996 pp.8–9.

Streets of Hope Chapters 1 and 2

R. Epstein. "Lighting the Beacon" (IAF in NYC). *City Limits.* March 1995, pgs. 18–24; and "Spiritual Improvement" (on the Harlem Congregation for Community Improvement). City Limits. Feb. 1996 pp. 14–19.

A. Durnois "Organizing a Community Around Health." SOCIAL POLICY 1,5 Jan. Feb. 1971.

T. Mizrahi Madison. "The Struggle for Partnership in Health Service Planning." HEALTH LAW PROJECT LIBRARY BULLETIN. Nov. 1978.

City Limits Special Issue on *Community Organizing: The Power to be Heard.* August/September 1993. Features articles on ACE in Central Harlem; East Brooklyn Congregations; ACT UP; Community Alliance for the Environment (Hasidic/Latino community coalition); ACORN; Northwest Bronx Community and Clergy Coalition; the Umma Group in Flatbush.

IV: Steps in Developing A Community Organizing Campaign Focusing on the External

Kahn, Chapters 3 "Organizations;" 4 "Constituencies;" 5 "Issues;" 8 "Strategy;" 10 "Tactics"

Bobo, Kendall and Max, Part 1: *Direct Action Organizing* (Chapters 2-5;7).

G. Speeter, *Power: A Repossession Manual.* Chapter IV: Taking Action.

V: Steps in Building an Organization: Focusing on the Internal

Recruiting and Motivating Membership

Cultivating and Developing Leadership

Kahn, Chapters 2 "Leaders," 6 "Members;" Chapter 18 "Culture"

Bobo, Kendall and Max chapter 10 and 11.

G. Speeter, *Power: A Repossession Manual* Chapter III: How Structure 8 Develops Power.

S. Burghardt, *The Other Side of Organizing* "From Leadership Development to Critical Consciousness" Chapter 5.

VI: Specialized Skills

A. Gathering and analyzing information: The role of research, and data collection and dissemination as organizing tools

Kahn, Chapter 9.

Bobo, Kendall and Max, Chapter 19.

Warren and Warren. Chapter 8: Neighborhood Diagnosis.

Rubin and Rubin Chapter 8 "Information for Mobilization and Social Action." pgs. 156–186.

B. Organizing and Running Meetings

Kahn, Chapter 7 "Meetings"

Bobo, Kendall and Max, Chapter 12 "Planning and Facilitating Meetings."

E. S. Rainman, R. Lippitt, and J. "Designing Participatory Meetings" from *Taking Your Meetings Out of the Doldrums.* San Diego, University Associates, 1988.

C. Community Relations, Outreach and Publicity

Kahn, Chapters 12 "Communication," 13 "Media;" Chapter 16 "Unions."

Bobo, Kendall and Max Chapters 13 "Being a great public speaker," Chapter 14: "Using the Media" Chapter 16 "Working with community organization boards," Chapter 17 "Religious organizations" and Chapter 18 "Working with unions."

VII: Allies and Adversaries: Cultivating Support and Minimizing Opposition

A. Coalition Building

Kahn, Chapter 15.

Bobo, Kendall and Max, Chapter 9.

Rosenthal and Mizrahi "Advantages of Coalition-building" in Austin and Lowe, *Controversial Issues in Communities and Organizations.*

Mizrahi and Rosenthal, "Managing Dynamic Tensions in Social Change Coalitions" in T. Mizrahi and J. Morrison(Eds.) *Community Organization and Social Administration.* Haworth Press, 1993.

B. Handling Opposition and Obstacles

L. Staples "The Seven D's of Defense" in *Roots of Power*

D. Jones. "Not in my Community: The Neighborhood Movement and Institutionalized Racism." *Social Policy* 13 (2) 1979, pp. 44-46.

R. Lipsyte "Coping: The NIMBY Wars: View From the Backyard. *NY Times,* Feb.6, 1994; "Coping: NIMBY Wars II: The View From the Other Side. *NY Times,* April 3, 1994.

VIII. Focusing on the Organizer: Thriving For the Long Haul

Bobo, Kendall, and Max, Chapter 25.

C. Hyde. "Commitment to Social Change: Voices from the Feminist Movement." *Journal of Community Practice* 1(2)1994 pgs. 45–64.

J. Hollender with L. Catling, *How To Make the World a Better Place: 116 Ways You Can Make A Difference.* W. W. Norton, 1994.

IX: Contemporary Organizing Issues and Models

A. Hybrid and New Organizing Models

S. Burghardt, "Community Building" *Hunter Update Alumni Newsletter* Spring, 1995.

J. D. Clapp, "Organizing Inner City Neighborhoods to Reduce Alcohol and Drug Problems." *Journal of Community Practice* 2 (1)1995 pp 43–60.

C. Bradshaw, S. Soifer, and L. Gutierrez. "Toward a Hybrid Model for Effective Organizing in Communities of Color." JOURNAL OF COMMUNITY PRACTICE. 1 (1) 1994 pp. 25–41.

S. Early & L. Cohen. "Jobs with Justice: Building A Broad-based Movement for Workers' Rights." *Social Policy.* Winter 1994 pp. 7–17

B. Race, *Class and Gender Issues in Organizing*

G. Delgado, *Beyond the Politics of Place: New Directions in Community Organizing in the 1990s.* Applied Research Center, 1994.

"Race, Cultural Diversity and Organizing." *The Neighborhood Works* June/July 1995. (whole issue).

M. Adamson, *Politics Unusual.* Applied Research Center, 1996. (Case studies of progressive organizing to counter the "right" wing.)

B. Joseph et al. "A Foundation for Feminist Organizing" in *Women on the Advance.* Education Center for Community Organizing, 1991.

L. Gutierrez. "A Feminist Perspective on Organizing with Women of Color," in F. Rivera and J. Ehrlich (Eds). *Community Organizing in a Diverse Society.* Second Edition. Boston: Allyn & Bacon, 1995.

Also in Rivera and Ehrlich book are articles on organizing in different ethnic communities including Native Americans, Chicanos, African-Americans, Puerto Ricans, Chinese-American, Japanese American, Filipino-American, Central American, and Southeast Asian.

See also RACEFTLE and *Third Force* (published by Center for Third World Organizing) for articles relevant to race and gender.

Supplemental Bibliography
(Books and Articles relevant to community organizing written by members of the Hunter C.O.D. Collaborative)

S. Burghardt. *Organizing for Community Action.* Sage Publications. 1982.

S. Burghardt. *The Other Side of Organizing.* Schenkman Publishers, 1983.

Freudenberg, N. *Not in Our Backyard: Community Action for Health and the Environment.* Monthly Review Press: New York, 1984.

Charles Green and Basil Wilson. T*he Struggle for Black Empowerment.*

Steve Johnston and other Hunter Faculty. *A Guide to Sources of Information in New York City, Second Edition.* 1992.

Paul Kurzman (Ed.) *The Mississippi Experience.*

Terry Mizrahi. *Organizing for Better Community Health: Programs and Strategies for Consumer Health Groups.* National Clearinghouse for Legal Services, 1978.

Terry Mizrahi and John Morrison, Eds. *Community Organizing and Social Administration: Advances, Trends and Emerging Principles.* Haworth Press, 1993.

Jan Poppendeick. "Policy, Advocacy and Justice: A Case for Food Assistance Reform." in D. Gil and E. Gil (Eds.) *Toward Social and Economic Justice.* Cambridge Mass. Schenkman, 1985, pp. 101–131.

Jan Poppendeick. *Bread Lines Knee Deep in Wheat: Food Assistance in the Great Depression.* Rutgers, 1985.

Ruth Sidel, *Women and Children Last.*

Ruth Sidel, *Urban Survival.* U. of Nebraska Press.

Ida Susser. *Norman Street.* Oxford University Press, 1982.

Ida Susser. "Union Carbide and the Community Surrounding It: A Case in Puerto Rico." *International Journal of Health Services.* 15 (4) 1985 pp. 561-583.

Ida Susser. "Women as Political Actors in Rural Puerto Rico: Continuity and Change." in F. Rothstein and M. Blim (Eds.) *Anthropology in the Global Factory.* Bergen and Garvey, 1992, pp. 206–220.

COMMUNITY ORGANIZING SKILLS FOR UNDERGRADUATE C.O.D. PROGRAM AT HUNTER COLLEGE:

I. Organizing and Planning Skills

- able to develop and engage people in groups
- capable of organizing and running a meeting
- able to represent the organization

II. Interpersonal Skills

- able to work with different types of people
- able to understand how to motivate and involve people in change
- able to observe, listen, and hear

III. Analytical Skills

- able to understand the issues, philosophy, and styles of the organization
- able to gather and use data and information
- able to understand different types and models of organizing and advocacy

IV. Administrative Skills

- able to keep records
- able to communicate verbally and in writing
- able to use time productively

V. Political Tactics and Strategies

- able to understand and analyze power structures
- able to understand and develop relevant tactics
- able to understand the impact of gender, race, ethnicity, sexual orientation on organizing process and outcomes

VI. Personal Characteristics and Professional Values

- able to take initiative and self-directed
- able to ask for help, support, guidance
- able to make responsible decisions
- able to demonstrate integrity
- able to identify with clients/community/constituency

Civil Engineering 571, Traffic Flow Theory University of Utah

CIVIL ENGINEERING #571, TRAFFIC FLOW THEORY

Dr. Peter Martin, Civil Engineering
University of Utah
Fall, 1995

1. Students in the class provide a needed service: The Millcreek Lion's Club and the County of Salt Lake have approached me requesting that I work with them to address traffic control problems in the Millcreek neighborhood. Traffic routed improperly has become a safety issue and has greatly contributed to the deterioration in the neighborhood especially for seniors and children. Too much traffic on neighborhood streets has cut off access by foot and isolated parts of the neighborhood from what used to be a more cohesive unit.

2. The service experience relates to the subject matter of the course: In traffic engineering, you teach students that you need to inhibit speed and flow of traffic in residential areas. The opportunity to apply these concepts will teach students how to go about getting into the community, how to work with residents, community organizations and governmental entities. There aren't classes in engineering that teach students how one goes about talking to people in a community about their needs. But engineering graduates need to be more than just fine technicians. They need to understand that their design solutions will influence human beings and affect the character of a neighborhood and this is part of what the service in this class will do.

3. Activities in the class provide a method or methods for students to think about what they learned through the service experience and how these are related to the subject of the class: Preliminary classroom designs will be compared with those developed after contact with the community. Students will be required to write about how their designs have been influenced by community concerns.

4. The course offers a method to assess the learning derived from the service. Credit is given for the learning, and its relations to the course, not for the service alone: Students will assess the learning derived through peer group evaluation of projects and presentations. These presentations will be given in a community forum and critiqued by other students in the class, the County Engineer and the community.

5. Service interactions in the community recognize the needs of service recipients, and offer an opportunity for recipients to be involved in the evaluation of the service: The community first came to me, presenting the needs. Students will work continuously with the residents to understand the problems, then to design traffic solutions. Finally, students will present their findings and solutions to the Community and the County in public meetings and will get feedback from both as to how to improve their projects.

6. The service activities are aimed at the development of the civic education of students: Civic education will be enhanced through the exposure of the students to the complex interaction between small local groups and local governments. Community residents have expressed dissatisfaction with the County Engineer's Office and the County has expressed frustration that it does not have the resources to deal with traffic problems at the neighborhood level. Students in this course will serve as a liaison, helping both the neighborhood and the County to understand and solve these traffic problems.

7. Knowledge from the discipline informs the service experiences with which the students are involved: Students will see firsthand how a decision about street A will affect street B, and they will have the opportunity to get the residents' response to their design solutions. Cold, hard engineering principles will be tempered by the practicalities of dealing with the community. Students will learn the technology in the classroom and apply it to the community, but they will come to understand that there's much more to traffic engineering than technology.

8. The class offers a way to learn from other class members as well as from the instructor: Students will work together in small groups. These groups will then work on different aspects of the traffic engineering problems and solutions. Each group will do presentations in class as well as at community forums, coming together to create the entire project. There will be de-briefing sessions back in the classroom afterwards.

PREREQUISITES

It is assumed that each of you have completed CvEn 370 and CvEn 420. These courses dealt with:

- CvEn 370 Transportation Engineering - An introduction to planning, design and operation principles and practices of transportation systems.
- CvEn 420 Urban Systems - An introduction to urban land use planning, urban system models and various quantitative planning techniques.

COURSE OBJECTIVES

Transportation studies encompasses a wide variety of disciplines. The Traffic Engineering course has been designed to provide you with an insight into traffic control and management techniques. The syllabus states: Application of traffic control devices and management techniques for improving traffic flow and safety.

The learning should equip you to:

1. Have a basic understanding of the principles of traffic flow theory .
2. Acquire a critical view of traffic design guides and manuals.
3. Develop your own independent analyses of simple traffic problems.
4. Acquire an understanding of the way traffic engineering relates to community issues.

YOUR INSTRUCTOR

If you have a problem which troubles you enough to want to seek help from your instructor, the best and quickest way to communicate is through electronic mail, so try that first.

COURSE TEXT

The course will adhere closely to the following text: Adolf D. May, *Traffic Flow Fundamentals,* Prentice Hall, 1990. (I strongly advise you to have access to your own copy for the duration of the course). The book should be supplemented with your own notes. There are several other good texts which may be useful for supplementary reading:

Garber NJ & Hoel LA, *Traffic and Highway Engineering,* West Publishing, St Paul. MN.

1988 Yhisti, C. Jotin, *Transportation Engineering: An Introduction,* Prentice Hall, Englewood Cliffs, NJ, 1990.

Morlok, E.K., *Introduction to Transportation Engineering and Planning,* McGraw Hill Inc., New York, 1978.

Oglesby CH & Hicks RG, *Highway Engineering,* (4th Edition) John Wiley & Sons, New York, 1982

Wright PH & Paquette RJ, *Highway Engineering,* (4th Edition) John Wiley & Sons, New York, 1982

Wright, P.H., and Ashford, N.J., *Transportation Engineering: Planning and Design,* (3rd Edition) John Wiley & Sons, New York, 1989.

REQUIREMENTS

Your grade will be influenced by how well your reports meet the following requirements:

Write clearly, and don't be afraid to state the obvious. Use the third person passive in the past tense

Write your reports so that a Freshman Civil and Environmental Engineering student could understand them. Don't ramble or repeat yourself (waffle). Remember: "Quality triumphs over Quantity."

Don't make things up.

Avoid slang.

Be your own editor—check your reports yourselves and don't let your Instructor be the first to read them.

Staple or bind all sheets together.

Words are tools. Use the correct tool for each job.

All reports must be typed.

Clearly state the goals and objectives of the report.

Describe the background to the subject matter, i.e. put the report into context.

Provide a brief historical review.

Numerical work should be tabulated where appropriate, e.g. if more than one set of similarly obtained or treated figures are being dealt with. Ensure that tables are not spread over two pages —start a table on a fresh page, if necessary, to avoid this.

Number and title all tables, and refer to them by number in the text of your report, e.g. when discussing your results. State clearly your units in all numerical work. State clearly, in the appropriate section, what graphs have been plotted and/or used.

The Discussion section shows how you interpret your findings. It is the place where you demonstrate your understanding of the field and how the views and feelings of the local community influence your recommendations.

The Conclusions section addresses the introduction by stating the outcome of the exercise. This section is provided to answer the reader question: "what does it all amount to?"

State plainly the answers to the objectives, posed in the introduction.

The References part enables readers to follow-up your work. All material referred to should be listed giving chapter, author, date, full title and publisher. Here you show where you located the source of your expected results.

The Appendix is a collection of all the miscellaneous items which should be in the report, but which would spoil the flow of the main sections.

The grading will be a two stage process. An initial draft will be submitted and criticized. The better the initial draft, the more incisive the suggestions will be, so strive to submit your initial draft in its most mature form. Failure to submit an initial draft will inevitably result in a lower score for the final report. A ceiling score of 75% will be applied to final reports which have not been preceded by initial reports.

Late final reports will not be graded.

Append your annotated interim report to your final report.

COMMUNITY PROJECT BRIEF: SPEED PROBLEMS IN MILLCREEK

The good people of East Evergreen Avenue, Millcreek have a traffic problem. A posted speed limit of 25 mph seems to be consistently ignored by drivers making speedy short-cuts. The Salt Lake County Engineers Department measured speeds along the road using pneumatic tube detectors. Their data is attached. Analyze the data and write a technical report, which shall be submitted to the Millcreek Lions Club. You must address the following general issues:

Is the speed limit being broken?

Has there been a change in speed and volume since the 1986 survey?

Your analysis should take the form of:

> Graphical representation of the data - plotted distributions, cumulative frequency plots
>
> Time Mean Speeds
>
> Space Mean Speeds
>
> Modal Speeds
>
> Median Speeds
>
> Standard Deviations

Comment on the nature of the speed distributions

> Assess the adequacy of the 3 sample sizes assuming a confidence level of 95% and bound on error of +/-1 mph

REPORT FORMAT

1. Title Page: This should include the assignment number, the title, the class name, the due date and your name.

2. Executive Summary: Succinctly identify the nature of the study, the motivation for the study, the general characteristics of the methodology, and the principle conclusions and recommendations (3-4 paragraphs).

3. Background: Describe in more detail the nature of the study, the questions being addressed, the theoretical basis for the analysis, and any other pertinent background information (About a page).

4. Approach: Describe in moderate detail what you did, with specific reference to the theoretical justification for your work (About a page).

5. Results: Present your results in a summarized form that is easy to follow, using summary tables and charts where appropriate. Detailed work sheets and voluminous interim results should be banished to an appendix, or omitted altogether, if this helps to improve legibility. Include any recommendations and their justification (About a page of text, plus any tables and figures).

6. Appendices (if needed).

The first part of this project addresses the technical aspects of the traffic problem. You are required to provide a detailed typed report. You will have to research the topic thoroughly by a library study and by making contact with industrial and commercial organizations in the field. You should review and reference all published material. You may wish to contact manufacturers for trade literature. In essence, your report will:

- review the historical development

- describe current techniques

- point to the future

The second part of this project will expose you to the effect of introducing your designs to the local community. The product of this exercise will be a report that has been modified by those nontechnical issues so important to traffic engineering.

If you discharge this assignment effectively, you will:

- have learned how to gather technical and commercial information from a variety of sources

- be skilled at using a contemporary "electronic" library

- understand how and why there is so much more to traffic engineering than just engineering

There follows a list of topics and issues which are provided to guide you in the compilation of your reports. Although wide ranging, it should not be considered exhaustive.

PARAMETERS

Speed categories and classifications

Accident records

History

When did the "problem" emerge?

What attempts have already be made?

The Community Group

How do community pressure groups work? What are their resources?

What is their status?

How effective have they been in the past? What drives them?

How are they constituted?

Who are the officers?

What are the characteristics of the organization?

How many people?

Where do they live?

Where do they work?

The Government Engineers

How does the Engineering Department function?

What are their resources?

What is their legal status?

What is their budget?

How are they constituted?

Who are the officers?

How do they relate to City and State organizations?

Data Accuracy and Precision

Accuracy

What degree of error is associated with the systems?

What are the variables which influence control?

Precision

How repeatable are the measurements?

Costs

capital

installation

operation training

English 107: Technical Report Writing
Hibbing Community College

ENGLISH 107: TECHNICAL REPORT WRITING

Hibbing Community College
Lois Schmidt, Instructor

CATALOGUE DESCRIPTION

The practice of technical writing, ranging from the simple memorandum to the long, complex technical research report. The course is designed for students in professional, technical and scientific programs. Prerequisite: English 106 or equivalent.

THEME

"Understanding the role of writer and citizen through service-learning"

TEXT

Technical Writing, Seventh Edition by John M. Lannon

MATERIALS

3 1/2" disk; journal notebook; student guide

COURSE OBJECTIVES

1. To prepare effective documents, visuals and presentations by knowing purpose, audience, constraints of the situation, and strategies for organizing and presenting information.

2. To reinforce writing and revising as a process.

3. To learn to analyze reports, technical documents, and articles for clarity, credibility, development and control of purpose, logic, ethics and bias.

4. To develop skills to collaborate effectively in the workplace like: careful listening, self-directed learning, considering divergent points of view, consensus building, and acceptance of group and instructor evaluation.

5. To apply necessary procedures for primary and secondary research.

6. To reflect on and evaluate critical thinking, problem solving processes and group processes as a means of: approaching writing problems in the workplace and approaching issues relating to civic interaction.

7. To experience community involvement as a means of understanding the role of an informed citizen.

This course has two goals. The first is to help you become a better writer. Over the next ten weeks, you will spend a lot of time writing—both inside and outside of class—and will come to understand the challenges of a work environment. To foster this understanding, the class will become a work community wherein we model relationships that sustain any community—shared power, valuing differences and communicating in a way that values the voices of others.

The second goal is for you to become more sensitive to the number of communities to which you belong and to the ways your activities in these communities reflect your role as a citizen. To this end, you are required to spend 20 hours in community service during this course. By being involved in community service, you will be involved in the everyday lives of persons who may be cornered by very limited social and economic choices, and your experience with them is authentic as you work with them to change their circumstances.

Your service work is, itself, a project in writing as well. As you write about your community service-learning experiences, you will have an opportunity to reflect on your role in this community and how you and others sustain it. Through this experience you will do more than develop insight and skills useful in the world of work. You will become a better prepared citizen able to bring about change in your community.

Hibbing Community College has arranged a number of settings where students can complete this service requirement. Your hours at your site will be negotiated between you and the agency or institution.

STATEMENT OF INTEGRITY

As I conscientiously prepare course lessons, I expect students to also conscientiously prepare assigned readings, exercises and major assignments; to be punctual and responsible; to confer with me on issues or problems they or I deem relevant to their performance as a student; to be courteous and respectful to others and their ideas so as to create a healthy learning environment.

Your success in the course depends almost entirely on you. You must be responsible for turning in assignments on time, for contacting me or your agency supervisor if you need help, for making sure things are as you assume they are. I am here to support and assist you. Students are encouraged to discuss their individual needs with the instructor.

COURSE REQUIREMENTS

1. Attend class and be punctual. This is a writing workshop, and many of the activities cannot be replicated outside of class. In addition, your peers will need your feedback and participation in group activities. Finally, this class will rely on your discussion and participation. Being a member of our work community means attending regularly.

2. Do all the reading for the course. Text: A reference for the skills and concepts needed to sustain a work community and to create technical documents, essays, and other peer work.

3. Type all writing assignments except for your journal.

4. Complete all assignments.

   a. **Journal:** In a 8.5 x 11" spiral notebook, keep a journal as a record of your reflections on your community service experience. A journal handout will provide you with the general structure, and the course handout and class discussions will provide a weekly focus.

   b. **Peer Editing Activities:** Since work in real life often depends on collaborative efforts, you will be assigned to a four student editing group at the beginning of the quarter. You will learn to edit your own writing—an ultimate goal of the course—by editing the writing of your peers. You will also be relying on your peers for some of the information and effort needed to complete projects.

   c. **Simulation Assignment:** This assignment is designed to simulate the multiplicity of writing modes you will encounter in life beyond college. Two assignments will follow a simulation game that centers on a controversy that must be resolved. You may adopt the persona of any of the people involved in the controversy and will present his/her concerns in a statement at an open meeting. Assignments include: a definition report and a recommendation report. In each case, the class will reach consensus on the purpose, audience and length of each assignment.

   d. **Final Project:** Your final project will be a report prepared for your community service-learning agency which involves both primary and secondary research. Be observant. Listen to members of the agency to discover problems they consider significant. You will begin this project by submitting a proposal and later a progress report. After completing your research, you will complete an analytical report and submit a copy to me and later to your service-learning supervisor (or other appropriate audience).

   e. **Final Examination:** Essay on your Community Service-Learning.

WEEK 1: **Orientation to Technical Report Writing**

Discussion: Who writes for a living and what are the consequences of selected products?

Orientation to community service-learning, citizenship and service, and its effect on community.

Journal Focus: What is "community?" What are ones I belong to and how do they reflect my values? When have my values been in conflict? How does my "community" depend on me?

WEEK 2: **Service-Learning Placement**

Introductions and forms

Writing Exercise: Description and Audience Profile

Readings in Text: introductory chapters

Journal Focus: What is the mission at my service site? How will I be a part of it? How are differences apparent in my service site? What is my reaction?

WEEK 3: **The Persuasive Problem**

Readings in text: purpose, audience, strategies for selecting format and organization.

Writing: audience profile/Persuasive Letter

Journal Focus: Examine your reflective listening skills at the service site. What result did you anticipate? Are there barriers to applying this skill?

WEEK 4: **Simulation Assignments**

WORKSHOP: Definition Report and Opening Statement

Readings in text: gathering evidence, research and writing and developing your ideas

Journal Focus: What are the political constraints and realities (time, organizational, ethical) at your service site? How do they affect the work of the agency?

WEEK 5: **Considering the Analytical Report**

Strategies for choosing a topic

WORKSHOP: Recommendation Report

Readings in text: revising for emphasis, voice, format, including graphs and other visuals

Journal Focus: Seek feedback at your service site, particularly concerning your final analytical report. What are the messages you receive? Are service receivers (clients) able to provide input or to seek feedback? Do they seem voiceless?

WEEK 6: **Mid-Quarter formative evaluation of Service-Learning Writing**

Proposal for final project

Readings: research and writing, continued

Journal Focus: Use techniques for observing and recording behavioral and attitudinal elements as you reflect on your service experience.

WEEK 7:   **Final Project—Secondary Research**

WORKSHOP: gathering evidence, developing ideas and documenting sources

Journal Focus: What changes can you identify in your perception of the clients at your service site? What social issues impact the work of your agency? What are obvious causes of these problems? What causes may not be obvious?

WEEK 8:   **Final Project—Progress Report**

WORKSHOP: drafting the Progress Report

Drafting and revising the Analytical Report

Journal Focus: Reflect on your role in your peer group and in any groups with which you work at your service site. Use the checklist provided in class to organize your thoughts.

WEEK 9:   **Final Project**

WORKSHOP: polishing and editing the Analytical Report

Journal Focus: Did you effect positive change at your service site? What skills did you use? Have your values changed or become more clearly defined? How have your goals been affected? Your social or political awareness?

WEEK 10:   **Final Project delivering to agency seeking agency feedback**

Final Examination: Reflection on community service-learning work

GRADING

Final grades will be based on an averaging of the following: Class assignments, including the process description; Recommendation Report Proposal and Progress Report; Analytical Report; Reflection Essay and Journal.

JOURNAL QUESTIONS

1. Recall a successful learning experience. Describe what happened and explain why you were successful. What was the effect of this successful experience?

2. Recall a difficult or impossible learning experience. Describe what happened and explain why it was difficult. What was the effect of this unsuccessful experience?

3. Why have you earned the grade recorded on the assignment which has just been returned? Are there external causes to be considered?

4. Describe your reaction to the service-teaming tutoring project. What is your belief about your possible success? What will make it difficult?

5. Explain your writing process. How do you go about completing a writing assignment? What distracts you? What helps you when you are stuck? Where and when do you work best?

6. What strengths do you bring to your peer group? What keeps you from contributing to the group?

7. Describe your tutee and the classroom in which you work? Use all your senses to capture the scene.

8. Describe your work with your tutee. What is difficult for you and what is easy? When does your tutee have the most difficulty? What seems easy for him or her?

9. After describing your activity as a tutor, assess whether the tutoring hour was a successful or an unsuccessful learning experience. Use the criteria discussed in class.

10. Is your tutee an optimistic or a pessimistic learner? What messages, body language or situations confirm your assessment?

11. What skills do you use most during the tutoring hour? Describe situations in which you are viewed as a leader by the students?

12. Describe your attempt to confirm or dispute the tutee's learning messages. Then describe the effect on the learning climate. (Look for clues in your tutee's face, body language, comments or attention to the task.)

JOURNAL WRITING GUIDELINES

One useful way of keeping track of what you are learning is to keep a personal journal. Writing in a journal will help you think your experiences and gain insight into what they mean.

A journal is a series of entries. You will have one or two entries per week, and entries may take different forms. However, a few ingredients are essential. Do not edit as you write. Instead, write your thoughts freely, without regard for spelling or punctuation. Editing may be done later, if you wish. The point is not to stop the flow of your thoughts. Be candid and use your senses and observational skills. As a result, your writing will become more interesting.

Your journal is a reflective activity which allows you to grapple with problems and frustrations; it allows you to think about the way you think and about the way you organize your time and pursue tasks; it allows you to identify your accomplishments and positive learning experiences. In other words, in this Journal, you can chart your growth both academically and personally.

1. As you complete journal prompts given in class, follow the specific directions given for each. (12 points)

2. When completing a journal entry during your tutoring project, use the following format: Record a journal entry each time you tutor. Take a few minutes soon after the tutoring session (no longer than a few hours later) so that your reflection will be as accurate as possible.

    A. Begin with an objective description, including the place, date and hours worked. Indicate what happened in a brief factual account. Do not include any opinions. This part of the entry will be a few lines. (2 points)

B. Then interpret. Respond to the focus question given in class. Think of this as a focused free write in which you put down everything that seems pertinent to the question. This part of the entry will be a paragraph or more. (5 points)

C. Describe what the experience means to you. Use emotion words (happy, surprised, frustrated, etc.) to describe your feelings. Add other information that seems important to you. I have included a few questions below that you might use in this section. This part will be a paragraph or more. (5 points)

1. What's the best thing that happened today?

2. What skills did I learn/practice?

3. How do others see my role?

4. Did I receive any compliments/criticisms? What did I learn from this?

5. What kind of person does it take to be a successful tutor?

6. How does tutoring help the community?

Strategic Planning in Health Services
Portland State University

PA 510/PHE 510: STRATEGIC PLANNING IN HEALTH SERVICES

Portland State University
Sherril B. Gelmon, Dr.P.H.
Associate Professor of Public Health
Departments of Public Administration and Public Health Education
Room 237, School of Urban and Public Affairs

COURSE DESCRIPTION

This course introduces general concepts, models and theories of strategic planning, and develops them in terms of applications in the health services industry. Through participation in a community-based strategic planning process, students will gain experience and some expertise in the planning, decision-making and conduct of strategic planning.

PREREQUISITES

There are no formal prerequisites for this course. However, students are strongly encouraged to have taken PA 570: Health Administration or PA 510: Health Systems Organization prior to taking this class, as certain knowledge related to the delivery of health services acquired in these classes will be assumed for all students as a baseline of understanding. If you have not successfully completed either of these classes, please discuss this with me within the first week of the quarter. Certain work experience may be appropriate to provide the necessary baseline knowledge.

LEARNING OBJECTIVES

The learning objectives for each student to achieve by the completion of this class are:
- to understand basic concepts, models and theories of strategic planning;

- to apply these concepts, models and theories to health services delivery and gain an understanding of special applications to the health services industry;

- to develop proficiency in the application of these concepts, models and theories through participation in a community-based strategic planning project;

- to develop skills in working with a community partner to define and meet their needs with respect to the planning project;

- to develop or enhance skills in interviewing, synthesis of findings, and presentation of recommendations;

- to reflect on the role of community service in achieving professional goals; and

- to develop or improve skills in working and learning in groups.

METHODS OF EVALUATION

There will be multiple methods of evaluation that will determine both your course grade and the evaluation of the course itself.

1. **Evaluation of Students**

   The course grade will be determined as follows:

   Short assignments. 40%

   Group project and presentation. 40%

   Class participation and reflective journal 20%

2. **Evaluation of Course and Professor**

   I am eager to receive your feedback on the class, and I will conduct brief process evaluations periodically throughout the class to solicit your input. On the basis of your comments, we will make "mid-course corrections" as necessary to ensure that the class meets your needs and is responsive to your suggestions, while still fulfilling the course objectives set out above.

   As well, a final evaluation of the course and the professor will be conducted during the last class session. At the conclusion of the course, students will be asked to determine the extent to which they have accomplished each of the specified learning objectives in their own learning.

REQUIRED AND SUPPLEMENTAL READINGS

The required textbook for this course, available at the PSU bookstore is:

John M. Bryson. *Strategic Planning for Public and Nonprofit Organizations: A Guide to Strengthening and Sustaining Organizational Achievement.* Revised Edition. San Francisco: Jossey-Bass Inc. Publishers, 1995.

You may also wish to purchase the workbook to accompany the text; this is available at the PSU bookstore and is optional:

John M. Bryson and Farnum K. Alston. *Creating and Implementing Your Strategic Plan: A Workbook for Public and Nonprofit Organizations.* San Francisco: Jossey-Bass Inc., Publishers, 1998.

You are also expected to obtain a copy of the *Oregon Benchmarks* if you do not already have one.

One other book will be used extensively to supplement lecture material. You are not required to buy this book, but may wish to use it from time to time for reference:

Henry Mintzberg. *The Rise and Fall of Strategic Planning.* New York: The Free Press, 1994.

Finally, a list of useful "core" books on strategic planning is appended to this syllabus. You are encouraged to reference these books for additional information and relevant examples.

DESCRIPTION OF MAJOR ASSIGNMENTS

1. **Short Assignments (40% of course grade)**

   There will be two short assignments to address material covered in the readings and in class. The first will focus on material covered in class to date, primarily drawing on the Bryson book and other material discussed in class. The assignment will be handed out in class on January 27, and will be due at the beginning of class on February 3. It will be returned on February 10. The second assignment will involve a structured critique of an article describing a strategic planning process. The assignment will be handed out in class on February 17, and will be due at the beginning of class on February 24. It will be returned on March 3.

   The first assignment will be a focused critique of material covered to date; you will be asked to respond to specific questions, using course readings and class notes. No additional research will be required. The second assignment will involve choosing one of a set of specified articles to critique, and then following an assigned format for the analysis. It will involve choosing the article you wish to critique and obtaining a copy of the article (from either the PSU or OHSU libraries), and then drawing upon course readings and class notes to complete the assignment. Each assignment response should be typed, double-spaced using a 10 or 12 point font, proofread for spelling and grammar, and 4-5 pages in length. Late assignments will result in marks being deducted. Each assignment is worth 20% of the course grade.

2. **Group Project (40% of course grade)**

For this course this year, we will be working with Legacy Health Systems as our primary community partner, and through its office of Community Programs we will assist a number of community-based agencies loosely affiliated with Legacy. There are over 25 of these agencies which have an affiliation with the Legacy system, and are housed on one of their campuses. The goal of this project is to help to plan a process for assessing the effectiveness of Legacy's partnerships with these organizations. This process will provide information which will help the organizations and Legacy itself in determining the nature and scope of their continuing affiliations. You will work with your partner organization to determine their specific goals depending on their mission and needs, and within the context of their current affiliation with Legacy.

The class members will form teams of two or three, and in the second class session you will choose the organization you will work with. One team will work directly with Legacy's Director of Community Programs to plan the corporate-level project, while all others will work with a specific community-based organization. The available organizations will be described in class on January 6; you will have the opportunity to identify your working partner and your preferences for organization, and group assignments will be made by the professor and handed out in class on January 13. This group project will provide an opportunity to apply material covered in a class to an actual strategic planning project. It also provides an opportunity to provide service to a community partner and to reflect on this service as part of your professional activities.

Each class group will determine the process to be used in completing this project, develop interview questions for key informants (or other mechanisms for information collection), prepare a standardized interview protocol, conduct key informant interviews, and as appropriate prepare documentation to assist the community partner in its planning. You will have the opportunity to discuss your group's process in class on a number of occasions. You will probably need to meet with the community partner at least three times: at the beginning of the project to obtain baseline information, during your work to verify progress and obtain additional information, and at the end of the project to present your findings. You will then need to review your findings, synthesize them, and prepare 2 products: a group presentation to the class and a group paper.

The 40% of course grade will be allocated as follows: 15% for the group presentation, and 25% for the group paper. Presentations will be made in class on March 3 and March 10. Each presentation will be 15 minutes in length, followed by 15 minutes of discussion. Presentations should address the focus of the group and identify the organization assisted in the process, review the planning process used by the group, identify individuals interviewed, present key themes emerging from the interviews, outline the content of the group's findings, and make recommendations for the organization for next steps in planning. A particular emphasis should be given to how the individual plan will fit into the overall plan to accomplish the goal of this project. Group members will complete a confidential peer evaluation for 5%, and 10% will be an evaluation of the group presentation as a whole by the professor (all students in a group will receive the same value out of the 10%).

Papers are due in my office by 4:00 p.m. on Thursday, March 13. One paper will be submitted for the entire group, and all group members will receive the same grade. The paper should be typed, double-spaced using a 10 or 12 point font, proofread for spelling and grammar, and no more than 20 pages in length (not including appendices). The paper should be a narrative expanding material covered in the presentation. References should be used as appropriate, but the majority of information will be derived from data collection and class content. Each student will also be expected to write a one to two page statement reflecting on their own experience in this project providing community service in the context of academic and professional responsibilities; these reflection statements should also be appended to the group paper.

3. **Class Participation and Reflective Journal (20% of course grade)**

Twenty percent of the grade will be allocated to class participation and the completion of a reflective journal. The class participation component includes preparation for each class session, active participation in discussions, and general involvement in class activities. Participation in the class sessions is an important part of your learning—to reflect on the reading and thinking you are doing related to the course content, to engage in discussions with your classmates and professor, and to ask questions and seek answers from all participants in the class.

The reflective journal is intended to provide you with additional opportunities to consider how community-based learning experiences shape your own learning as well as contribute to your personal and professional development. Three journals will be submitted, on January 22, February 10, and March 3. Each journal entry should be between two and four pages in length, and should be typed and proofread. Specific guidance about the focus of the journal will be provided in class. The journal entries themselves will not be graded; rather, the development of reflective skills as evidenced in the journal will contribute to the grade for class participation.

We will also do group reflection as a class in the final two sessions. These will facilitate discussions about your own observations on community-based learning as well as considering the role of planning in health services in the future based on your experiences in the community.

You are expected to attend all class sessions; the proportion of course grade allocated to class participation will reflect your level of participation and demonstrated learning. Readings listed for each session should be completed before that session so that you may draw upon them in the class discussions. If you must miss a class, please let me know in advance so that we may discuss how you may catch up on missed material.

EXPECTATIONS

A course syllabus can be considered as a contract between the professor and the students. This syllabus includes all expectations for performance in the class, and you should now understand what is required of you, and the deadlines for assignments. If you have questions about any of these expectations I encourage you to discuss them with me sooner rather than later. Any changes in the course requirements or schedule will be communicated in class. I will try to be accommodating of personal crises that affect attendance or submission of assignments in terms of working out suitable and fair arrangements for grading but also wish to be fair to all students in the class.

COURSE SCHEDULE

The following is a schedule of class topics, readings, and assignments. All readings are from the required textbook.

January 6   Course overview
The nature of planning
Definitions of strategic planning
Overview of group projects

January 13   Models of the strategic planning process
READ: Chapters 1 and 2; Resource D
Getting started with planning
Clarifying missions and mandates
Establish working groups and determine group process

January 20   No class; Martin Luther King holiday: Journal due to my office by Wednesday, January 22nd 6:00 p.m.

January 27   Leadership roles
Environmental assessment
Assumptions about planning
READ: Chapters 3, 4, and 5; Resource A
Assignment #1 handed out; Journal #1 returned

February 3   Identification of strategic issues
Stakeholder management
READ: Chapters 6, 11; Resource B
Assignment # 1 due

Feb. 10   Formulating strategies and plans to manage and respond to the issues
Challenges to the planning process

READ: Chapter 7; Resource C

Journal #2 due

Assignment #1 returned

Feb. 17   Establishing a vision

Linking planning and improvement efforts

READ: Chapter 8; Resource E

Assignment #2 handed out Journal #2 returned

Feb. 24   Overcoming barriers to strategic planning

Relating planning to daily work

Pitfalls in strategic planning

Implementation of plans

Next steps after the plan is adopted

Assignment #2 due

READ: Chapter 9

March 3   Group presentations

Group reflection: Is there a future for planning in health services?

Assignment #2 returned

Journal #3 due

March 10   Group presentations

Group reflection: Is there a future for me in health services planning as a career direction?

Course evaluation

Journal #3 returned

Group papers are due in my office by 4:00 p.m. on Thursday, March 11th. Graded papers and final marks will be available after March 19th.

SUPPLEMENTAL BOOKS ON STRATEGIC PLANNING

This is an introductory list of books; many other fine works exist which you may also find useful for reference purposes.

Duncan, W. Jack, Peter M. Ginter and Linda E. Swayne. *Strategic Management of Health Care Organizations.* Second edition. Cambridge, MA: Blackwell Publishers, 1990.

Hyman, Herbert Harvey. *Health Planning: A Systematic Approach.* Rockville, MD: Aspen Systems Corporation, 1982.

Nutt, Paul C. *Planning Methods for Health and Related Organizations.* New York: John Wiley & Sons, Inc., 1984.

Quinn, James Brian, Henry Mintzberg and Robert M. James. *The Strategy Process: Concepts, Contexts and Cases.* Englewood Cliffs, NJ: Prentice Hall, 1988.

Shorteil, Stephen M., Ellen M. Morrison and Bernard Friedman. *Strategic Choices for America's Hospitals: Managing Change in Turbulent Times.* San Francisco: Jossey-Bass Inc., Publishers, 1990.

Current Issues in Immigration Law
Iona College

BLW 302SL: CURRENT ISSUES IN IMMIGRATION LAW

Iona College

Dr. J.L. Yranski Nasuti

Winter Session (Iona in Mission)

Office: 85 Beechmont Avenue, New Rochelle, New York

TEXTS

- Helewitz, Jeffrey, United States Immigration Law, Pearson Publications Company, 1999.

- Reading Packet

COURSE OBJECTIVES

The purpose of this course is to provide an introduction to the basic issues underlying U.S. immigration law. Topics covered will include the history of immigration law; the law relating to admission, naturalization, removal, and removal procedures; and the legal issues concerning refugees, asylum seekers, illegal immigrants, and undocumented workers. However, since this is an IONA IN MISSION COURSE, most of the class will be conducted from various locations in Tucson, Arizona, Nogales, Arizona, and Nogales, Mexico. It is expected that the immigration issues covered will be done in large part in the context of immigration from Mexico. In addition, since the course is also a SERVICE-LEARNING COURSE, each student will have the opportunity, upon returning from Mexico, to do field work with a nonprofit organization that is concerned with immigration Issues.

At the conclusion of this course the student should understand:

1. The primary legal sources for U.S. immigration and naturalization law—the U.S. Constitution, treaties, statutes, administration rules and regulations, and judicial decisions;

2. The historical events which shaped U.S. immigration law and policy (with special emphasis on the events relating to immigration from Mexico and Latin America);

3. The legal basis for federal regulation of immigration and naturalization;

4. The administrative structure of immigration law;

5. The different requirements for obtaining immigrant and non-immigrant visas;

6. The process by which the government may refuse to admit or may remove immigrants from the United States;

7. The requirements for applying for refugee or asylum status;

8. The requirements for applying for citizenship and naturalization status;

9. The legal problems raised by illegal immigration and undocumented workers; and

10. How to apply immigration law to service-learning activities.

PLAN AND REQUIREMENTS

This course is going to require the student to absorb a great deal of material in a relatively short period of time. Consequently it will be essential that the student read all assigned materials at the beginning of the sessions in which they are due. As always, the degree and quality of participation throughout the course (including the student's openness to learning through immersion into a different context and culture) will be considered in the determination of the student's final grade.

The course requirements will consist of: 1) a journal reflecting on your daily experiences in Arizona and Mexico; your reactions to the readings and specific immigration laws; and your own personal family immigration history; 2) a term paper on an issue relating to immigration law; 3) twenty hours of service at a placement site in the United States; and 4) a journal recording your activities at, and reactions to, your service placement site. Each requirement will be worth one-quarter of the final grade.

MAJOR UNITS OF INSTRUCTION

At Iona College

SESSION 1 Orientation session to explain the scope of the course, the general requirements for living and studying in Tucson, Arizona and the squatters' village in Nogales, Mexico. Distribution of material on necessary travel gear and health concerns.

SESSION 2 Background to U.S. immigration law: Early case law; restrictive statutes; quota laws; the Immigration and Nationality Act of 1952 and later amendments; the Immigration Reform and Control Act of 1986; the Immigration Act of 1990; the Personal Responsibility and Work Opportunity Act of 1996; and the Illegal Immigration Reform and Immigration Responsibility Act of 1996.
The operation of the federal agencies responsible for the administration of immigration law: The Department of Justice, the Department of State, the Department of Labor, the Department of Health and Human Services, and the United States Information Agency.

Ethical Discussion Issues: Moral issues in support of and in opposition to a policy of "open-door admission. The global effects of an "open-door" policy.

SESSION 3 Admissions: Availability of immigrant visas for family-sponsored immigrants, employment based immigrants, diversity immigrants, and refugees; availability of non-immigrant visas for students-scholars and business-entrepreneurial non-immigrants. Admission procedures for non-immigrant admission, immigrant visas and visa petitions, adjustment of status, and parole.

Denial of Admission and Removal: Grounds for denial of admission and removal. Procedures and relief from denial of admission and removal.

Ethical Discussion Issues: Sham marriages and sham labor certifications.

At Borderlinks in Tuscon, Arizona
SESSION 4 Illegal Immigration and Undocumented Aliens: Reasons for, and impact of, illegal immigration; the Immigration Reform and Control Act (sanctions on employers of undocumented aliens and antidiscrimination provisions).

Ethical Discussion Issues: Exploitation of undocumented workers.

SESSION 5 Refugees and Political Asylum: Definition of "refugee" under U.S. law and international law; meaning of "nonrefoulement"; over-seas refugee programs; political asylum and the "well-founded fear of persecution" requirement; detention and interdiction of asylum seekers.

Ethical Discussion Issues: New asylum claims based on gender.

At Iona College
SESSION 6 Conclusions: Community meal. Reflection on the Iona in Mission experience and preparation for the service placements. Viewing of movie, *El Norte*.

EXPERIENTIAL ACTIVITIES IN NOGALES, MEXICO AND NOGALES, ARIZONA
A distinctive feature of this Iona in Mission Service-Learning course is the fact that most of the group experiential learning will take place in Nogales, Mexico. After our preliminary sessions on campus, we will fly to Phoenix, Arizona and travel by van to the Borderlinks house in Tucson, Arizona. Borderlinks is a nonprofit organization that is concerned with educating people about the problems of life along the U.S./Mexican border. Two members of the Borderlinks staff will accompany us throughout our week in Arizona and Mexico.

In Tucson, we will meet with people who have emigrated from Mexico and other parts of Latin America. We will also have an opportunity to talk with representatives of church groups involved in the Sanctuary Movement in the late 1980s and early 1990s. Finally, we will be given an overview of recent events in Mexico from a political and economic perspective.

The next day we will travel south to Nogales, Arizona where we will cross the border (for the first time) into m-exico. A major part of our experiential learning will come from our homestays in Nogales, Mexico. We will be the guests of a number of families living in one of the many squatters' villages which have sprung up in the hills overlooking the city. Our accommodations will range from extremely modest to rough. The homes that we will stay in will most likely be built out of a combination of cardboard, cinder blocks, tires, and metal sheeting. None of the homes will have running water or functioning toilets. Some will have only one room, others may have two, or perhaps, three rooms. Most families will include at least one member who works in a maquiladora. All families will know of people who have legally or illegally immigrated to the United States. Food will be prepared by our hosts and will primarily consist of beans and tortillas. In January, it can get very warm in Nogales during the daytime—and very cold at night. This will be especially meaningful for us since our nights will be spent in sleeping bags in homes without any central heating.

During our time in Mexico, we will have the opportunity to observe the conditions which explain the push/pull factors for immigration to the United States from Mexico. We will visit at least one foreign-owned maquiladora and speak with management representatives. Later in the week we will have an opportunity to talk with maquiladora workers about their working experiences. The president of the Nogales Chamber of Commerce will meet with us to discuss the less profitable Mexican owned businesses along the border. We will also have an opportunity to go to some of the local grocery stores to find out how far a maquiladora worker's wages can go towards purchasing staple items. In addition, we will visit one of the many squatters' villages which are growing further out from the center of the city . . . where less crowded living space is exchanged for greater isolation and more danger at night. We will also meet with Mexican health workers to discuss the medical consequences of the environmental pollution in the region. Finally, we will have contact with union organizers and religious workers.

While in Nogales, Mexico, we will cross back over the border a number of times for meetings with officials of the United States government including representatives from the Immigration and Naturalization Service, Customs, and the Border Patrol. They will talk about the responsibilities of their particular agencies and the concerns that they have in implementing the immigration and customs laws. We will also have an opportunity to discuss some of the problems involved in patrolling a border.

READING ASSIGNMENTS

> SESSION 1 READING PACKET: "Travels Into America's Future—Mexico and the Southwest," R. Kaplan, *Atlantic Monthly,* July 1998.
>
> "To Live in the Borderlands Means You . . . ," by G. Anzaldua.
>
> "Snapshots from the Edge: A Report from the U.S./Mexican Border," K. Clarke, *Salt of the Earth,* May/June 1997.
>
> Map of the U.S.-Mexican border region from *The Troublesome Border,* O. Martinez.
>
> "Useful Statistics on Mexico," Human Rights Watch.
>
> "NAFTA's Impact on Mexican Agriculture and Rural Life," S. Suppan, Institute for Agriculture And Trade Policy.

"Chiapas: An Uprising Born of Despair," M. Renner, *World Watch,* Jan./Feb. 1999.

SESSION 2 HELEWITZ: Chapter 1, History and Administration of U.S. Immigration Law, pp. 1-50.

SESSION 3 HELEWITZ: Chapter 2, Citizenship and Nationality; Chapter 3, Immigrant Categories; Chapter 4, Nonimmigrant Categories; Chapter 5, Admission to the United States; and Chapter 6, Removal Prior to Entry into the United States, pp. 51-146.

SESSION 4 READING PACKET: "It's a Secret: Economics Is All About Values," E. Teninty, Equal Means, Winter 1991.

"Clinton, NAFTA and the Politics of U.S. Trade," K. Hansen-Kuln, NACLA Report on the Americas,Sept./Oct. 1997.

"The Failed Experiment: "NAFTA at Three Years," Institute for Policy Studies, 1997.

"The Border," G. Smith and E. Malkin, *BusinessWeek,* May 12, 1997.

"The Gilded Cage: The Allure of Nogales' Maquillas After the Peso Crash," J.E. Reilly, *The Tucson Weekly,* Dec. 5-11, 1996.

"Factory Tests for Pregnancy in Mexico Draw Criticism," T. Steller, *The Arizona Daily Star,* Feb. 1, 1998.

"Making Links Across the Border," D. La Botz, *Labor Notes,* Aug. 1994.

"Union Vote in Mexico Illustrates Abuses," S. Dillon, *New York Times International,* Oct. 13, 1997.

"Bridging the GAP: Exposing the Labour Behind the Label," B. Jeffcott and L. Yanz, *Our Times,* Feb. 1997.

"To Explore NAFTA's Future, Visit Nogales," *National Catholic Reporter,* Jan. 7, 1994.

"Bashing Immigrants Won't Save Environment," Gomez, San Francisco Chronicle, Nov. 17, 1997.

"Masters of the Game—How the U.S. Protects the Traffic in Cheap Mexican Labor," W. Graham, *Harper Magazine,* July 1996.

"Baiting Immigrants—Women Bear the Brunt," J. Light, The Progressive, Sept. 22, 1996.

"Who's Killing the Women of Juarez?" C. Bowden, *Talk,* Sept. 1999.

SESSION 5 HELEWITZ: Chapter 8, Refugees and Asylum, pp.147-172.

SESSION 6 READING PACKET, "INS Bigger than FBI, Prisons Bureau," I. Ibarra, *The Arizona Daily Star,* Jan. 27, 1998.

"U.S. Border Patrol/Tucson Sector Productivity Recap 1991-1996" U.S. Border Patrol, 1997.

"America Puts Up Chain Links Along a Once Friendly Border," H. La Franchi, *The Christian Science Monitor,* Feb. 13, 1996.

"Militarizing the Border," *Covert Action Quarterly,* Spring 1996.

"Borderline Shootings: Two Cases This Year Raise Questions About Military's Role on Rio Grande," T. Herrick, *Houston Chronicle,* June 22, 1997.

"Border Patrol Reinforcements to be Sent to Porous Sectors," W. Branigin, *The Washington Post,* Oct. 8,1997.

"Churches' Call to 'Love the Stranger' Includes Illegal," D. Ramirez, *Arizona Daily Star*, Feb. 17,1995.

"A Catholic Framework for Economic Life," Bread for the World (1998).

"AFSC Perspectives on Immigration Policy," American Friends Service Committee, July 1997.

SERVICE-LEARNING ACTIVITIES IN THE UNITED STATES

The service component of this course may be satisfied in a variety of ways. Possible placements will include:

1. **Catholic Charities, Immigration Department, N.Y., N.Y.**
   Students interested in the legal processing of claims may assist staff attorneys by completing intake applications for clients and by doing research on country specific claims for asylum.

2. **Lawyers' Committee for Human Rights, N.Y., N.Y.**
   Students interested in issues involving refugee and asylum cases may volunteer to work on specific regional issues.

3. **The Center for Immigration Rights, N.Y., N.Y.**
   Students interested in legal process issues may volunteer to be court watchers at removal hearings.

4. **Bonita Springs Project, Bonita Springs, Fla.**
   Students interested in working with migrant workers may spend spring break working with the Christian Brothers' community in Florida.

5. **Iona College After School Program, New Rochelle, N.Y.**
   Students interested in working with immigrant families (many of whom are from Mexico) may become involved in language and naturalization tutoring programs.

Management 377
Organizational Behavior
University of Evansville

MANAGEMENT 377 - ORGANIZATIONAL BEHAVIOR

Instructor: Dr. Nancy Leonard
University of Evansville
Office: 207 Hyde Hall
Fall Semester 1997

COURSE DESCRIPTION

Organizational behavior is the study of human behavior, attitudes, values and performance within organizational settings. It is an interdisciplinary field, which draws on social and clinical psychology, sociology, labor relations, anthropology, industrial engineering, and industrial psychology. We will be discussing and experiencing the theory, methods and principles of these diverse disciplines to learn about individual perceptions, values, and learning styles; group structure and dynamics; and organizational processes that occur on a daily basis within any social gathering. These processes include, but are not limited to, communications, decision-making, leadership, power and politics, conflict, stress management, and change.

The major objectives of this course include:

1. To expose you to the basic issues and literature in organizational behavior

2. To help you apply this knowledge in a work setting in order to experience organizational behavior concepts as well as gain an understanding of the concept of social responsibility.

3. To help you improve your analytical, decision-making, and interpersonal skills.

REQUIRED TEXT

Schermerhorn, J.R., Hunt, J.G., and Osborn, R.N., 1995. *Basic Organizational Behavior.* New York, NY: John Wiley & Sons, Inc.

In addition to the text for this course, you will be required to beg, borrow, or buy a number of tools (i.e. a hammer and a tape measure).

Throughout the semester, discussion topics will be posted to our class discussion group on the Internet. In order to participate in the discussions, you will need to subscribe to the class group. The list-serv name is mgt377. To subscribe, send a message to majordomo@evansville.edu. In the text area type subscribe mgt377. Group topics are appropriate for the discussion group, personal messages should be sent directly to individual e-mail accounts.

SOCIAL RESPONSIBILITY AND SERVICE-LEARNING

In many business administration courses, you are taught that a corporation's first responsibility is to share-holders and specifically to increasing shareholder wealth. This perspective is often seen as in conflict with the concept of social responsibility.

In today's business environment the demands for social responsibility placed on contemporary organizations by an increasingly sophisticated and educated public are stronger than ever. It is therefore important for organizations to fashion an approach to social responsibility the same way that they develop any other business strategy. Social responsibility is a major challenge to managers, and requires careful planning, decision making, implementation, and evaluation.

One common view of social responsibility is that a business' sole responsibility is to shareholders and that socially responsible activities such as social improvement programs should be determined by law, by public policy, and by the actions and contributions of private individuals. They feel that the government, via legislation and allocation of tax revenues is better qualified to make decisions concerning social improvement programs and that businesses contribute by being profitable and paying their taxes. Some people, including the famous economist Milton Friedman, argue that expecting organizations to become involved in social reform will undermine the United States' economy by detracting from the basic mission of business: to earn profits for owners. A second view of social responsibility is based on the belief that society is entitled to more than the mere provision of goods and services and that at a minimum, businesses must be accountable for the ecological, environmental, and social costs incurred by its actions. Proponents of this view support corporate contribution to charity as socially responsible behavior.

A third view of social responsibility is that socially responsible behaviors should be anticipatory and preventive rather than reactive and restorative. In this case, a socially responsible organization seeks solutions to social problems. Managers in organizations that subscribe to this view of social responsibility apply corporate skills and resources to problems ranging from run-down housing to youth employment and small business creation. This level of social responsibility on the part of organizations moves managers and their organizations away from the traditional position of singular concern with economic means and ends.

Because managers often define social responsibility for an organization and determine what is "socially responsible behavior," it is increasingly important for business administration programs to provide you with the opportunity to experience socially responsible activities and to gain self awareness of your own perspective on social responsibility. In this class, this experience will involve a community service project. The goal of this community service project is to allow you to generate your own data about the concept of social responsibility. The class format will allow you to observe and share your personal reactions to what you have experienced. By incorporating a community service component which focuses on social responsibility into this course, I hope to:

1. Help you gain self awareness of your own perspective on social responsibility.

2. Increase your awareness of the impact of social responsibility on interpersonal relations, decision making, managing change, and other key managerial and organizational behavior functions.

3. Help you develop a concern for both what is produced and how that happens, balancing stockholder interests, family support, and community responsibility.

4. Help you become socially responsible business leaders and corporate citizens, who recognize the importance of the corporate sector taking a socially responsible perspective.

5. Develop a spirit of partnership with the community, a belief that through shared effort, teamwork and widespread participation, both the organization and the community will benefit.

COMMUNITY SERVICE PROJECT

As a basis for discussion and experience, we will form a construction company. The task assigned to this company is to build a house! Our company will manage the construction cycle for a Habitat for Humanity home. Habitat for Humanity International and Habitat of Evansville seek to eliminate poverty housing and homelessness around the world, and to make decent shelter a matter of conscience and action.

My goal is to provide you with the opportunity to work as an "organization" and deal with the behavioral issues which arise. These issues may include, but not be limited to, group development, communication between group members and outside organizations, motivation and social loafing, decision making, ethics, leadership, and performance evaluation.

Because the project will be an ongoing project, the weekly activities involved in organizing the effort needed to build a Habitat house will provide the basis for class discussion and application of the concepts presented in the textbook.

Because we will be working on Saturday, we will not have class on Wednesday. On Saturday, we will have two shifts. The first shift will work from 8:00 a.m. until noon. The second shift will work from 11:00 a.m. until 3:00 p.m. This will allow you to make arrangements for your other Saturday obligations (i.e. sports workouts, part-time jobs, etc.). The overlap between 11:00 a.m. and noon will allow the site supervisors to coordinate their efforts and the morning crew to show the afternoon crew the "ropes."

You will be required to keep a personal log of your observations and feelings concerning the project. These logs will form the basis of class reflection and discussion, application papers, and a personal evaluation assignment at the end of the semester.

GRADING POLICY

Final course grades will be assigned to each student at the end of the semester based on performance in the following areas:

"Building" Attendance and Participation 20%

Class Attendance and Participation 20%

Peer Evaluation 30%

Application Papers 10%

Personal Log 10%

Personal Evaluation Paper 10%

Total 100%

Early in the semester, we will create the Peer Evaluation Forms based on the following criteria:

Quality of Work Quantity of Work Attitude Responsibility Reliability Any other criteria which we, as a class, determine to be important.

Peer Evaluation Forms will be due each Monday. Application Papers will be due periodically during the semester. Personal Logs will be due on October 10th and November 24th so that I can read them and provide feedback over Fall Recess and Thanksgiving Break. The Personal Evaluation Paper will be due on the last day of class.

ORGANIZATIONAL STRUCTURE

As a class, we will decide on the organizational structure needed to accomplish our task. As a basis for discussion, I am proposing the following structure:

President

Vice President

Treasurer

Records/Pictures/Historian

Secretary

Afternoon

Morning site foreman & Afternoon site foreman (rotating positions)

Ordering/Supply

Family committee

Public relations committee

Utilities/permits/inspections committee

Human safety volunteer

Resources

Time cards

Conflict/dispute resolution

Committee

Attendance

Insurance

Safety Issues

Emergency Response

First Aid

TQM Committee

Quality Control

The Executive Board will consist of the officers and a representative from each committee. The Executive Board and any other individuals who would like, will meet with Steve Peters and myself on Monday evening to be sure the committees understand what must be accomplished during the week in order to be prepared for the following Saturday.

Kineseology 325L
Motor Development Laboratory
California State University-Northridge

KIN 325L - MOTOR DEVELOPMENT LABORATORY (1 UNIT)

California State University - Northridge
Instructor: Jennifer L. Romack, Assistant Professor
Office: KN285
Office Hours: MTWTh 11:00 a.m. - 12:00 p.m., or by appointment.
Tuesday and Thursday Sections, 1:30 - 3:50 p.m.

COURSE DESCRIPTION

A service-learning experience designed to understand and apply concepts of motor development while fulfilling a need in our community.

PURPOSE OF THE SERVICE-LEARNING EXPERIENCE

Occasionally we learn important lessons by EXPERIENCE. One type of experience is found through giving in your community. In modern times this giving is too often limited to money donations. The act of giving one's time and energy as a service to another seems to have fallen out of fashion among many people. In addition, in the process of giving, significant lessons can be learned that directly relate to course content. The purpose of this lab experience is to facilitate the process of giving of yourself and learning through community service. Service-learning is the opportunity to integrate the abstract elements of this course with the concrete aspects gained in the larger community setting. Another benefit of service-learning is the insight you gain into yourself and others. In fact, you may find you sense of interconnectedness with others is strengthened. The intent of our service-learning experience in lab, therefore, is for you a) to provide a needed service, and b) to relate the service-learning content to the subject matter of motor development.

SERVICE-LEARNING OUTCOMES

At the completion of this course, the student will be able to:

Learning Outcome 1: Understand and Apply Knowledge

1. conduct an internet and database search on a motor development topic that is related to a community need.

2. develop the ability to think critically, problem solve, and synthesize knowledge gained through community experience with motor development principles and concepts.

3. develop skills in measuring, interpreting, and presenting data that demonstrates the fulfillment of a community need.

4. observe motor behavior in a normal, diverse, or special population.

5. apply a quantitative or qualitative assessment of movements patterns via observing static images, video records, or real time performance.

6. evaluate and apply ecological theory to motor development.

7. plan, complete, and assess a motor development project relevant to his or her community experience.

Learning Outcome 2: Develop Identity and Values

1. assume responsibility for a community project.

2. appreciate the value of motor development.

3. develop autonomy and independence.

4. recognize societal stereotypes and systems of inequity affecting motor development and work to change them.

Learning Outcome 3: Develop Community Awareness and Practice Community Engagement

1. demonstrate an understanding and appreciation of community diversity.

2. develop problem-solving and decision-making skills in community settings.

Learning Outcome 4: Demonstrate a Commitment to Life-long Learning and Action

1. assume new experiences and unfamiliar roles, taking risks and accepting challenges.

2. improve student recognition of importance of communication.

3. use a variety of ways to articulate information, for example, oral, written, email, and visual.

COURSE CONTENT

I. Introduction to Service-Learning

II. Application of Motor Development Terminology and Theory

III. Physical Growth and Maturation

IV. Observing and Assessing Movement Skills and Correlates of Motor Development

V. Examining Biological and Sociocultural Factors that Influence Motor Development over the Lifespan

ASSESSMENT/EVALUATION

1. *40% Service-learning Experience*

   A. Preparation for Service Experience

      1. Attendance and Participation

      2. Tuberculosis Shot

      3. Email Account

   B. At least 15 Hours of In-service Hours

   C. Service Project Site Supervisor Evaluation

   D. Group Evaluation

   E. Instructor Evaluation

   F. Preparation for Poster Presentation

      1. Attendance

      2. Peer Evaluations

II. 60% Reflective Journal (see attached description)

REFLECTIVE JOURNAL GUIDELINES

You should write in your journal (a) to record the process of planning and completing your project, (b) after each interaction with your service partner, and (c) to address any impact assignments. Entries should be in handwriting. For each reflective entry include the date and time. When writing in your journal, use fictitious names when referring to any individuals. This maintains the confidentiality of all persons involved. Each journal entry should be composed of three steps. Each step should be written in its specified color (see below).

BLUE: The activities you've undertaken for either the project or an impact assignment. A key to this process is objectivity. This is when you see like a camera, recording only what is seen without any judgments or preconceived ideas. Don't interpret what is observed.

RED: Thoughtful analysis of the experience. Describe what you felt about the encounter, share all of the joys, successes, frustrations, anxieties, boredom, setbacks, challenges, surprises, etc.

GREEN: Evaluate the experience relative to what is currently being presented in lecture. Connect what we are learning in class with either the impact assignment or the experience you are having at your site. Use information from your textbook to support what you discuss. Underline the concept/theory and give the exact page number(s) in the text where the concept/theory is stated.

Pay close attention to technical errors like margins, spelling, grammar, and punctuation. Neatness does count!

Political Science 120-04
United States Government
University of Pennsylvania-Bloomburg

Pol Sci 120-04: United States Government

Bloomsburg University of Pennsylvania
Instructor: Dr. Diana G. Zoelle
Department of Political Science
Fall 1999

SCOPE OF THE COURSE

The academic substantive focus of this course is integrated with students' service experiences in local and state agencies. The service opportunity provides insight into the practical application of particular national policy areas. Of course, in some cases, the responsibility and oversight of the implementation of programs has been shifted to state or local government. This is also salient to our investigation. This type of experiential learning enhances students' awareness of issues which may affect their lives or the lives of those close to them and empowers them if they choose to advocate political change or reinforce efforts to maintain certain programs. It prepares them to be better citizens.

Students complete two (2) hours of volunteer work each week for ten (10) weeks of the semester. They also review and reflect upon their service through keeping a journal of their experience. Their experience is integrated with academic readings and discussions in class in which we attempt to analyze the basis for, and the practical functioning of, the organization and its providers.

Individual and group informal, in-class presentations are encouraged.

Students enrolled in US Government 120-04 may consider making longer commitments to their service organizations. However, there is no mechanism in place with which to encourage their continued efforts. Also, we have no fourth credit option as yet, but the possibility is in the planning stages. Should the fourth credit option become a reality, the in-class presentation of an analytical essay could become a formal requirement.

The service experiences offered to the students are chosen for their relationship, however distant, to the political agenda or practical policies of national government. Part of the mandate of the student is to identify and critique the operative politics and policies. Future development of the program may take the form of a second semester course in American Public Policy in which students may further explore the specific policy issues they have investigated in this preliminary course. Each student may either continue working in the substantive area chosen in the first semester or move to one that presents itself as more critical or interesting to them. Whichever option they choose, the student's first requirement in the second course will be to outline the proposed investigation.

CLASS MEETINGS

Class discussions serve three main purposes:

1. The first few sessions serve as an orientation to the service-learning experience and dissemination of service information;

2. Subsequent class meetings will, in general, be discussions of general material, accented by students' own reflections on their experiences as they relate to the material (at the instructor's urging and possibly with the instructor's collaboration, at first);

3. Classes are, thus, a vehicle for dissemination of general knowledge about government, but also a venue for students to make observations about the relationship between theoretical constructions and practical realities.

DIRECTIONS IN RESEARCH

Guiding questions related to students' service experience and the reflexive nature of their endeavor are:

1. What do you consider to be the most pressing need of the population you are serving?

2. How can the needs you have identified be more effectively met by government agencies or non-governmental organizations with the support of government?

3. How could more direct services be provided to the population you are serving?

4. Can the clients, themselves, affect the level of service they are being provided? (i.e., Could they organize to lobby government?)

REQUIRED READINGS

American Government and Politics in the New Millennium, Stewart et al.
The Washington Post

These readings describe the current social contexts within which government programs and policies are carried out and discuss the relative effectiveness of advocacy groups and the service organizations that focus on particular issues.

SCHEDULE OF READINGS

We will receive the weekly edition of *The Washington Post,* for which reading students are responsible on an on-going basis. I try to arrange discussions so they will have the weekend to relax and enjoy reading the paper.

AUG. 31	Intro: How Do Political Scientists Know What They Know?
SEPT. 7, 9	Chapter One: The Language of Political Science
SEPT. 14, 16	Chapter Two: Constitutional Beginnings
SEPT. 21, 23	Chapter Three: Federalism: Theories of Governing
SEPT. 28, 30	Chapter Four: Public Opinion, Political Culture and Political Socialization
OCT. 5, 7	Chapter Five: Political Parties
OCT. 12, 14	Chapter Six: Campaigns and Elections
OCT. 19, 21	Chapter Seven: The Media
OCT. 26, 28	Chapter Eight: Interest Groups
NOV. 2,4	Chapter Nine: The Congress
NOV. 9	Chapter Ten: The Bureaucracy
NOV. 11	NO CLASS. PROFESSOR ATTENDING CONFERENCE.
NOV. 16, 18	Chapter Eleven: The Presidency and Leadership
NOV. 23	Chapter Twelve: The Judiciary
NOV. 25	NO CLASS. THANKSGIVING DAY.
NOV. 30 & DEC 2	Chapter Thirteen: Civil Liberties
DEC. 7, 9	Chapter Fourteen: Civil Rights

WRITTEN ASSIGNMENTS

Students keep analytical journals throughout the semester and will discuss their observations at designated times throughout the semester. Each will also compose a one-page abstract of his/her entries (type-written) for in-class presentation and discussion.

COURSE GRADE

30% of the course grade relies on the student's satisfactory conclusion of the service work, a journal, on-going, spontaneous discussion of experience as it connects with the general course material and a short presentation of journal reflections and/or analyses.

50% of the course grade relies on satisfactory completion of 10 unannounced quizzes on the course reading material, lectures and videos.

20% of the course grade relies upon participation in class which will be partially determined by reading questions that students bring with them to class and which may be collected at any time by the instructor.

Journals are due no later than the last day of class: Thursday, December 9, 1999.

SERVICE OPTIONS

The value of the service experience is in finding an appropriate service organization. Each student works in an organization concerned with a specific policy area, such as:

Human Rights Policy
Women's Center
Migrant Community Project

Health Policy
Adopt-a-Grandparent
Columbia-Montour Area Agency on Aging
American Cancer Society
COMPEER - to be a fiend to someone with a mental illness

Education Policy
Bethesda Day Treatment Center
Head Start—Millville
Big Brothers/Big Sisters
Juvenile Probation

U.S. GOVERNMENT

The course, US Government, provides a solid base for the types of service that students at Bloomsburg University find available to them. It is also a substantively sound format for reflection upon what government does and does not do for its citizens. Readings are structured to reinforce learning within the service opportunities. The range of service opportunities is selected so that students can make strong connections between the substance of the course and their experiences in the field. By working closely with the Director of the SOLVE program which serves as a clearinghouse between students and the organizations they might potentially serve, we can maximize the experience for the students and for the populations they are serving.

Bloomsburg is a small community in a rural area of northeastern Pennsylvania. When students come here as freshmen, they almost invariably feel some sense of isolation and loneliness. The course's service component provides a medium for students to group together and do cooperative work or to connect with the community individually. However they choose to arrange their work, this experience offers them the opportunity to form lasting bonds and navigate the first couple of semesters at Bloomsburg more easily. Because the students in US Government are usually freshmen, the course and its service component provide a positive beginning to their academic experience. Because they are usually political science majors, they are more likely to follow their service experience with some aspect of political inquiry to which they will bring a deeper, more nuanced understanding of the far-reaching functions, but also the particular limitations, of government policies and programs.

I find that students respond positively to the idea that their service enhances in them an ethic of service that will be an invaluable asset to them and their future communities given the increasing emphasis on less, rather than more, government involvement in domestic social and welfare services.

Dr. Diana G. Zoelle
Professor of Political Science
Bloomsburg University of PA

Psychology as a Social Science Indiana University- Purdue University Indianapolis

Recitation Syllabus
Indiana University-Purdue University Indianapolis
Robert Bringle, Ph.D.
R144, T 11-12:15, LD 014
Spring, 2000

REQUIRED TEXTBOOKS

Rings, S.L., & Kremer, J.F. (2000). *Introductory psychology: Psychology as a Social Science* (8th ed.). Indianapolis, IN: Psychology Department.

COURSE REQUIREMENTS

All students are expected to complete the following recitation requirements:

1. Attend and participate in all recitations.

2. Read course materials.

3. Bring completed tickets to the beginning of class meetings.

4. Take and pass quizzes.

5. Participate in community service a minimum of 2 hours/week for 12 weeks (5-6 hours per week for Freshman Community Service Scholars) at School 44, Riverside Academy, 2033 Sugargrove Ave. (approx. 4 blocks north, 3 blocks east of Bush Stadium).

6. Complete assignments related to the community service.

LEARNING PSYCHOLOGY

My job is to prepare you for examinations. In addition to the quizzes and going over the textbook, we will be doing other learning activities.

- Be prepared

- Be prepared for anything

- Be willing to participate

If you are still seeking more help:

- Attend mentoring

- Make an appointment with me

- Study the glossary more

- Attend mentoring

- Schedule time to study: more studying ===> more learning

- Outline chapters

- Attend mentoring

- Form a study group

- Do not study where you eat and sleep (try a library, any library!)

- Bring questions to recitations

- Join a study group

Let me know if you need help

- I have an open office door and I am around much of the time

- I have available hours in addition to my office hours

- I have an interest in seeing you do well

- I have voicemail, leave a message

- I have email, leave a question

- I have time, come see me

- I have some answers

- I have patience

But remember:

- You are responsible for determining your level of commitment to your education and you are responsible for your performance in this course.

- I am committed to helping you. But, don't ask me to be more interested in your education than you are.

SERVICE-LEARNING

Service learning provides an opportunity for students to actively participate in organized community service experiences and to relate these experiences to course content through reflection activities. Introductory psychology is particularly well-suited to provide a perspective from which to learn from community activities. The combination of experiences (service, course content) provides an opportunity for students to better understand their own relationship to their communities, to feel that they have contributed to a community-based program, and to explore personal and professional issues in ways not typically available in traditional courses. All students will complete 3 hours of service at School 44 each week.

EVALUATION

I. Examinations

Examinations are taken on computers in Room SL 070A (see pp. viii-ix, xi of textbook). You may take each examination twice—with the better grade counting toward your final grade. Each examination has a closing date and time. Do not wait until the end of the examination period to take the test—>there will be lines!! The examination is turned off at 5 P.M., whether or not you are in line to take it and whether or not you are in the middle of taking the examination.

Testing hours are:
- Monday through Thursday: 9 to 9

- Friday and Saturday: 9 to 5

- Sunday: 11 to 5

You must have an IUPUI OneCard to enter the test room.

You must have an IUPUI OneCard displayed when taking a test.

Each of the five tests has 50 multiple-choice questions and a short essay for 5 points. Most of the essay questions on the test will come from the "Putting It All Together Section" of the study guide. Immediately after taking the test you will receive feedback on the number of multiple-choice questions that you answered correctly. The essay portion will be graded within 2 days after you take the test.

Although there are 55 possible points on each examination, assume that the examination has 50 possible points (with 5 bonus points possible from the essay) and grades are based on the following scale:

A . . . . 45+

B . . . . 40+

C . . . . 35+

D . . . . 30+

If you cannot take the examinations outside of class, then drop the course.

THERE ARE NO MAKE UP EXAMINATIONS. If you miss an examination, you can replace that score with a cumulative final at the end of the semester which is based on the 10 assigned chapters of the Study Guide only (no lecture material) plus the appendix. The cumulative final, which is entirely multiple-choice questions, is given during the same time period as Exam 5. Only those persons who have missed an examination can take the cumulative final. If you miss two examinations, drop the course.

II. Recitation

Recitation is worth 100 points toward your course grade.

A. 50 POINTS ARE BASED ON PERFORMANCE ON QUIZZES

There will be 13, 10-item quizzes based on the study guide and lectures.

YOU MUST HAVE A TICKET TO TAKE A QUIZ.

Your ticket will be completion of an assignment distributed the previous week.

If you miss the previous class, you still need a ticket for the next class. You may either (a) pick up the assignment from me on a subsequent day, or (b) do all of the study guide materials for the assigned chapter.

If you get 6 or more questions correct on a quiz, you pass!

If you get fewer than 6 correct, it's a goose egg.

50 of the 100 recitation points are awarded on the basis of the following schedule:

6 or fewer passes . . . . 00 points

7 or 8 passes . . . . 35 points

9 or 10 passes . . . . 45 points

11 to 13 passes . . . . 50 points

THERE ARE NO MAKE-UPS ON QUIZZES.

A missed quiz is a dropped pass.

B. 50 POINTS IS BASED ON 4 MINI-PAPERS AND A FINAL PAPER WRITTEN ABOUT YOUR COMMUNITY SERVICE

> 4 mini-papers and final paper . . . . 50 points
>
> 3 mini-papers and final paper . . . . 40 points
>
> Anything less than the above . . . . . 00 points

1. **Journal:** A journal provides an opportunity for students to describe service activities while they are fresh, reflect on those activities, and relate psychology course content to the service activities. Journal entries should be long enough to capture the important aspects of the experiences. A split-entry journal format, with description on the left side of the page and analysis (i.e., connections to psychology material) on the right side of the page, is a good way to structure journal entries and will help you write the mini-papers. Journals will not be collected during the semester—they are for the student's benefit and provide an important resource for completing the writing assignments.

2. **Mini-Papers:** The mini-paper will be a minimum of 3 pages, double-spaced, typewritten with the following sections:

   a. **Description (1 page).** This section is a narrative of events, interactions, decisions, successes, problems, and plans that occurred during your service. It can include not only a descriptive account of events, but also your thoughts and feelings about these events.

   b. **Analysis (1 page).** The analysis section includes connections between your service experience and material from the B104 textbook, lectures, and recitations. In this section, you should cite theories, theorists, concepts and research findings that you find useful in analyzing and understanding the events at your service site. HINT: Go through the glossary, and page through the text and study guide, and you will discover connections that can be made.

   c. **Application (1 page).** The application section relates the course work and your service experiences to your personal life. In this section, you can comment on insights that the connections in the Analysis section provide you regarding your relationships to others, your career plans, and your goals, dreams, values, and growth.

   The paper must have a cover page that includes your name, student ID #, and section #.

   Note: Late papers will not be accepted.

3. **Final Paper:** The final paper will be a minimum of 15 pages, double-spaced, typewritten with the following sections:

a. **Description (5 pages).** This section is a narrative of events, interactions, decisions, successes, problems, and plans that occurred during your service. It can include not only a descriptive account of events, but also your thoughts and feelings about these events.

b. **Analysis (5 pages).** The analysis section includes connections between your service experience and material from the B104 textbook, lectures, and recitations. In this section, you should cite theories, theorists, concepts and research findings that you find useful in analyzing and understanding the events at your service site. HINT: Go through the glossary, and page through the text and study guide, and you will discover connections that can be made.

c. **Application (5 pages).** The application section relates the course work and your service experiences to your personal life. In this section, you can comment on insights that the connections in the Analysis section provide you regarding your relationships to others, your career plans, and your goals, dreams, values, and growth.

The paper must have a cover page that includes your name, student ID #, and section #.

NOTE: Late papers will not be accepted

III. Final Grades

There are 350 points in the course: 250 points from examinations (5 x 50 points) and 100 from recitation (50 points from quizzes and 50 points from reflection papers). Final grades are based on the following scale:

A . . . . 315 to 350

B . . . . 280 to 314

C . . . . 245 to 279

D . . . . 210 to 244

F . . . . <210

1. You may access the points you have accumulated from examinations via: http://test.psych.iupui.edu/student_access.asp

IV. Extra Credit

Students may earn 15 extra credit points in the course, but no more than 12 points in any one way:

1. Students who regularly visit School #44 and actively participate in tutoring/mentoring will earn 12 points extra credit (be sure to sign-in at the front desk in the main office).

2. Participating in research (see p. x of textbook).

3. Written reports (see pp. x-xi of textbook).

4. Three-in-a-row: Students may earn 1 point per chapter if they accumulate 20,000 points. These bonus points will be automatically listed in the grade book. Access the game via: http://test.psych.iupui.edu/3inarow/

V. Fourth Credit

Students enrolled in this service-learning recitation may elect to enroll in B292, R185 for an additional 1 credit hour.

VI. Cheating

You should know that I hate academic misconduct. If you are caught cheating, all your passes on quizzes up to that point turn into zeros.

NOTE: Reproduction or dissemination of material in the videotaped lectures is prohibited without the written permission from the Psychology Department.

RECITATION SCHEDULE

Aug 29   Introduction, etc.
[NOTE: Withdraw with full refund before Aug 30th, 6 P.M.,]

Sept 5   History and Personality
Chapter 1, Lecture 1
Beginning of class: Quiz #1
Bring your ticket to class

Sept 12   Learning
Chapter 2, Lecture 2
Beginning of class: Quiz #2
Bring your ticket to class

Sept 19   10:45: Meet at School 44, Riverside Academy,
2033 Sugargrove Ave. (4 blocks north, 3 blocks east of Bush Stadium)

Sept 26   Human Development
Chapter 3, Lecture 3
Quiz #3, bring ticket to class (last reminder!)

Oct 1   Examination 1 over chapters and lectures 1 & 2 closes at 5 P.M.
      (if you're smart you did not wait until now)

Oct 3   Stress and Health
      Chapter 4, Lecture 4
      Quiz #4

Oct 10   Review—Quiz #5
      Mini-paper #1 due

Oct 17   Psychopathology
      Chapter 5, Lecture 5
      Quiz #6
      [Can withdraw with advisor's signature with grade of W through Oct 17th]

Oct 22   Examination 2 over chapters and lectures 3 & 4 closes at 5 P.M.

Oct 24   Psychotherapy
      Chapter 6, Lecture 6
      Quiz #7

Oct 31   Review—Quiz #8
      Mini-paper #2 due

Nov 7   Research
      Chapter 7, Lecture 7
      Quiz #9

Nov 12   Examination 3 over chapters and lectures 5 & 6 closes at 5 P.M.

Nov 14   Intelligence/Assessment
      Chapter 8, Lecture 8
      Quiz #10
      [Can withdraw with advisor's signature and instructor's signature through Nov 14th]

Nov 21   Review—Quiz #11

Mini-paper #3 due

Nov 28   Social Psychology

Chapter 9, Lectures 9a & 9b

Quiz #12

Dec 3   Examination 4 over chapters and lecture 7 & 8 closes at 5 P.M.

Dec 5   Industrial/Organizational

Chapter 10 + Appendix,

Quiz #13

Lecture 10

15-page paper due

All extra-credit due

Dec 17   Examination 5 over chapters and lectures 9 & 10 closes at 5 P.M.

Cumulative make-up final (based on 10 chapters + Appendix from the textbook, but not the lectures) closes at 5 P.M. NOTE: The cumulative make-up final can be taken only if one of the five examinations was missed.

Sociology 211
Human Community and
Modern Metropolis
Augsburg College

SOCIOLOGY 211: HUMAN COMMUNITY AND MODERN METROPOLIS

The City As Text: Reading And Understanding Communities And Neighborhoods In The Twin Cities And U.S.
Augsburg College, Mpls, MN
Garry Hesser, Ph.D.

I. **"Reading" A Community Through A "3m" Lens: Methods, Models And Milieu**

   A. Methods and techniques of investigation and inquiry: sociology as a social science/empirical

      1. Gathering Relevant, Existing Information (Data)

      2. Observation (often as a Participant)

      3. Interviewing and Asking Good Questions

      4. "Knowledge About" and "Acquaintance With" Continuum

   B. Models: lenses or frameworks (theories and concepts)

      1. Sociological Perspective: where the individual [agent] and social forces/history converge

      2. Poets Ecosystem

      3. Structuration: Theory for Community/Social Systems

      4. Horizontal and vertical relationship: within and between open systems & locality-relevant functions (Warren)

      5. Conflict Theory

      6. "New Urban Sociology": Political Economy and Structuration Theory/Agency

C. Milieu: context and comparison for reading a city:

Neighborhoods, Minneapolis, Twin Cities

Variations in perception & interaction

Structuration in the 20th century

- Deindustrialization

- Global economy

- Decentralization/suburbanization/sprawl

- Immigration, ethnicity, & race

Government: democracy at work & on trial

Independent sector: public-private partnerships

II. **The Community As Text: Practice Makes Perfect (Or Better])**

A. Seward-Milwaukee Avenue: case study of change

B. Triangulating: observing, poets, interviewing and conversing

1. Field study Neighborhood: Cedar-Riverside, Phillips, Seward, Lyndale, Powderhorn

2. Minneapolis

3. Twin Cities region

C. Locality relevant functions/horizontal relationships

1. Met by your field site organization

2. Other organizations meeting L-R-F's

D. Participant observation and critical analysis (DIE)

E. Connecting the text (the community) to the text (*City Lights*)

F. Community leaders and "agents": structuration at work

III. Application & Integration of Field Study, Course Concepts, and Content

Leading A Community: The City As A Text
A "3M"/Triangulation Approach

Methods & Techniques
(ka & aw)
-Existing Information/Data
-Observation
-Interviews

models: lenses/frameworks
(theories and concepts)
-Poets Ecosystem
-Social systems/LRF's
-Vertical and Horizontal Patterns
-Political Economy/New Urbanism
-Agency and Structuration
-Conflict/Competition

Region-community-city-neighborhood
[e.g., MPLS, NHD, MPLS, REGION]

Milieu: context and comparisons

Neighborhoods, Minneapolis, Twin Cities

Variations in perception & interaction

Structuration in the 20th century

• Deindustrialization

• Global economy

• Decentralization/suburbanization/sprawl

• Immigration, ethnicity, & race

Government: democracy at work & on trial

Independent sector: public-private partnerships

Reading the city-community-region as a text: assumptions

1) You and I can discover and explore that "invisible" highway called social organization (social structure, culture, & institutions).

2) Communities, like all social organizations, are the result of social-economic forces and human activism ("agency").

3) Reading and understanding communities (and all social organizations and institutions) can liberate and empower people for effective citizenship and community building.

4) Reading and understanding communities is significantly enhanced by developing skills in research methodology, theories and concepts, and comparative knowledge and information, enabling us to understand:

-What is happening?

-Why is it happening?

-Who benefits the most and the least from the way things are?

-Why is that the case?

-If one wanted to change things to improve the quality of life for more residents of the community, what public policies and actions would be required?

5) Healthy people (and communities) are growing and helping others to grow. (Robert Theobald)

HUMAN COMMUNITY AND MODERN METROPOLIS
Sociology 211 (City Perspective)
Fall, 2000

Have you ever wondered why some cities and neighborhoods are such desirable places to live and others are not? Well, sociologists contend that there are "social facts" or "social forces" that explain the "making," "sustaining," and "unmaking" of communities, whether suburban, rural, or central cities. This course is designed to help you think with a "sociological imagination" so that you will understand communities better and be a more informed and more active citizen in the future.

All of us live out our lives in communities. But, like fish in water, we take communities for granted, seldom taking the time or developing the tools to understand how to "read a community" and learn how the institutions around us create and mold us into the persons we are becoming.

This class will ask you to make use of your own experiences as you question and enlarge your understanding of the human community and social institutions. The objectives for this class include

- learning how to read a community using basic concepts and methods of sociology;

- learning how to understand communities as social systems which are a part of larger systems;

- learning to be a "participant observer" and gather important information helpful in "reading a community," often using an approach we will call "triangulation";

- improving your ability to learn with and from other persons, including your classmates;

- learning how to utilize existing information from organizational and government materials;

- applying the concepts and ideas of urban and community sociology to better understand what you are learning about Mpls, the Twin Cities and other major metropolitan areas; and

- enhancing your understanding and practice of citizenship and community service skills.

To begin this journey, I would like for you to think about what some sociologists have written:

> "...to begin to solve the daunting problems [facing our times], let alone the problems of emptiness and meaninglessness in our personal lives, requires that we greatly improve our capacity to think about our institutions. We need to understand how much of our lives is lived in and through institutions, and how better institutions are essential if we are to lead better lives....One of the greatest challenges, especially for individualistic Americans, is to understand what institutions are—how we form them and how they in turn form u—and to imagine that we can actually alter them for the better. [p.5]...
>
> "Americans often think of individuals pitted against institutions. It is hard for us to think of institutions as affording the necessary context within which we become individuals; of institutions as not just restraining but enabling us; of institutions not as an arena of hostility within which our character is tested but an indispensable source from which character is formed. [p.6]...
>
> Indeed, the great classic criteria of a good society—peace, prosperity, freedom, justice—all depend today on a new experiment in democracy, a newly extended and enhanced set of democratic institutions, within which we citizens can better discern what we really want and what we ought to want to sustain a good life on this planet for ourselves and the generations to come." [p.9]

ROBERT BELLAH, ET AL, THE GOOD SOCIETY, 1992

TEXTS AND READINGS

Phillips, *City Lights,* 2nd Edition (required)

Warren, "The Community as a Social System" (Reserve)

Gist and Fava, "Human Ecology/POETS" (Reserve)

"Structuration: Agency and Social Forces" (Reserve)

Grams, "Learning by Participating" (Reserve)

State of City, 1996, 1997 & 1998 (Reserve and loaner copies)

Neighborhood Profiles, Reports, Newpapers, KTCA-ch 2 and Local TV News, KNOW-FM [91.1]

The Face of the Twin Cities: Another Look, United Way Report (Reserve)

"Metropolitan Blueprint," Metropolitan Council (Reserve)

 "Making One Community Our of Many" (Reserve)

"Sprawl: Its Nature, Consequences, Causes," Henry Richmond (Reserve)

GRADING AND EVALUATION

Midterm Exam (10/25) 25%

Final Exam (12/18 @ 1:00 see ACTC calendar). 25%

Field Study Journal/Written Assignments. 50%

Cumulative Friday Journal Applications (averaged) 25%

Field Study Application-Integration Paper (12/13) 15%

Class Presentation on Neighborhood (12/6-12/13) 10%

CRITERIA FOR GRADING

1) *See college catalogue for what a 4.0, 3.0, 2.0, 1.0, etc. mean at Augsburg;* but, basically, students who achieve the basic requirements should expect to receive a passing grade of a 2.0. Grades above that will require "going the extra mile" in some or all elements of the course.

Note: Review College Catalogue for meaning of 4.0 [consistent excellence], 2.0 [demonstrates basic competence]; 3.0 has elements of excellence, etc.

2) *What is required to perform satisfactorily in this class?*

In general, being a full time student means that you devote at least 40 hours a week to your courses, i.e., at least 10 hours a week to this particular course. Students who receive grades of 4.0 on particular assignments and the course itself will almost always spend that much time on the course and will demonstrate a thorough understanding of each of the elements of the course, including how they relate to each other. Students receiving a 4.0 will be able to use the course content to offer reasonable explanations of why cities and communities are the way they are and how communities affect their residents the way they do. They will be able to demonstrate their understanding in the various written and oral opportunities for evaluation, including the collaborative efforts of the group(s) in which they work. They will demonstrate a thorough understanding of the readings, class presentations/discussions, and field study neighborhood.

3) *On the first day of class* we will discuss and decide upon other expectations and criteria for evaluation and course grading.

4) *Attendance and active participation are essential for this course.*

If it is necessary to miss class, you are responsible for finding out what you missed and for any information provided on that day, including collaborative work which your group is expecting. (Note: "Bonus points" for regular attendance, increasing your Friday Field Journal average the more "perfect" your attendance.)

5) *Late assignments will be lowered one grade for each day they are late, e.g., 4.0 to 3.5; 3.0 to 2.0, etc.*

6) *The college policy on Honesty and Plagiarism [see Student Guide] is the norm for this course.* Each student must sign a statement at the beginning of the class promising to adhere to the policy. You are expected to do your own work where the assignment indicates, but collaboration and mutual assistance is also expected in conjunction with many assignments. If unsure, ask instructor.

7) *If you have any special needs or challenges,* please discuss them with me as soon as is possible so that accommodations can be made to enable you to be successful in this course.

CLASS SCHEDULE AND ASSIGNMENTS

MONDAYS: "*The City as a Text:* Field Study Hours and gathering information to understand what your neighborhood, Mpls and the Twin Cities are like and why things are the say they are.

WEDNESDAYS: Text Reading Assignments—read and come with questions and ready to discuss

FRIDAYS: "Putting It All Together"—Connecting your Field Study and the Concepts of Sociology

Integrative and application Journals due at beginning of class each Friday…

NOTE: C=Class Assignment

A=Assignement

WEEK #1   HOW CAN WE UNDERSTAND THE MAKING AND UNMAKING OF CITIES?

Wed-9/6   Seeing the Community as a Text to "Read" and Understand: Going Beyond the Obvious

C: Field Trip to Milwaukee Avenue: What can be learned by observation?

Sign up for meeting with professor in small groups: Wednesday and Thursday

Fri-9/8   Getting the Course into Focus

A: Read pp. 1-6 of the syllabus carefully

Complete: Friday Journal #1 & bring to class (return visit to Milwaukee Avenue area?)

Column #1 Monday Field Notebook

Complete biographical sheet and bring to meeting with professor in Memorial 430

Meet for 15-20 minutes (small group) with professor—"Getting acquainted"

-What is your most memorable experience ("KK") with or in a city?

-What makes it memorable or important?

C: Group Reflection on Milwaukee Avenue: What can you learn from observations/data?

-What did you and other classmates see and observe on the field trip?

-Why do you and your classmates think that Milwaukee Avenue is the way it is?

Lecture: Milwaukee Avenue as a Case Study for course—Intro to "analytical concepts"

-POETS Ecosystem ("Human Ecology"): Description and Interpretation

-Warren: Horizontal and Vertical Relationships Between Social Organizations

-Social Structuration: Agency and Social Forces

-Conflict Over Scarce Resource

Introduction to Field Study Options

-Field Study Through Service-Learning: Reciprocity and Experiential Education

Alternatives described and explained: Q & A followed by rank ordered choices

Monday Field assignment: "Triangulating on Cedar-Riverside"

WEEK #2	READING THE COMMUNITY: WITH A LITTLE HELP FROM OTHERS
Mon 9/11	"Looking for the Whole Elephant: "Triangulation" with Multiple Observers A: Explore one of four quadrants of Cedar Riverside as assigned and, if possible, with another classmate (or friend), stopping in at least one business/"busy place" -Complete "Field Notebook #2 (column #1) in Field Study Journal: I (Mondays) -Read "PROJECTS 2 & 3" (p.23): How do they compare to this assignment? C: Reading a City: Four Quadrants of Cedar-Riverside -What can you learn from the observations of others (same and different quadrants)?
Wed 9/13	"How Can We Understand Communities (or Anything, for that Matter)?" A: City Lights, ch 1 - "The Knowing Eye and Ear" "Friday" Journal #2 (Review Chapter 1 and "write for new insights") C: Knowledge About and Acquaintance With: Overlapping Pathways to Knowledge -Introduction to "Triangulation": Theories, Disciplines, Observers, "KA" & "AW" to expand KK, KDK, & DKDK

-Dyad exchange of journals to learn more from another colleague

-Orientation by Site Supervisors/Contact Persons and Placement Sign Up/scheduling

- Background information by Site Supervisors: Bring Questions

Fri 9/15   NO CLASS: "RELEASE DAY" FOR FIELD STUDY ("banking" time)

Cf. October 6; November 3; November 10; December 8

WEEK #3 -   9/18: EXPANDING YOUR AW AND KA: TRIANGULATING FOR "THICKNESS"

Mon 9/18   ABSORBING/GATHERING ALL THE "AW" THAT YOU CAN FROM EXPERIENCE

A: Walking (plus busing, driving...) tour of your Field Site Neighborhood "quartile"

-Two hours of exploring, including 30 minutes in a restaurant(s), business

-Complete Field Journal #3

C: Triangulation

-Exchange Field Study Notebooks and expand your initial understanding

(Begin to "thicken" your understanding by learning from your colleagues)

-Class discussion about "epistemology" and ways of knowing: KK, KDK, DKDK

-"You have to DIE in order to learn"-Description, Interpretation(s), Evaluation

Wed 9/20   SOCIOLOGY IS A NECESSARY, BUT NOT SUFFICIENT, PERSPECTIVE

A: CL, ch. 2 - "Thinking About Cities: Triangulating and Interdisciplinary Approaches"

Suggestion: Review and Know Key Terms (something to do for each chapter)

C: Communities as Social Systems: Vertical and Horizontal Patterns as Social Forces

-See Warren's "Communities as Social Systems"—(Reserve) for review/examples

Fri 9/22   NEIGHBORHOODS ARE VERY COMPLEX REALITIES

A: Review ch. 2 and write Journal entry discussing how Sociology and one other discipline can expand your understanding of the neighborhood site you have chosen

C: "Structuration and the Sociological Perspective: Agency and Social Forces"

"Across the River": Washington DC as a case study for Community Ecosystems
-"Human Ecology: POETS Ecosystem" (see Reserve Reading for more examples)
-"Triangulating using Sociological Perspective (and other disciplines)"
-Assignments/Division of Labor in Field Study Groups for Field Notebook #4

WEEK #4   9/25: POSING THE QUESTIONS & SEEKING "THICKER" UNDERSTANDING

Mon-9/25   GATHERING ALL THE "KA" THAT YOU CAN FROM EXISTING DATA

A: Making Use of Existing Information: Field Notebook #4

-Read the material you are assigned for your Neighborhood (on Reserve in library)

-Writing legibly, using the Field Notebook categories, record the information you find and consider to be critical to an understanding of the neighborhood

-Use both sides of your Field Notebook page, remembering that each reading will have more information for certain categories/sections than others,

i.e., some sections will be filled to overflowing and others nearly empty.

-Review materials given to you at orientation on 9/17

C: Meet with core group to create a "POETS Ecosystem understanding of your neighborhood, with attention to Vertical and Horizontal Relationships, Conflict, etc.

Overview of "Posing the Questions" and Objectives of the Course

Wed 9/27   POSING THE QUESTIONS USING THE SCIENTIFIC METHOD

A: CL, ch. 3

C: "How can Sociology [augmented by other disciplines] help us understand communities?"

How can we understand cause and effect when it comes to urban change & challenges?

-Public and private initiatives: "agency" as an independent variable

-Case study, Suisun City, CA/Roxbury, MA—testing hypotheses from Warren, et al.

Fri 9/29   TESTING HYPOTHESES IN THE REAL WORLD OF URBAN NEIGHBORHOODS

A: Journal #4 using elements of POETS/H/V or other "theories" as possible "independent variables"/causes to explain or interpret what you have described

C: Exchange journals with "core" group; discuss and expand your KK, KDK, DKDK

Class discussion on "Doing Sociology" and the "causes of" neighborhood change and the "operating theory" of the organization where you are doing service-learning

-"Holding Ground: The Rebirth of Dudley Street," continued: "Thicker Analysis"

-What "independent variables"/causes might explain these successes [POETS/V/H]?

WEEK #5	10/2 - DEEPER UNDERSTANDING BY "DISCOVERING THE RULES/NORMS"
Mon 10/2	"MICRO ANALYSIS: "UP CLOSE AND PERSONAL" INTERACTION

"MICRO ANALYSIS: "UP CLOSE AND PERSONAL" INTERACTION

A Participant Observation through Service-Learning

Grams, "Learning By Participation" (Reserve)-use "status," "role," "def'n of situation"

Do Field Study #5 using status, role, def'n of situation to explain a specific interaction N.B. Go beyond the obvious since "social reality is rarely what it first seems..."

C: -Exchange essay with colleague(s)

-Discuss "participant observation" as a research technique for "discovering rules"

-Introduction to "Discovering the Rules" & "Holding Ground" (applications)

Wed 10/4   A: CL, ch. 11 (Friday Journal # 5 optional)

C: Lecture-Discussion of "Discovering the Rules": Understanding Residents of Nhds

Video Clips that illustrate "taken for granted"; structuration; micro & macro

How can an "outsider" understand why others are doing what they are doing or why things are the way they are & how do you learn enough to be an "insider"? (N.B. How does everyday interaction illustrate/reveal "operating theories"?)

"Holding Ground": Dudley Street in Boston

Fri 10/6   NO CLASS

A: FIELD STUDY/SERVICE-LEARNING TIME [3 hours]

HOMECOMING WEEKEND [October 7: 10-12:30 Brunch at Hesser-Homans]

WEEK #6 -   10/9--IS A SENSE OF COMMUNITY POSSIBLE NOW AND IN THE FUTURE, GIVEN THE DIVERSITY AND DIFFERING PERCEPTIONS & EXPERIENCES

Mon 10/9   MICROANALYSIS: DIFFERENTIAL PERCEPTIONS & PERSONAL SPACE"

A: 1) Repeat the PO Field Study (#6) assignment using concepts and ideas from ch 11 to explain and interpret what you have described, "going beyond the obvious" by giving some attention to the idea that "reality is socially constructed" and that most explanations require combining MICRO- and MACROANALYSIS for a "thick" understanding.

Suggestion: Take a look at Projects 1 & 2, p. 319, for examples of how sociologists do "micro" and "macro" analysis of "everyday/taken-for-granted" behavior.

C: Share your written assignment and explanations with core group and report to entire class what you think are some of the most important "rules of behavior" in your neighborhood, including your best explanations as to why people behave as they do.

Wed 10/11   A: CL, ch. 5, pp. 117-120; 138-140 [including key terms];

CL, ch. 16, 451-454; 463- 471 ["EXPERIENCING…" to "ENVIRONMENTAL PSYCH"]

C: How is it possible to sustain "human community" when people's "perceptions" and sense of "social space" is so varied? How does the S in POETS relate to this? How does this contribute to the "making and unmaking" of your neighborhood/hometown?

What difference do attitudes, perceptions and values make to you? Your neighborhood?

-"Neighbors: Conservation and Change"-differential perceptions & urban community

Fri 10/13   A: Journal #6 applying ideas of chapters to neighborhood; review ch 5 & 16

C: Exchange in "secondary" groups and compare and learn from each other and what difference do they make [structuration theory/horizontal rel'ps]?

Lecture/Discussion: "Structuration Theory" according to Giddens and Flanagan

-A Framework for understanding the making and unmaking of urban community

-Applications and connections to Boston and Minneapolis

WEEK #7   10/16 HORIZONTAL & VERTICAL FORCES: ECONOMY AND REGIONALIZATION

Mon 10/16   STRUCTURATION THEORY & AGENCY HYPOTHESIS: IN HISTORICAL CONTEXT

A: Changing the Level of Analysis: Understanding Minneapolis
Collaborating to learn from existing data (Monday #7) All read: NRP Primer & Introduction Assign: State of City, 1998 to 3 colleagues: 1-3) Sections 1-3; 4-6; and 7-9; 4) County and City Extra 1998/1999 [REF HA203 C68] & www.ci.minneapolis.mn.us, www.nrp.org, www.mcda.org 5) Places, Towns, & Townships [HA203 P63] & Metro Sections of newspapers

N.B. Each team member does ONLY ONE with all four/five covered by team; use back of page, too

C: Letterman's Top Ten List for Minneapolis (Field Study Team)

Minneapolis Past as a "Social Force": Ecosystem and Structuration

Wed 10/18   MACRO AND MICRO REALITIES THAT INTERSECT TO EXPLAIN ECOSYSTEMS

A: CL, ch. 4, pp. 94-109 (beginning with "Manchester, England..."), [skim pp. 84-93]

CL, ch. 15, pp. 432-435 ("NEW PERSPECTIVES")

C: Reflecting on Urbanization and our Multinucleated Region: "Structuration" Up Close

Case Studies: New York and LA

Fri 10/20   MACRO & MICRO CONTINUED

A: Journal

C: Chattanooga, Tennessee: A Case Study that illustrates structuration theory

Midterm essay questions

WEEK #8   10/23—PUTTING IT ALL TOGETHER [for the first time]

Mon 10/23   REVIEW AND CONSOLIDATE UNDERSTANDING ABOUT URBAN COMMUNITIES

A: Review readings and exercises to date & "take-home" Midterm questions

Review "Key Terms" from each assigned reading for matching part of exam

C: Discuss the "take-home" essay questions for mid-term

Work together in core group to assist each other in preparing for mid-term exam

Questions and Answers

Wed 10/25

A: Review and prepare for Midterm Exam: Essay and Matching (from Key Terms)

C: Mid-Term Exam (essay test with questions selected from take-home questions)

Blue Books provided; Honor Code in effect (sign name on blue book cover)

Fri 10/27

A: MID-TERM BREAK

C: NO CLASS

WEEK #9

10/30—LOCAL AND GLOBAL FORCES: REGIONAL/SUBURBANIZATION

Mon 10/30

CAN THERE BE A SENSE OF COMMUNITY IN A MODERN METROPOLIS?

A: Field Study #8—A collaborative inquiry: "TRIANGULATING" ON OUR REGION

Complete the Field Notes assignment (#8) reflecting/speculating on how the regional realities can be explained using structuration theory-vertical-horizontal-agency and how this metropolitan reality affects the city of Minneapolis and your neighborhood

Note: Plan ahead for field study interviews by 11/10 for 11/13-due date (nhd staff/residents)

C: Exchange field notebook within your neighborhood-core group; discuss in small group

"Sprawl: Its Nature, Consequences, Causes," Henry Richmond

Posing the Question: "Can or Should Anything Be Done About Suburban Sprawl?"

Wed 11/1

MAKING CONNECTIONS IN A METROPOLITAN COMMUNITY?

A: CL, ch. 6, pp. 145-150 (skim pp. 151-158); 159-164 (including Key Terms)

CL, ch. 7, pp. 167-176 (skim 177-183); 184-188

Review: CL, ch. 15, pp. 434-435 (from "The Multinucleated" to "Where People Live")

C: CAN THERE BE A SENSE OF COMMUNITY IN THE METROPOLITAN COMMUNITY?

-Public Policy as Agency: Metropolitan Council; Fiscal Disparities; Liveable Communities Act

-"Growth Options for the Twin Cities Metropolitan Area: Metropolitan Blueprint"

-"Back From the Brink": Portland Case Study in regional planning/transit/down town

cf, "Sprawl: Its Nature, Consequences, Causes," Henry Richmond

Again, the Question: "Can or Should Anything Be Done About Metropolitan Sprawl?"

Fri 11/3	NO CLASS: FIELD STUDY/SERVICE-LEARNING TIME/CATCH-UP

Note: Plan ahead for 11/13 interviews with neighborhood residents [see Field Study #10]

-2 DIFFERENT PEOPLE FOR EACH PERSON IN THE GROUP

Nov. 7	VOTE.............VOTE.............VOTE...............VOTE

WEEK #10	11/6—THE IMPACT OF THE NATIONAL AND GLOBAL ECONOMY

Mon 11/6	HOW CAN YOU EXPLAIN THE "MAKING, SUSTAINING AND UNMAKING" OF YOUR NEIGHBORHOOD USING THE THEORETICAL FRAMEWORKS & DATA YOU HAVE?

A: Taking Stock and Hypotheses Re: Making, Unmaking and Sustaining: Field Study #9

What 10 social/structural forces and agency best explain the "making and unmaking..."?

C: Taking stock of your neighborhood's ecosystem, horizontal and vertical forces, agency...

"Letterman's Top Ten Social Forces that best explain your neighborhood. Group

Wed 11/8	THE IMPACT OF CHANGES IN THE ECONOMY ON CITIES AND PEOPLE

A: CL, ch. 15, pp. 421-423 (Column 2 to "THE INTERNAL STRUCTURE OF CITIES")

CL, ch. 17, pp. 505-508 (to Identifying Basic Sectors)

CL, ch. 18, pp. 535 ("LOCAL OCCUPATIONAL STRUCTURES")-546

C: "Surviving the Bottom Line: Living on the Fault Line"—Impacts on Cities and Families

Case Study: San Diego [#2040]

Cf. Suisan, CA & Chattanooga, TN: Planning/agency in the "new era"

Fri 11/10   NO CLASS: FIELD STUDY/SERVICE-LEARNING TIME/CATCH-UP

WEEK #11   11/13—ETHNICITY AND IMMIGRATION (digging deeper into the "P" in POETS)

Mon 11/13   A: Field Study #10

Interview 2 "oldtimers" about the changes in the population in the neighborhood, the city and the metropolitan region during the past "decade"/few years.

-write one page summary of key changes, strengths, good things, & challenges

-"filling in the blanks" of KDK, DKDK for neighborhood report

-checking out what you think you know [KK] about the neighborhood

C: Exchange findings in core group

Consolidating your understanding about the "making, sustaining and unmaking..."

Migration: Old and New

Wed 11/15   DIFFERING MIGRANT EXPERIENCES IN THE U.S.

A: CL, ch. 8—"Movin' On," pp. 201-222 (including Key Terms)

CL, ch. 10, pp. 286-287 ("Ethclass and Gender")

C: "Give Me Your Tired, Your Poor" or Pluribus vs. Unum

What is it Like to Migrate to the Twin Cities in the 1990's?

"Tibetans in Minnesota", KTCA Reports

Fri 11/17   WHY DO THE EXPERIENCES VARY SO MUCH & SO WHAT?

A: Journal #10 connections to chapters 8 and 10: DKDK, KK, KDK

C: Exchange and learn from each other; class discussion

Division of Labor for Monday Assignment (#11)

WEEK #12	11/20ff--IDENTITY CRISIS: HOW MUCH DO RACE AND ETHNICITY MATTER?
Mon 11/20	A: Begin to consolidate your Field Study for the Report on Your Neighborhood Field Study #11

WEEK #12   11/20ff--IDENTITY CRISIS: HOW MUCH DO RACE AND ETHNICITY MATTER?

Mon 11/20

A: Begin to consolidate your Field Study for the Report on Your Neighborhood Field Study #11

-Bring outline(s)of your sections to class to share with your group and get feedback

Re-visit your previous Monday Field Assignments, the Neighborhood Files, State of the City & City and County Data Book (REF HA202 A36; HA203), et al as you create an outline of what you know about the "making, sustaining, and unmaking" of your neighborhood.

C: Exchange outlines and identify KDK that needs attention for final paper & presentation

"Minneapolis Past": Social Class, Race and Ethnicity as Social Forces

Where Macro and Micro converge

"IDENTITY CRISIS": HOW MUCH DO RACE AND ETHNICITY MATTER?

Wed 11/22

RACE AND ETHNICITY: THE CONTINUING "AMERICAN DILEMMA"

A: CL, ch. 9, pp. 228-251 (including Key Terms)

CL, ch 15, pp. 435-438 (from "Where People Live" to "What People Live In.)

C: Can American cities and society survive and/or transcend our "Identity Crisis"?

"Race Space: What Really Drives Metropolitan Growth?"-Jon Powell

Fri 11/24

THANKSGIVING HOLIDAY: HAPPY TURKEY DAY!

WEEK #13

GETTING THINGS DONE: AGENCY TAKES ALL LEVELS OF GOVERNMENT: LOCAL, STATE, AND FEDERAL (You guessed it, another Triangulation

Mon 11/27

A: Continue to consolidate your Field Study for the Report on Your Neighborhood

Field Study #11

-Bring completely revised outline(s) to class to share with your group and get feedback

Review your previous Monday Field Assignments, the Neighborhood Files, State of the City [G1429 M51] & City and County Data Book [REF HA202 A36; HA203], et al, as you do an expanded and revised outline of your sections with a focus on what you and your group know about the "making, sustaining, and unmaking" of your particular neighborhood

N.B. Complete your field study hours by Friday of this week

C: Exchange outlines and identify KDK that needs attention for final paper & presentation

Introduction to Theories about "community power"

Wed 11/29	"The Skeleton of Power" as a Framework/Context for "Getting Things Done"
	A: CL, ch. 12, pp. 332-336; 343-355 (beginning with "The Context of Local Government")
	C: Social Forces and Agency: Power, Influence and Coalitions
	Met Council, Fiscal Disparities Act, Highway 55, IS94 and LRT: Local Parallels
Fri 12/1	CASE STUDIES OF EFFECTIVE PUBLIC PRIVATE PARTNERSHIPS & AGENCY
	A: Journal with Field Study hours completed and approved by supervisor
	C: Portland Suisun, Chattanooga, Roxbury, Anacostia DC, et al]
	-15 minutes in group for feedback and discussion of profile: KK, KDK, DKDK
	-Creating Coalitions: People Who Are Making a Difference [Guest speaker/ video]
WEEK #14	MAKING AND SUSTAINING COMMUNITIES: WHOEVER SAID THAT AGENCY WAS EASY OR SIMPLE?
Mon 12/4	A: Bring a Draft of your Sections for the Report on Your Neighborhood
	C: Planning your group's class presentation
Wed 12/6	"It's Messy, But Agency Can Happen If You Mix Idealism and Realism"
	A: CL, ch. 12, pp. 355-360;
	Ch. 14, pp. 387-392; 407-409 [beginning with "Case Study Concluded..."]
	"Conflict or Consensus: 40 Years of MN Metropolitan Politics," Rep. Myron Orfield
	C: Public Policy Options for the Twin Cities and Other Metropolitan Areas

| Fri 12/8 | NO FORMAL CLASS: TIME TO MEET WITH YOUR GROUP & PLAN REPORT |

Fri 12/8   NO FORMAL CLASS: TIME TO MEET WITH YOUR GROUP & PLAN REPORT

WEEK #15   THE MAKING AND UNMAKING OF MINNEAPOLIS NEIGHBOR-HOODS

Mon 12/11   A: Revise and complete written Neighborhood Profile-Analyis

C: 1st and 2nd Neighborhood Groups: Neighborhood Profiles Presentation

Note: Use Overheads, Powerpoint, handouts, video clips for professional presentation

Wed 12/13   A: Completed written paper due for each neighborhood group/collaboration

C: 3rd and 4th Neighborhood Group: Neighborhood Profile Presentation

Fri 12/15   PUTTING IT ALL TOGETHER: CELEBRATION OF OUR DISCOVER-IES & SERVICE

A: Review City Lights and course; Organize Answers for Final Exam

C: Work in core groups on Final Exam questions; general class discussion

Discuss Conclusions reached in papers and Final Exam Questions (Review TBA)

FINAL EXAM: HON 216-Mon, Dec 18 @1:00; SOC211 Wed, Dec 20—10:15-12:15 p.m.

FIELD STUDY THROUGH SERVICE-LEARNING

Assignment

Every student in Human Community and Modern Metropolis [Soc/Hon 211] is expected to do field work in one of the neighborhoods surrounding Augsburg.* This entails assisting in a neighborhood oriented organization, in active collaboration with 3–4 other students from the class, and will involve you in a minimum of 15 hours during the semester. The actual distribution of these hours is to be worked out with our contact at the agency in ways that are mutually acceptable to you and the needs of the agency and should include at least one committee meeting/Board Meeting with an important agenda to observe and learn from.

*Talk with me by 9/11 if you need an alternative to field study

Assumptions

-   Understanding and knowledge requires personal experience, as well as factual information and abstract reflection and generalization, i.e., research and theories;

- In order to achieve this level of understanding of contemporary urban realities, it is necessary to experience first hand some of the every day realities of persons and social organizations that make up the city;

- In addition, the personal experience is enhanced by preparation and a growing knowledge about the neighborhood and its urban context, including changes that are taking place;

- Such a field experience, which necessarily involves the personal and professional lives of other people, is a privilege that requires:

  - Reciprocity

  - Collaboration, and

  - Appreciation for diversity, including gender, race, ethnicity, social class, values and life styles.

Objectives and Desired Outcomes

As the semester proceeds, it is my hope that all of us involved in this course will achieve the following:

1. A thorough and accurate knowledge of the social, organizational and physical make-up of "your" neighborhood, with a focus upon what "makes, unmakes and sustains" it;

2. A knowledge of the major internal ("horizontal") and external ("vertical") trends and changes that have taken place in "your" neighborhood, city and region since 1950;

3. A growing appreciation for these internal and external factors that help to explain why this neighborhood [and the city] are the way they are, including the impact that these social realities have upon the people, families and social organizations that live and operate within their "boundaries";

4. A knowledge of the history and structure of the organization where you are helping, including a growing awareness of how the organization interacts with and affects other organizations and realities in the neighborhood, city and region;

5. A growing awareness and appreciation for citizens, professionals and organizations that are having a positive impact ("agency") on the quality of life and the public issues and challenges facing the community;

6. An understanding of how this particular neighborhood compares to other neighborhoods in the Twin Cities, the nation and the world; and

7. A growing understanding of what is happening in most urban areas across the United States, why these trends are occurring, who benefits the most, and what alternatives are possible or desirable.

Summary

The provision of assistance to the organization makes it possible for students to assume a legitimate role in the everyday life of the organization. In addition, this service enables the student to give something back to the neighborhood and organization for the opportunity to be a "participant observer." The combination of first-hand experience and factual knowledge about one neighborhood (and an organization within it) will be the basis for learning about the trends and challenges facing U.S. cities and communities.

Web Site Design and Management
San Francisco State University

WEB SITE DESIGN AND MANAGEMENT

San Francisco State University
Kristen Gates
DAI 575.1 - Schedule No. 12294
DAI 575.5 - Schedule No. 12316
Spring 2000

I. OVERVIEW

This class is designed for the student who has experience with HTML and basic site building and focuses on user interface, navigation design, and information architecture. These issues are discussed in lively lectures/seminar setting, using real-time interaction with live Web sites. With a strong emphasis on community service and group learning, teams of students design and build fully functioning Web sites for Bay Area organizations. In addition to the team project, students independently create five Web site projects: 1) Low Bandwidth/Browser Safe Color and Background Titles; 2) Site Navigation; 3) Tables for Optimizing Graphics; 4) Web Animation and 5) Frames.

Prerequisites

- Senior or graduate level standing

- DAI 626 Computer Graphics

- DAI 475 Exploring the World Wide Web

- Portfolio evaluation: (substitution for DAI 626 and DAI 475)

- Evidence of HTML experiences. Web page development using HTML or editor. Visual design experiences using PhotoShop or related software. Web Site URLs, Interactive projects.

- E-mail account (SFSU) with remote Internet access.

- Consent of the instructor.

Mission Statement: Design and Industry Mission Statement

Educate a culturally diverse population of students through interdisciplinary problem solving activities about technology related industry.

This education is provided through experiential, hands-on, up-to-date curriculum that offers liberal arts and technical skill courses.

Conflict Resolution

Conflicts or disagreements between student(s) and/or instructor must be addressed in the following order: 1) Instructor; 2) Department chairperson and 3) Dean.

Plagiarism

Plagiarism and cheating will not be tolerated. Academic dishonesty will result in a failing grade for this course and will be reported to the University.

Attendance

Attendance is required. Your attendance and active participation in class discussion and activities are a crucial part of your learning process. In order to provide the best learning environment, you need to be present in class. Excessive absences and/or late arrival will severely impact your ability to learn the course goals. Therefore, two unexcused absences will lower your final course grade one full letter. Of course, should an emergency arise for which you can provide proof, those absences will not be counted against you.

II. RATIONALE, PURPOSE, AND TARGET AUDIENCE FOR THIS COURSE

The San Francisco Bay Area is widely regarded as the birthplace of the interactive media industry, and when it comes to job creation, Interactive Media is San Francisco's fastest growing industry. A recent study commissioned by the City of San Francisco, revealed that the interactive media industry employed 35,000 people in 1997. That is an increase of 69 percent over the pervious year (MDG.org, 1997). Skills essential to the Interactive Media industry include: graphic and digital artists, writers, programmers, animators, interface designers, content developers, production specialist, technical consultants, content designers, producers and project managers.

This course is intended to prepare future Web designers, producers and interactive media artists entering the Interactive Media Industry. This course is also intended to respond to the needs of senior standing undergraduates and graduates in all majors with the desire to: 1) adapt Web based design and management skills to their particular field of study; 2) increase their awareness of the Interactive Media Industry and 3) for those students looking to participate in a design course with a community service-learning component.

The primary target audience of this course is senior standing and graduate level Design and Industry students. This course is open to all majors.

III. COURSE FORMAT

A lecture/laboratory format utilizing software demonstrations/instruction by instructor and students. Emphasis placed on problem solving "hands-on activity" utilizing Power Macintosh computers and related hardware resources will constitute primary in-class activity. Teaching and learning methods will include reading and written assignments, lecture and discussion, large and small group work, individual student presentation, student critiques, and case studies. Attendance is required.

IV. CLASS SCHEDULE

575.1 Class meets for 3 hours Tuesday and Thursday evening from 6:10 PM to 8:55 PM. Each class will have a 15-minute break at midpoint. You are expected to attend all class meetings. Attendance is required. 575.5 Class meets for 6 hours, Saturday from 9:10 - 12:00 and 1:10 -3:55. Attendance is required

V. GENERAL COURSE OBJECTIVES

The learning experience in this course with the selected topics should enable each student:

1. To learn professional design principals necessary to create effective Web sites.

2. To gain experience using Dreamweaver 2 and Photoshop software programs.

3. To learn how to integrate images, sound, and video into Web site design.

4. To gain insight and understanding concerning the interrelationship between digital design issues and outline principles.

5. To be introduced to roll-overs, behaviors and style sheet capabilities.

6. To develop an understanding regarding how Web masters maintain their sites.

7. To gain experience working as a member of a design team.

8. To learn project management skills.

9. To improve their oral communication and visual presentation skills though a variety of class presentations and assignments.

10. To integrate academic study, community service field work with structured reflection and interdisciplinary problem solving activities, integrating university and experiential community service-learning.

Key Concepts Examples

Some examples of Key concepts taught In the course are listed below.
Background Tiles - Cascading Style Sheets - Color Aesthetics
DHTML - Flowcharts - Frames - GIF Animation - Imagernaps
Information Architecture - Low Bandwidth Graphics - Navigation
Project Management - Rollovers - Strategy - Storyboards - Tables
Transparent Art - Web Typography

VI. REQUIRED TEXT BOOK

Textbooks are available in the school bookstore, retail bookstores and online via lynda.com books (http:www.lynda.com) or amazon.com (http://www.amazon.com).

Required Text: *Deconstructing Web Graphics. 2*
by Lynda Weinman and Jon Warren Lentz
New Riders Publishing ISBN:1-56205-859-2

Designing Web Graphics. 3
How to Prepare Images and Media for the Web
by Lynda Weinman
New Riders Publishing ISBN: 1-56205-715-4

Dreamweaver 2 - H.O.T.
Hands-On Training
by Lynda Weinman
Peachpit Press ISBN: 0-201-35452-7

Suggested Text: *Yale CAIM Web Style Guide*
Available at the school bookstore or online at http://info.med.yale.edu/caim/manual/

VII. REQUIRED CONSUMABLES

1. Two Zip Disks for project files

2. Binder with dividers for Project Book and Class Notes

3. Tracing Paper Pad 11 x 14

4. Pens and Pencils

See Materials List
Required Text and Consumables:
Estimated cost: $161

VIII. EVALUATION METHODS

1. Letter Grade Scale:

A . . . . 90 – 100%

B . . . . 80 – 89%

C . . . . 70 – 79%

D . . . . 60 – 69%

F . . . . 59% and Below

2. Reading reviews and other written assignments and Student presentations/review of readings

3. Individual Web Page

4. Midterm Exam and Practice

5. Term

6. Team Project and FieldWork

In progress and final oral report(s) by team members regarding total site and individual contributions. Includes Team Project Report: a written report detailing your Design Team Project and activities.

7. Project Book

Notes, flowcharts, storyboards, design docs, etc. for Individual and Team projects.

8. Plagiarism: Plagarism and cheating will not be tolerated. Academic dishonesty will result in a filing grade for this course and will be reported to the University.

IX. DESCRIPTION OF WRITTEN ASSIGNMENTS, PROJECTS AND PROJECT BOOK ITEMS

1. **Bibliography "My Favorite Web/Multimedia Resource"**

Bibliography with one paragraph description. Cost (if any).

Bring hard copy to class and post to DAI listserv at dai575-1@sfsu.edu

Siegel, D. (1997). *Secrets of Successful Web Sites.* Indianapolis, IN: Hayden Books. Cost: $49.99

This example uses the APA style of documentation.

2. **Written Assignments   Reading Assignment**

Written assignments must be word-processed and due at beginning of class. Use this format for all assigned readings. Assignment not to exceed one page per chapter. Late assignments will not be accepted.

Name:
Date:
Assignment No.:
Chapter:

Item 1. What were the major points learned from this chapter profile.

Item 2. List at least one outstanding feature, concept or technique that I will apply to my own Web design and/or Web site and why.

3. **Listserv**

DAI ListServe Assignment

Post URL to the class List serve (dai575-1 @sfsu.edu)

Name: Date:

This week, the hot URL I recommend is URL:and why (design, layout, content, technique, etc.).

Use entire URL address (e.g. http://dai.sfsu.edu) in your post.

See Example

4. **Individual Web Projects**

Students will independently create 6 Web site projects incorporating the following:

Create an SFSU student Web site; 1) Low Bandwidth/Browser Safe Color and Background Titles; 2) Tables for Optimizing Graphics; 3) Site Navigation; 4) Frames; 5) Web Animation; 6) Forms; and 7) DHTML.

Web Project No. 0:	Create SFSU student Web site
Resource Materials:	public-html folder & Index.htm page. In-class project
Web Project No. 1:	Create Low Bandwidth /Browser-Safe Color and Background Tile.
Resource Materials:	Chapters 4 & 6 - Designing Web Graphics
Web Project No. 2:	Tables for optimizing graphics and page layout.
Resource Materials:	Chapter 13 - Designing Web Graphics
	Chapter 2 - Deconstructing Web Graphics
Web Project No. 3:	Site Navigation. Design a navigation theme for your site.
Resource Materials:	Chapter 10 - Designing Web Graphics
Web Project No. 4:	Create a Frames addition to your Web Site.
Resource Materials:	Chapter 10 - Designing Web Graphics
	Chapter 10 - HTML for World Wide Web
	Chapter 14 - Creative HTML Design Navigation
Web Project No. 5:	Web Animation -Animated GIF and Javascript Rollover.
Resource Materials:	Chapter 14 - Designing Web Graphics
	Chapter 3 - Deconstructing Web Graphics
	Chapter 15 - Creative HTML Design JavaScript
Web Project No. 6:	Forms
Resource Materials:	Chapter 6 - Dreamweaver 2 Hands-On-Training
Web Project No. 7:	DHTML
Resource Materials:	Chapter 23- Designing Web Graphics
	Chapter 13 - Dreamweaver 2 Hands- On-Training

Midterm Exam: There will be a midterm exam at Week 10. The midterm will cover readings, class demonstrations and discussion. The test will have the following types of questions:

1) Several short-answer definition questions

2) Matching examples to concept or principle

3) Web design software task

   Midterm Date: March 30, 2000

   April 1, 2000

4) Term Paper

   There will be a term paper having a minimum of 5 pages. Paper topic will focus on the Internet/Web and related technology. Instructor will approve paper topic.

   Due Dates: DAI 575.1 -April 27, 2000

   DAI 575.5 -April 29, 2000

5) Team Project

   Web Site Development for Bay Area Organization/Community Service-Learning Component

   A) Student Responsibility
      Students, working in teams, will be required to complete a Web site design and development for an organization located within the greater Bay Area. The student team will meet with the organization to develop the time line for achieving the goals and produce the organizations' Web site. The time spent on the Web site design will be a minimum of three hours per week in addition to regular scheduled class time.

   B) Student Reflection, Report and Evaluation
      In addition to keeping a Project Book documenting the your team project, you will be required to provide in-class updates on the organization's Web site—discussing issues experienced. At semester end, you will give an oral and written report detailing your work on the organization's Web site and reflection upon the organization itself. The above components will be incorporate into your grade for Team Project and Field Work participation.
      Student Participation in the Community Service Model is required—and will be detailed in the class outline and course description. Students will be given a choice, from several organizations, as to the project(s) they work on. Also, students may submit recommendations of organizations seeking Web site design services.

6. Project Book

Students are required to keep a "Project Book." This is a binder/portfolio of the students work over the entire course. Lecture notes, handouts, homework assignments, group work, individual Web and team project notes and reflection. The Project Book and Project Report are due during final examination.

Women's Studies 350
Lasell College

WS/IDS 350: THE PUBLIC SPECTER: FEMINIST REPRESENTATIONS OF THE AFTERLIFE

Lasell College
Dr. Kerrissa Heffernan
Tuesday-Thursday: 4:00-6:00pm; Wolfe 207

COURSE DESCRIPTION

This course will examine ghost stories as a vehicle for the social and cultural concerns of women. Through readings, discussions and service students will explore how ghost stories provide a rich insight into the experiences of women and the social, political and economic forces that affect them.

COURSE INTRODUCTION

This course will utilize literature, art, film and historical record to examine representations women construct of death and the afterlife and the relationship of these representations to social movements of the times (American women, 1860-1920). We will examine these representations as a response to the social, cultural and economic forces that denied women a more traditional public response and contrast these responses with the contemporary social condition of specific populations of women. To better grasp content and meaning, students will participate in a service-based research project at the West Newton/ Waltham Burial Ground repairing monumentry, researching community events evidenced in monumentry and creating a resource for the community of women's history.

READINGS

The books listed below are required reading. It will be important for your understanding and interpretation of this course that you follow the timetable listed in the Course Outline. In addition, the readings will provide a common base for questions and discussions during class. The Reserve Reading List refers to a more expanded range of sources that you might find useful for pursuing topics in greater depth.

This class is reading intensive and much of the class discussion will build upon previous assignments, as such I expect you to complete all readings in a timely manner.

Course Reading Packet

Restless Spirits: Ghost Stories by American Women 1872-1926 – Catherine Lundie

Beloved – Toni Morrison

The Woman Warrior – Maxine Hong Kingston

In addition, students will identify a series of readings to support a specific interest they have related to the course service project.

COURSE GOALS

Students who have successfully completed this course should be able to demonstrate their understandings of:

- The Spiritualism movement in America in the late 19th and early 20th centuries.

- Ghost stories as allegories for the social, political, economic and cultural concerns of women.

- The ways a feminist perspective can inform images of the afterlife.

- The literary tools women authors have used to convey the psycho-social importance in a ghost story.

- How women's community history is conveyed at Newton/Waltham Providence Burial Ground.

- Cemeteries as public spaces that contribute to the health of a community and serve as sites that illustrate the social, political, economic and cultural concerns of women.

COURSE OBJECTIVES

Students who have successfully completed this course should be able to:

1.) Identify and analyze the cultural tensions between material and spiritual conceptions in late 19th century America and how those gave rise to the Spiritualism movement.

2.) Identify and analyze the social and cultural anxieties evidenced in course assignments.

3.) Identify and analyze representations of women evidenced in readings, lectures, service and related assignments and how those representations continue to resonate and influence contemporary images of women.

4.) Identify, define and utilize metaphor, religious iconography and motif.

5.) Analyze specific community events that impacted women in Newton/Waltham as evidenced in the Burial Ground.

6.) Explore the conditions under which a cemetery serves as a public space.

Ways students will demonstrate Objectives 1-6:

1.) One paper in which students research and analyze the Spiritualism Movement.

2.) Students will address this competency as part of a large service and research project. The project will include a writing component and a presentation.

3.) Students will keep a weekly journal in which they reflect upon representation of women in course assignments.

4.) Students will be asked to identify and interpret literary tools in class discussion and in weekly journal assignments.

5.) Students will address this competency through a community-based, action research project.

COURSE REQUIREMENTS

- Students and the instructor are required to attend class.

- Complete all assigned readings within the time allotted by the weekly calendar.

- Participate in class discussions and group activities.

- Successfully complete course service project (action research project).

- Successfully complete a course journal and community proposal.

ATTENDANCE POLICY

Students are required to attend all classes since group participation and discussion are critical in this course. In case of illness or emergency, the student should contact the instructor before class. If it is necessary to miss class, the student is responsible for seeking assistance from other students or the instructor to make-up work. This should be done in a timely manner. Excessive absences in the course could result in failure.

COURSE GRADE

Course grades will be determined in the following manner:

- 30% Class attendance and participation

- 20% Journals

- 20% Midterm service proposal

- 30% Final Project

SERVICE PROJECT/COMMUNITY-BASED ACTION RESEARCH PROJECT

Working with the American Gravestone Society at the Newton/Waltham Burial Ground, we will repair tombstones and in the process research events in the Greater Boston area history that are evidenced through inscriptions on tombstones and monuments (e.g., influenza outbreak of 1918). Working in 2 groups the class will compile a series of essays that describe the community history of a particular section of the Burial Ground within an agreed upon time period (e.g. 1880-1920). The essays must include a ghost story or legend that is connected to the Burial Ground and explain what social and cultural norms the story reflects. Students will present their works to relevant and agreed upon organizations and neighborhood associations (e.g., the West Newton Neighborhood Association).

Field Notes
Human Community
and Modern Metropolis
Augsburg College

HUMAN COMMUNITY AND MODERN METROPOLIS

Honors 216
Field Study
Garry Hesser, Ph.D.
Augsburg College
Friday Journal
Fall 2000

Connecting the readings and the field study/service involvement
Reflections and critical analysis to "thicken" and deepen understanding from field study/participant observation

Name_____

Campus P.O.#_____

Phone#_____Email_____Field Site: _____

FIELD STUDY THROUGH SERVICE-LEARNING
Assignment
Every student in Human Community and Modern Metropolis [Soc 211/Hon216] is expected to do field work in one of the neighborhoods surrounding Augsburg. This entails assisting in a neighborhood oriented organization, in active collaboration with 3–4 other students from the class, and will involve you in a minimum of 15 hours during the semester. The actual distribution of these hours is to be worked out with our contact at the agency in ways that are mutually acceptable to you and the needs of the agency.

Assumptions

- Understanding and knowledge requires personal experience, as well as factual information and abstract reflection and generalization, i.e., research and theories;

- In order to achieve this level of understanding of contemporary urban realities, it is necessary to experience first hand some of the every day realities of persons and social organizations that make up the city;

- In addition, the personal experience is enhanced by preparation and a growing knowledge about the neighborhood and larger urban context, including the changes that are taking place;

- Such a field experience, which necessarily involves the personal and professional lives of other people, is a privilege that requires:

  - Reciprocity

  - Collaboration, and

  - Appreciation for diversity, including gender, race, ethnicity, social class, values and life styles

OBJECTIVES AND DESIRED OUTCOMES

As the semester proceeds, it is my hope that all of us involved in this course will achieve the following:

1. A thorough and accurate knowledge of the social, organizational and physical make-up of "your" neighborhood (city and region) as an Ecosystem;

2. A knowledge of the major trends and changes that have taken place in "your" neighborhood, city and region since 1950, with a growing understanding of "structuration" and "agency";

3. A growing appreciation for the internal and external relationships and "social facts" that help to explain the "making, sustaining and unmaking" of the neighborhood (and the city), including the impact that these social forces have upon the people, families and social organizations that live and operate within their "boundaries";

4. A knowledge of the history and structure of the organization where you are helping, including a growing awareness of how the organization interacts with and affects other organizations and realities in the neighborhood, city and region;

5. A growing awareness and appreciation for the professionals and organizations that are having a positive impact ("agency") on the quality of life and the public issues and challenges facing the community;

6. An understanding of how this particular neighborhood compares to other neighborhoods in the Twin Cities, the nation and the world; and

7. A growing understanding of what is happening in most urban areas across the United States, why these trends are occurring, who benefits the most, and what alternatives, including public policies, are possible or desirable.

SUMMARY

The provision of assistance to the organization makes it possible for students to assume a legitimate role in the everyday life of the organization. In addition, this service enables the student to give something back to the neighborhood and organization for the opportunity to be a "participant observer." The combination of first-hand experience and factual knowledge about one neighborhood (and an organization within it), combined with information from existing sources, interviews, and the insights of colleagues, will be the basis for learning about the making, sustaining and unmaking of U.S. cities and communities.

*Talk with me by 9/11 if you need an alternative to field study.

PARTICIPANT OBSERVATION/SERVICE-LEARNING

Site Sheet Record of Hours Spent Serving

Student's Name/P.O. Number/Phone: _____

Site/Organization: _____

Site Supervisor's Name: _____

	Site Visit Date	Hours Served	Supervisor's Initials
1.			
2.			
3.			
4.			
5.			
6.			
7.			
8.			
9.			
10.			
11.			
12.			
13.			
14.			

Note: This sheet should be current when you turn in journals 4, 8, & 11.

MAKING CONNECTIONS BETWEEN THE FIELD STUDY AND THE COURSE
Milwaukee Avenue Field Visit [#1]

    I.   **Description**: If you were to write home telling your parents or best friend about Milwaukee Avenue, what would you tell them? (keep it factual, i.e., "empirical"):

    II. **Interpret**: At this point in the course, what might you tell them that would "explain" how this neighborhood came to be the way it is:

    III. What **new insight**s have you gotten from the field visit to Milwaukee Avenue?

        -What surprised you about Milwaukee Avenue?

        -To explain why Milwaukee Avenue is the way it is, what are 4–5 important things you think you need to know?

MAKING CONNECTIONS BETWEEN THE FIELD STUDY AND THE TEXT
City Lights, ch 1 (#2)

    I.   **Description**: Describe an experience or observation from your field study surveillance of Cedar-Riverside.

       [Note; your choice of what to describe should illustrate or be related to this week's reading (approx 100 words):

II. **Interpret/Explain** what you described above, using the key ideas and concepts of KA & AW from the chapter. (Note: Underline concepts and phrases from text to highlight the application; 200–300 words.)

III. What **new insights** have you gotten from the field and text?

-Surprises? [DKDK]

-Expansion of what I thought I knew about the neighborhood? [KK]

-New Questions I have as a result of observations? [KDK]

MAKING CONNECTIONS BETWEEN THE FIELD STUDY AND SOCIOLOGY
City Lights, ch 2 (#3)

I. **Description:** Describe an experience/observation/conversation from your field site neighborhood visit.

Note: Describe something which illustrates or is related to this week's reading, i.e., gives you an opportunity to show how Sociology and one other discipline can increase understanding (approx 100 words).

II. **Interpret/explain** what you described above, discussing how Sociology and one other discipline can help you to understand or explain different aspects about what you have described above: (Note: Underline concepts and phrases from text to highlight the application; 200–300 words.)

III. What **new insights** have you gotten from the field and text?

  -Didn't Know I Didn't Know (surprises)?

  -Expanded what I thought I knew/opportunity to apply knowledge (Knew I Knew)?

  -New Questions (Things I Know I Don't Know)?

MAKING CONNECTIONS BETWEEN THE FIELD STUDY AND THE TEXT
City Lights, ch 3 (#4) (Note: Field site "time sheet" needs to be filled out and signed today)

  I. **Decription:** Describe what your organization does to improve the quality of life in the neighborhood, making use of the orientation you received on 9/17, annual reports, conversations, observations, etc. (approx. 100 words):

  II. **Interpret/explain** what you described above, using the key ideas and concepts from the chapter. (Note: Formulate your "interpretation" with at least two hypotheses that might explain why your organization does what it does, i.e., its "operating theories" about what makes for sustainable communities. Suggestion: Use POETS/Horizontal-Vertical/Structuration theories (approx. 200-300 words).

  III. What **new insights** have you gotten from the symposium, especially regarding the scientific method?

  -DKDK?

  -KDK?

  -KK?

MAKING CONNECTIONS BETWEEN THE FIELD STUDY AND THE TEXT
City Lights, ch 11 (#5) OPTIONAL (if you want to raise your average; Due on Wednesday, 10/4)

    I. **Description:** Describe an experience or some important realities [KA] about your field site neighborhood or site which illustrate how important it is to "discover the rules" (and how difficult it often is.) (approx. 100 words):

    II. **Interpret/explain** what you described above, using the key ideas and concepts from the chapter to discuss how important it is for you to "discover the rules" that are "taken for granted" in the neighborhood and/or site. (Note: Underline concepts and phrases from text to highlight the application; 200–300 words.)

    III. What **new insights** have you gotten from the field and text?

        -DKDK?

        -KDK?

        -KK?

MAKING CONNECTIONS BETWEEN THE FIELD STUDY AND THE TEXT
City Lights, chs 5 & 16 (#6)

    I. **Description:** Describe an experience, observation or information [KA] from your neighborhood field site, which illustrates how different "senses of place" can make a significant difference. (100 words):

II. **Interpret/Explain** what you described above, using the key ideas and concepts from the chapter. (Note: Underline concepts and phrases from text to highlight the application; 200-300 words.)

III. What **new insights** have you gotten from the field and text?

-DKDK?

-KDK?

-KK?

MAKING CONNECTIONS BETWEEN THE FIELD STUDY AND THE TEXT
City Lights, chs 4 &15 (#7) OPTIONAL (if you want to raise your average; Due Wed, 10/18)

I. **Description:** Describe an experience or some important realities [KA] about your field site neighborhood or Mpls. (Note: it might occasionally be newspaper/TV coverage of an event or issue which illustrates or is related to this week's reading.) (approx 100 words).

II. **Interpret/Explain** what you described above, using the key ideas and concepts from the chapters. (Note: Underline concepts and phrases from text to highlight the application; 200–300 words.)

III. What **new insights** have you gotten from the field and text?

   -DKDK?

   -KDK?

   -KK?

MAKING CONNECTIONS BETWEEN THE FIELD STUDY AND THE TEXT

City Lights, chs 6 & 7 (#8) — Remember: Field site "time sheet" needs to be up updated and signed today.

I.   **Description:** Describe an experience or some important realities (KA) about your field site neighborhood or Monday exercise which illustrates or is related to this week's reading (approx 100 words).

II. **Interpret/Explain** what you described above, using the key ideas and concepts from the chapter. (Note: Underline concepts and phrases from text to highlight the application; 200–300 words.)

III. What **new insights** have you gotten from the field and text?

   -DKDK?

   -KDK?

   -KK?

MAKING CONNECTIONS BETWEEN THE FIELD STUDY AND THE TEXT

City Lights, ch 15, 17, 18 (#9)—OPTIONAL (if you want to raise your average; Due 11/8)

I.   **Description:** Describe an experience or some important realities (KA) about your field site neighborhood or Mpls that illustrates the "vertical" influence of the national and global economy (100 words).

II. **Interpret/Explain** what you described above, using the key ideas and concepts from the chapter. (Note: Underline concepts and phrases—economy & social class—from text to highlight the application.)

III. What **new insights** have you gotten from the field and text?

-DKDK?

-KK?

-KDK?

MAKING CONNECTIONS BETWEEN THE FIELD STUDY AND THE TEXT

City Lights, ch 8 & 10 (#10)

I.   **Description:** Describe an experience or some important realities (KA) about your field site neighborhood or Mpls which illustrates or is related to this week's readings on migration and demography (approx 100 words).

II. **Interpret/Explain** what you described above, using the key ideas and concepts from the chapter. (Note: Underline concepts and phrases from text to highlight the application.)

III. What **new insights** have you gotten from the field and text?

-DKDK?

-KK?

-KDK?

MAKING CONNECTIONS BETWEEN THE FIELD STUDY AND THE TEXT
City Lights, ch 9 & 15; 10 & 18 (#11)—Due 12/1 ("Time sheet" must be completed and all hours completed.)

I. **Description**: Describe an experience or some important realities [KA] about your field site neighborhood or Mpls which illustrates or is related to this week and last week's readings on race, ethnicity class [approx. 100 words]:

II. **Interpret/Explain** what you described above, using the key ideas about race, ethnicity & class. (Note: Underline concepts and phrases from text to highlight the application; 200–300 words.)

III. What **new insights** have you gotten from the field and text?

-DKDK?

-KK?

-KDK?

MAKING CONNECTIONS BETWEEN THE FIELD STUDY AND THE TEXT
City Lights, chs 10 & 18 (#12)—Due 12/6

I. **Description:** Describe an experience or some important realities (KA) about your field site neighborhood or Mpls. (Note: it might occasionally be newspaper/TV coverage of an event or issue.) which illustrates or is related to this week's reading (approx 100 words).

II. **Interpret/Explain** what you described above, using the key ideas and concepts from the chapter. (Suggestion: In preparation for the final paper, focus on what you find in these chapters that helps you understand and answer items III and IV, i.e., vertical influences and public policies and "agency.")

III. What **new insight**s have you gottn from the field and text?

-DKDK?

-KK?

-KDK?

MAKING CONNECTIONS BETWEEN THE FIELD STUDY AND THE TEXT
City Lights, chs 12 & 14 (#12); OPTIONAL (DUE: 12/6) "Time sheet" must be completed.

I. **Description:** Describe an experience or some important realities (KA) about your field site neighborhood or Mpls. (Note: it might occasionally be newspaper/TV coverage of an event or issue) which illustrates or is related to this week's reading (approx 100 words):

II. **Interpret/Explain** what you described above, using the key ideas and concepts from the chapter. (Suggestion: In preparation for the final paper, focus on what you find in these chapters that helps you understand and answer items III and IV, i.e., vertical influences and public policies and "agency.")

III. What **new insights** and understanding have you gotten from the field and text?

-DKDK?

-KK?

-KDK?

The Capstone Capsule
Portland State University

THE CAPSTONE CAPSULE

Fall 2000
A fact sheet for students on the UNST Capstone Course at Portland State University

What is a Capstone course?

The Capstone course is the culminating course for Portland State University students as part of the General Education curriculum. The Capstone course has three primary objectives:

- It allows students to apply their area(s) of expertise to real issues and problems;

- It gives students experience working in an interdisciplinary team context;

- It empowers students to become actively engaged in their community.

Capstone courses are designed to build cooperative learning communities among students and contribute to student success. Students are required to engage in their type of community-based learning in order to enhance their ability to communicate and interact with diverse populations, as well as to further their capacity to think critically about the social, cultural, economic and environmental issues facing our society. Placement sites vary significantly, including educational institutions (a wide range of school systems), environmental organizations, for-profit businesses, on-campus organizations, and government and social service agencies.

A University Studies Capstone consists of a course or course series totaling 6 credit hours. In each Capstone, a team of students develops a strategy to address a problem or concern in the community and implements this strategy over one, two or three quarters of work. Each Capstone course will be designed in accordance with the educational objective of the course and the community issue being addressed.

Do I need to take a Capstone course?

If you began college during the fall of 1994 or after, you will be enrolled in the General Education curriculum and will therefore be required to complete a Capstone course before graduating from Portland

State. If you began college during the summer of 1994 or before, you have the option of following the distribution model, which was in effect at that time or the new General Education curriculum. If you choose to follow the new General Education curriculum, you will be required to complete a Capstone course. See an advisor in the IASC office, SMC 118, 725-4005, to discuss your options and to choose the plan which best suits your educational needs. *PLEASE NOTE, DURING THE 2000-2001 ACADEMIC YEAR: You can complete your Capstone course during your Junior or Senior year.

How do I register for a Capstone course?
For Capstones with course registration numbers (CRN) listed on this sheet or in the class schedule, you can register as you would for any other Portland State course.

CAPSTONES OFFERED FALL 2000

Teams of PSU faculty are developing major long-term partnerships with government agencies and community groups. If you have any questions about any of these courses, please contact the instructor directly. Capstone courses will be online the fall 2000 term.

UNST 421, crn 13530, Advanced Mentoring Group - 1, (2 credits)
Devorah Lieberman
This capstone course is aimed at helping PSU student mentors learn the skills required to promote life-long learning and leadership and to provide positive mentoring experiences for the youth participating in the Oregon Leadership Institute (OLI) program. OLI is a three-term, one Saturday per month program that offers high school students of Latino descent an opportunity to learn skills necessary to become effective leaders. Capstone students learn the mentoring process as well as intercultural communication skills and effective communication strategies.

UNST 421, crn 13506, Community Assistance and Family Safety Net - 1, (2 credits)
Bee Jai Repp
Students will work in conjunction with Services to Children and Families (SCF) in the community Safety Net Project for Marion County. Students will participate as mentors and advocates for families that are assessed by SCF as needing community resources. Students will receive extensive training on family intervention their first term; in winter and spring students will work in dyads and triads with a family that is assessed by SCF as potentially at risk. The goal for the Capstone is for students to assist families in building and sustaining a positive family environment. This capstone course is offered through the Salem Center.

UNST 421, ern 13513 & crn 14542, Design Process - 1, (2 credits)
Far Etesami and Douglas Hall.
Engineering design methodologies will be discussed as a framework for solving broadly defined technology problems. The course objective is to prepare students for proposing, conducting, and reporting of their capstone project: problem definition, customer and engineering requirements, prioritizing requirements, alternative generation and evaluation, and design implementation. There is a Mechanical Engineering and an Electrical & Computer Engineering section for the capstone.

UNST 421, crn 13535, Air Quality, Vehicle Emissions and Oxygenated Fuels - 1, (3 credits)
Robert O'Brien

Is global warming reduced with less fossil fuel burning? Are there direct or indirect health effects associated with different fuel composition? The Portland Metropolitan Area currently employs oxygenated fuels during the winter months as a means to reduce unhealthy vehicle emissions, particularly carbon monoxide. This capstone will study the effectiveness of this strategy along with other environmental and financial implications. A partial list of the issues involved are: effectiveness, cost and environmental implications. This course will also be offered Winter term 2001.

UNST 421, crn 13517, Asset Mapping: Portland Caring Community Capstone "Building Communities through Community Building" - 1, (3 credits)
Margrete Merrick

Capstone students will work with the Portland Caring Community. Students will identify and inventory "community associations" (neighborhood residents' talents and skills, local services, and institutions) as well as create an electronic database and electronic and hardcopy atlases using geographic information systems (GIS) technology to enhance the community building process. No technical expertise is required. Additional time is required outside of classroom participation. The course will also be offered Winter and Spring terms 2001.

UNST 421, crn 13544, Engineering Project Management - 1, (3 credits)
Scott Huff

This capstone concentrates on the engineering management process including owner-design professional-constructor relationships; procurement procedures; project evolution; contracts; dispute resolution; bonds; warranties; construction documents including specifications, cost estimating, planning, and scheduling; construction administration; group process and leadership. It is best suited for technical writing students, business majors, and others interested in project management and marketing. My second part of this capstone is offered Spring term as Civil Engineering Design.

UNST 421, crn 13510, Enhancing Youth Literacy: Service in K-5 Public Education - 1, (3 credits)
Mary Seitz

Capstone students research and document the literacy needs and resources of the Beach community, to design and produce a tutoring manual. Students will also organize and host a literacy night at the school for parents and others in the Beach community. The class will meet at PSU 1–2 hours per week to discuss readings on service-learning, education, and the status of on-going projects. Individual writing assignments will include a personal reflective journal, one book review each term, and a final reflective narrative.

UNST 421, crn 13512, Evaluating Diversity in Public Agencies: Washington County - 1, (3 credits)
Masami Nishishiba and Erin Saunders

Students will work with Washington County employees in conducting an evaluation of their Diversity Program. First, students will study the current Diversity Program that has been taking place at the County office and critically analyze its strengths and weaknesses. Then, together with the staff members at the Department of Support Services, students will devise and implement a plan for evaluating the current program. By the end of the course, based on the results of the evaluations, students and the County staff will jointly develop "benchmarks" for future evaluations of the Diversity Program.

LINST 421, crn 13537, Global Portland: IRCO - 1, (3 credits)
Lida O'Donnell
Students work with IRCO (International Refugee Center of Oregon), a community-based non-profit organization that provides assistance to immigrants from around the world: Africa, Asia, the Caribbean, and Europe. In the class students will examine refugee-related issues and reflect on the experience I journals and a final essay. In small groups, students will collaborate on developing communication, research and assessment skills, and work on projects addressing some of the needs of the agency. Students will sign up for a block of 3 hours per week on a specific day—either mornings from 8:45 – 12:00 or afternoons from 1: 15 – 4:30—to tutor vocational English in the Job and English Training (JET Plus) program.

UNST 421, crn 13515, Global Portland: Refugees- 1, (3 credits)
Lida O'Donnell
This capstone will provide students with rich opportunities to experience other cultures without leaving Portland. Students in the roles of tutors and mentors of English will help refugees, from many countries in Africa, Asia, the Caribbean and Europe on their way to self-sufficiency. As a group they will reflect on the experience; collaborate on developing communication, research and assessment skills; ascertain needs of the community agency and refugees and then design a project addressing the needs. Students will be matched with refugee families for weekly 2 hour tutoring sessions. This course will also be offered Winter term 2001.

UNST 421, crn 13514, Issues in Campus Health and Social Change - 1, (3 credits)
Sandra Franz, Layton Borkan, and Tim Hagge
This course provides students with an opportunity to connect and commit to a process that provides a greater understanding of social change as it relates to public health issues of the campus community. Working in teams, students will develop a health promotion strategy in one of the following content areas: sexual health, college survival skills, or alcohol use on campus. During the first term students will conduct a needs assessment and propose and design a strategy based on this assessment. This course will also be offered Winter term 2001.

UNST 421, crn 13522, Latin American Website Project - 1, (3 credits)
Anthony Granados
The students will conceptualize and design a website for the PSU Center for the Study of U.S.-Latin American relations. All topics that relate to Latin America will be covered. The project will be ongoing. It requires advanced interactive skills, the ability to transfer ideas into web reality and the self-discipline to finish the work. Students from professional majors, liberal arts, social sciences and humanities are welcome. This course will also be offered Winter term 2001.

UNST 421, crn 13529, Measuring the Effectiveness of Criminal Justice Interventions - 1, (3 credits)
Don Trapp

This Capstone will examine the efficiency of criminal justice programs in reducing recidivism, a standard measure of effectiveness in the criminal justice system, and the productiveness of these programs with regard to offender typology. Students will participate in all phases of a pilot evaluation project. Students will work in conjunction with evaluation staff and participate in data collection and analysis. Students will also participate in the oral and written reporting of project findings.

UNST 421, crn 13519, Multimedia Production - 1, (3 credits)
Robert Bremmer

The multimedia capstone course is designed to build teamwork and client relationship skills while developing a needed multimedia training product for a community client. Early in the term students will form teams working on 1) technical: graphics, video and computers, 2) creative: storyboarding, and scripting, 3) client liaison: determining and communicating clients' needs, and 4) quality assessment: assuring accuracy, timeliness and development of product scope. Ability with creative skills or computer skills is important, but not necessary. The course is very intensive, and participants are encouraged to plan accordingly to fit their other courses with this capstone. While course dates are adhered to initially, after the development of the teams, assignments can be worked on schedules developed by the individual team members, who then report to the whole class in session on a weekly basis. This course will also be offered Spring term 2001.

UNST 421, crn 13516, Neighborhoods and Watersheds - 1, (3 credits)
Barry Messer

This course focuses on addressing the health of cities with respect to the community stewardship of their watersheds. Students will be challenged to engage in a learning process of discovery and direct involvement in the essential elements that contribute to the health of Portland's watersheds. Student work will be incorporated into a "Shedding Water in Portland" publication. This course will also be offered Winter term 2001.

UNST 421, crn 13534, Opening Doors: Equity, the Library, and Learning Disabilities - 1, (3 credits)
Rebecca Black

Students will form research teams to investigate the impact that libraries have on people with learning disabilities. An important issue for this course to explore is what types of people with learning disabilities are utilizing Portland's libraries. Team members will then develop models for creating library access for those who currently are unable to use the facilities and to expand the accessibility for those people who use the library. This course will also be offered Spring term 2001.

UNST 421, crn 13511, Parent Mathematics Workshop - 1, (3 credits)
Lisa Ada Jian

Students work with elementary classrooms to observe teaching methods and participate as facilitators. They design lesson plans to present to parents that reflect what is being taught at appropriate grade levels. The final project is the presentation of a series of Parent Math Workshops. Students are responsible for advertising, organizing, and implementing these workshops. Three hours of community service per week is required.

UNST 421, crn 13536, Public Relations for Non-Profit Companies- 1, (3 credits)
Walt Amacher

This Capstone provides communications training for a selected organization, including: formation of an organizational communications program, creation of informational and promotional materials, and practical experience in working with the media. Students will learn basic communications theory and apply it to an organization. In addition to textbook materials and class presentations, this course includes guest lecturers and field trips to media outlets.

UNST 421, crn 13531, Small Business Consulting Capstone -1, (3 credits)
Brad Robertson

Students will provide assistance to not-for-profit and for-profit organizations located within the Portland metropolitan area. The goals are to assist organizations in becoming more stable and successful, and to provide opportunities for students to work in communities surrounding PSU. Projects will be identified through the Business Outreach Program and assigned to student teams for accomplishment over a two-term time frame. Students will learn to collaboratively provide needed assistance through multidisciplinary teams.

UNST 421, crn 14648, Stories From the Forest: Oral Histories of the Gifford Pinchot - 1 (3 credits)
Donna Sinclair

This Capstone is a two-term course in oral history. During fall quarter, the class will index and compile existing oral histories while learning oral history interviewing and research methods. During winter term, students will conduct oral history interviews with ex-forest rangers, fire lookouts, trail blazers, and others connected to the Gifford Pinchot National Forest before and after WWII.

UNST 421, crn 13542 & 13543, Us and Them: A History of Intolerance in America - 1, (3 credits)
Beth Stafford-Grodd

Through various mediums, students will explore events in our history when intolerance arose from the fear, suspicion, and anger of ordinary people—the same impulses that still cause discord today—and will be brought face-to-face with the negative and often tragic consequences of prejudice and hate; but they will also learn about the hope and heroism that true moral conviction inspires. Exposure to intolerance will include both historical and fictional accounts of the struggles of alienated groups throughout our country's history to the present time, and will lead to class discussions and writings reflecting on important issues the works evoke. Besides the required course work, you will engage in collaborative projects of your choice, which will consist of outreach activities in the community. I will provide more information on this in class, but you should be prepared to spend at least four hours per week outside of class to devote to your project. There will be two courses of this capstone offered Fall term.

UNST 421, crn 13532, Women in Transition: Portland WICS - 1, (3 credits)
Kristin Christophersen
This course will provide students a unique opportunity to gain hands-on experience in a collaborative research project with Women in Community Service, Inc. (WICS). We will conduct research and outreach to build a pool of resources for women entering employment after incarceration or unemployment. This course will also be offered Spring term 2001.

UNST 421, crn 13521, YWCA: Women's History- 1, (3 credits)
Patricia Schechter
Students will undertake a local women's history project related to the Portland Young Women's Christian Association. This Capstone will combine archival research and oral history interviews to produce a history of the Portland YWCA for their centennial celebration in 2001. Students with an interest in US history, urban institutions, feminist communities, social reform, race relations, and religion are encouraged to participate in the research project. This course will also be offered Winter term 2001.

UNST 421, crn 13526, Brooklyn Neighborhood History Capstone, (6 credits)
Cathy Alzner
In this Capstone course, students perform historical and architectural research of the Brooklyn neighborhood in southeast Portland. Students will conduct historical research, building inventories, and oral histories to help write a history of the neighborhood, which is striving to form an identity and redefine its business core in order to become an anchor for the community.

UNST 421, crn 13507, Collaborations: Portland Area Council of Camp Fire, (6 credits)
Heather Petzold
This course focuses on teaching Portland Public School youth the responsibility of discovering, evaluating and reflecting on the needs of their community by helping them incorporate their academic skills into a service-learning project. Students will teach the youth how to have respect for themselves and others as part of a community and will promote teamwork, leadership and problem solving skills, as well as instilling the desire to explore the social needs of one's community as an ongoing process. Students must be able to pass a background check in order to enroll for this Capstone course and will have to spend additional time outside of class in the community. Please contact instructor to determine available times. This course will also be offered Winter and Spring terms 2001.

UNST 421, crn 13520, Communication Education Outreach, (6 credits)
Gloria Totten
This capstone explores basic communication skill development and practice. Students will be required to work as an interdisciplinary team, researching information, practicing and presenting course material to peers and in an elementary school setting (grades K-6). This course will develop a resource manual for elementary education teachers which focuses on basic communication skills. Topics may include: listening, interpersonal, intercultural, small group, and public speaking skills. This course will also be offered Winter term 2001.

UNST 421, crn 13518, Connecting Diverse Populations: Immigrant and Refugee Consortium, (6 credits)

Kathleen Cushing

This capstone focuses on issues that prevent immigrant, refugee, and minority communities from adapting to demands placed on them by legal, safety, health and social aspects of American society: legal and societal views, race relations, health issues, ethnic diversity. Students collaborate with members of minority, immigrant, and refugee communities about common topics of interest.

UNST 421, crn 14367, Conservation Issues for Marine Mammals in the Northwest, (6 credits)

Deborah Duffield

This course will offer students an opportunity to investigate some of the marine mammal-human interactions that are seen along our coast. Class time will be used to acquaint the students to marine mammals and to the issues. Students can then choose to work with a local elementary or high school class to introduce that class to problems in our environment that affect seals, sea lions, porpoises and Whales; or create an articulation of a marine mammal for display; or develop pamphlets that can be distributed to our coastal communities increasing awareness of conservation issues in the marine environment. There are possibilities for special projects based on individual student skills and background.

UNST 421, crn 13533, Gay & Lesbian Archives, (6 credits)

Ann Mussey

The Lesbian Community Project is a community organization in Portland which, since its inception in 1986, has worked to create lesbian visibility, support a diverse community of lesbians in Portland, and respond to homophobic attacks on gays and lesbians. Students will research the history of lesbian and gay community organizations, delve into the archival records of the LCP, and conduct oral history interviews of LCP participants to create a history of the organization and its activities within the larger social context. This course will also be offered Spring term 2001.

UNST 421, crn 14307, Geology of the Northern Basin-and-Range Capstone, (6 credits)

Alex Ruzicka

Students will work as a group to study the geology of the northern Basin-and-Range province, in the vicinity of the Malhuer Field Station in southeast Oregon, and to assemble their findings into a pamphlet, web page, or map that is accessible to the general public. A field trip to the study area during the term is required. The exact form of the studies and project will depend on the interests and backgrounds of the students and the needs of the Malhuer Field Station. In addition, I would require one 4-day field trip to the Malhuer Field Station in the middle of the Fall term, Oct. 26-29.

UNST 421, crn 13538, Middle School Reading Group Facilitators, (6 credits)

James L. Martin

Capstone students will meet with Middle School teachers to read and discuss assigned works and then gather with the student groups assisting them with difficulties and stimulating conversations concerning the materials. The facilitators will generate questions and guide the discussions to fulfill the desired goals of the reading sessions, while maintaining a journal of successes, misconceptions, and complications of the reading group. This course is recommended for Portland State students interested in, but not limited to education, child development, and literature. Students should possess a desire to team, positive and professional attitudes, and be willing to make a time commitment of six hours per week.

UNST 421, crn 13523, Multimedia & Web Training, (6 credits)
Doug Christensen

This capstone focuses on creating multimedia for web-based training in large companies or organizations that provides instruction or information for a community partner. Students will work within one of three separate teams (Instructional, Creative, or Technical). Although no prior experience is required, students will be expected to develop some general technical skills and software application proficiencies related to their team areas of focus. This experience is meant to be fun, simulate real world work conditions, and significantly add to a student's resumé. This course will also be offered Winter and Spring terms 2001.

UNST 421, crn 13524, Salmon Corps Web Site Project, (6 credits)
Katy Barber

Students in this course will develop a website for Salmon Corps, a program comprised of five Northwest Native American tribes, the Columbia River Inter-Tribal Fish Commission, the U.S. Department of Energy, the U.S. Forest Service, and AmeriCorps and administered by the Earth Conservation Corps. The program focuses on salmon habitat restoration by working with at-risk youth to restore habitat in the Pacific Northwest. No previous web writing experience is necessary for this hands-on course.

UNST 421, crn 13541, Science Education in the Outdoors, (6 credits)
Lauri Shainsky

This course invites students with a keen interest in ecology, education, small business, or community-building to be of service with Wolftree—a growing non-profit organization whose mission is to serve people, their communities, and the Earth through science education in the outdoors. Students will learn about aquatic and terrestrial ecology, and apply their learning by teaching young people about the science discipline of ecology and science inquiry in the field. Students will be asked to participate in field instruction, class discussion, and a class project of their choosing. Students who attend this course must be able to spend at least one 8-hour block of time in the field per week (Tuesday, Wednesday, or Thursday) at our outdoor education facility. Students must have a passion for nature and young people, a sense of humor, and a desire for personal growth through service. This course will also be offered Spring term 2001.

UNST 421, crn 13509, Women's Oral Narratives - Girl Power, (6 credits)
Melissa Gilbert

This class will work with teen girls to raise their awareness of resources and activities in the Portland Area. We will conduct a series of rap sessions with teens and coordinate writing workshops in order to provide spaces for teen girls to think, talk, and write about current issues in their lives. We will also work with local teen agencies to build a local community coalition of organizations advocating on behalf of teen girls.

UNST 421, crn 13528, Writing and Community Capstone, (6 credits)
Vicki Reitenaur
This course is an investigation into what it means to build community through a shared experience of writing. Classroom work will include reading texts which contain both theoretical and practical inquiries around personal empowerment through the writing process, as well as explore the ways in which community may be built through a collaborative experience of the written word. Students will engage in their own group writing process, as well as partner with Write Around Portland to further its community writing projects. This course will also be offered Spring term 2001.

UNST 421, Community Psychology, (4 credits)
Erik Mankowski
Applications of basic psychological knowledge and methods to community problems are the focus of this capstone. Students join a working group which does service and research in the community, participating in the governance and decision-making process of the group. Students work in several field projects in cooperation with community agencies engaged in social service in the fields of health, education, corrections, welfare, and others. Students MUST register for PSY 480 or USP 407 fall term for this capstone course, UNST 421, winter and spring. See fall schedule for days and times offered.

These Capstone courses will begin Winter term 2001:
UNST 421, Albina Community Organization and Development, *James Mason*

UNST 421, Assessing the Needs of Academically Disqualified Students, *Mary Ann Barham and Dan Fortmiller*

UNST 421: Astronomy: The Final Frontier - An Interactive Website, *Erik Bodegom*

UNST 421, Caribbean Overseas Project, *Candice Goucher*

UNST 421, Collaborative Community Response to Family Violence, *Louise Bauschard and Margi McCue*

UNST 421, Community Based Volunteer Tutoring Program for the GEARS Program, *Pati Zimmerman*

UNST 421, Early Music Capstone, *Stephen Martin*

UNST 421, Effective Environmental Education, *Stephanie Wagner, Dir. of Education, Friends of Tryon Creek State Park*

UNST 421, Environmental Education Through Native American Lenses, *Dilafruz Williams*

UNST 421, Grant Writing for Non-profits, *Arthur Davis*

UNST 421, Group Performance Workshop, *James Eikrem.*

UNST 421, The Hambleton Project, *Wendy Cutler*

UNST 421, Homeless Families Capstone, *Gretchen Kafoury*

UNST 421, Impact on the Community: Portland State University's Impact on the Local Portland Metropolitan Area and State Economies, *Jennifer Shawcross*

UNST 421, Neighborhood District Revitalization, *Carl Abbott, Shanna Eller, and Sy Adler*

UNST 421, New Teacher Support, *Sam Henry*

UNST 421, Oregon Historical Society: The Radical Elders Project, *Sandy Polishuk*

UNST 421, Planning, Implementation, and Evaluation of a Health Fair at the University Park Community Center in North Portland, *Gene Stainbrook*

UNST 421, Program Evaluation for Volunteers of America Parenting Program, *Joy Rhodes*

UNST 421, Poverty in Your Community, *Anna Rockhill and Terri Greenfield*

UNST 421, Public Safety & Livability Concerns in NW Portland, *Joan Strouse*

UNST 421, Schools Uniting Neighborhoods, *William Becker*

UNST 421, Software Engineering, *Joseph Blotner*

UNST 421, Women in Community Service, *Cheryl Creel* (This capstone course is offered through the Salem Center.)

UNST 421, Youth Activism through the Arts, *Keisha Edwards and Linda Hummer*

These Capstone courses will begin Spring term 2001:

UNST 421, Lents Neighborhood History Capstone, *Cathy Croghan-Alzner*

UNST 421, Regional History Project, *Bill Lang*

Bibliography

BIBLIOGRAPHY

Battistoni, R. *Service-Learning and Civic Education.* Unpublished Paper, 2000.

Brant, Martha. "Last Chance Class" *Newsweek,* May 31, 1999, 133(22): 32+.

Coles, Robert. *The Call of Service.* New York: Houghton-Mifflin, 1993.

Cooper, David and Julier, Laura. "Writing and the Arts of Public Discourse: The Service Learning Writing Project." East Lansing, MI: Michigan State University/The Writing Center, 1995, pp. 7-14.

Eyler, J., and Giles, D. *Where's the Learning in Service Learning?* San Francisco: Jossey-Bass, 1999.

Fenstermacher, Barry. "Infusing Service-Learning into the Curriculum." In Kendall and Associates, *Combining Service and Learning: A Resource Book for Community and Public Service, Volume II.* Raleigh, NC: National Society for Internships and Experiential Education, 1990.

Gronlund, Norman. *Stating Behavior Objectives for Classroom Instruction.* London: The Macmillan Company, Collier-Macmillian Limited, 1970.

Heffernan, K. and Saltmarsh J. (eds). *Introduction to Service-Learning Toolkit: Readings and Resources for Faculty.* Providence, RI: National Campus Compact, Brown University, 2000.

Jacoby, Barbara and Associates. *Service-Learning in Higher Education: Concepts and Practices.* San Francisco, CA: Jossey-Bass, 1996.

Kretzman, John and McKnight, John. *Building Communities from the Inside Out: A Path Toward Finding and Mobilizing a Community's Assets.* Chicago: The Urban Affairs and Policy Research Neighborhood Innovations Network, Northwestern University, 1993.

Morton, Keith. "Issues Related to Integrating Service-Learning into the Curriculum." In Jacoby and Associates, *Service-Learning in Higher Education: Concepts and Practices.* San Francisco, CA: Jossey-Bass, 1996.

Perkins, David and Abbott, Robert. "Validity of Student Ratings for Two Affective Outcomes of Introductory Psychology. *Educational and Psychological Measurement,* Spring, 1982, 42(1): 317-23.

Schroeder, Charles. "New Students—New Learning Styles." *Change,* Sep-Oct., 1993, 25(4): 21–26.

Woodcock, Michael. *Constructing a Syllabus: A Handbook for Faculty, Teaching Assistants and Teaching Fellows,* Second Edition. Providence, RI: Brown University, 1997.

Walker, Tobi. *Service and Politics: The Lost Connection.* Paper prepared for the Ford Foundation, June 27, 2000.

Suggested Readings

BOOKS

AAHE's Monograph Series on Service-Learning in the Disciplines. Washington, DC: AAHE Publications, 1999.

Ayers, W., Hunt, J.A., and Quinn, T. (eds.) *Teaching for Social Justice.* New York: Teachers College Press, Columbia University, 1998.

Barber, Benjamin. *An Aristocracy of Everyone: The Politics of Education and the Future of America.* London: Oxford University Press, 1992.

Belenky. M., Clinchy, B., Goldberger, N. and Tarule, J. *Women's Ways of Knowing.* New York: Basic Books, 1986.

Bellah, R., Madsen, R., Sullivan, W., Swidler, A. and Tipton, S. *Habits of the Heart.* Second Edition. New York: Harper and Row, 1996.

Boyte, H. and Hollander, E. *Wingspread Declaration on Renewing the Civic Mission of the American Research University.* Providence, RI: Campus Compact, Brown University, June, 1999.

Bringle, Robert G., Games, Richard, and Malloy, Edward A. (eds.) *Colleges and Universities as Citizens,* Needham, MA: Allyn & Bacon, 1999.

Burbules, N. *Dialogue in Teaching: Theory and Practice.* New York: Teachers College Press, Columbia University, 1993.

Cooper, D., and Julier, L. (eds.) *Writing in the Public Interest: Service Learning and the Writing Classroom.* East Lansing, MI: Michigan State University, 1995.

Dass, R. and Gorman, P. How Can I Help? *Stories and Reflections on Service.* New York: Alfred A. Knopf, 1985.

Delve, Cecilia I., Mintz, Suzanne D., Stewart, Greig M. (eds.) *Community Service as Values Education, New Directions for Teaching and Learning,* No. 50, San Francisco, CA: Jossey-Bass, 1990.

Ender, M., Marsteller-Kowalewski, B., Cotter, D., Martin, L., and DeFiore, J. *Service-Learning and Undergraduate Sociology: Syllabi and Instructional Materials.* Washington, D.C.: American Sociological Association, 1996.

Eyler, Janet and Giles, Dwight E. Jr. *Where's the Learning in Service-Learning?* San Francisco, CA: Jossey-Bass, 1999.

Eyler, Janet, Giles, Dwight E., Jr., Schmiede, Angela. *A Practitioner's Guide to Reflection in Service-Learning: Student Voices and Reflections.* Nashville, TN: Vanderbilt University, 1996.

Friere, Paulo. *Education for Critical Consciousness.* New York: Continuum, 1973.

Friere, Paulo. *Pedagogy of the Oppressed.* New York: Continuum, 1990.

Gilligan, C. *In a Different Voice.* Cambridge, MA: Harvard University Press, 1982.

Grunert, Judith. *The Course Syllabus: A Learning Centered Approach.* Bolton, MA: Anker Publishing, 1997.

Honnet, E. and Poulsen, S.J. *Principles of Good Practice for Combining Service* and *Learning: Wingspread Special Report.* Racine, WI: Johnson Foundation, 1989.

Howard, Jeffrey (ed.) *Praxis I: A Faculty Casebook on Community Service,* and *Praxis II: Service Learning Resources for University Students, Staff and Faculty.* Ann Arbor, MI: Office of Community Service Learning, 1993.

Hutchings, P. and Wutdorff, A. (eds.) *Knowing and Doing: Learning Through Experience.* San Francisco, CA: Jossey-Bass, 1988.

Jackson, K.(ed.) *Redesigning Curricula: Models of Service-Learning Syllabi.* Providence, RI: Campus Compact, Brown University, 1994 (out of print).

Jacoby, Barbara and Associates. *Service-Learning in Higher Education: Concepts and Practices.* San Francisco, CA: Jossey-Bass, 1996.

Kendall, Jane et al. *Combining Service and Learning: A Resource Book for Community and Public Service. Vols. I and II.* Raleigh, NC: National Society for Internships and Experiential Education, 1990.

Kolb, David. *Learning Styles Inventories.* Boston, MA: McKerr, 1985.

Kolb, David. *Experiential Learning: Experience as the Source of Learning and Development.* Englewood Cliffs, NJ: Prentice Hall, 1984.

Kraft, Richard J. and Swadler, Marc, (eds.) *Building Community: Service Learning in the Academic Disciplines.* Denver, CO: Colorado Campus Compact, 1994.

Kupiec, T. (ed.) *Rethinking Tradition: Integrating Service with Academic Study on College Campuses.* Providence, RI: Campus Compact, Brown University, 1993.

Lovell-Troy, L. and Eickmann P. *Course Design for College Teachers.* Englewood Cliffs, NJ: Educational Technology Publications, 1992.

Maher, F. and Tetreault, Mary Kay Thompson. *The Feminist Classroom.* New York: Basic Books, 1994.

McKeachie, W.J., *Teaching Tips,* 8th Edition. Lexington, MA: D.C. Heath, 22, 1986.

Michigan Journal of Community Service Learning. Special Issue, Fall 2000. Ann Arbor: OCSL Press, The University of Michigan. (http://www.umich.edu/~ocsl/MJCSL/.)

Reed, Edward S. *The Necessity of Experience.* New Haven, CT: Yale University Press, 1996.

Rhoads, Robert A. and Howard, Jeffrey P. F. (eds.) *Academic Service Learning: A Pedagogy of Action and Reflection, New Directions for Teaching and Learning,* No 73, San Francisco: Jossey-Bass, 1998.

Science and Society: Redefining the Relationship. Providence, RI: Campus Compact, Brown University, 1996.

Service Matters: Engaging Higher Education in the Renewal of America's Communities and American Democracy. Providence, RI: Campus Compact, Brown University, 1998.

Shor, Ira. *Critical Thinking and Everyday Life.* Boston, MA: South End Press, 1980.

Stanton, T., Giles, D., Jr., Cruz, N. *Service-Learning: A Movement's Pioneers Reflect on Its Origins, Practice, and Future.* San Francisco, CA: Jossey-Bass, 1999.

Troppe, Marie. *Participatory Action Research: Merging the Community and Scholarly Agendas.* Providence, RI: Campus Compact, Brown University, 1994.

Warren, K., Sakofs, M. and Hunt, J. (eds.) *The Theory of Experiential Education.* Dubuque, IA: Kendall/Hunt Publishing Company, 1995.

When Community Enters the Equation: Enhancing Science, Mathematics and Engineering Education through Service Learning. Providence, RI: Campus Compact, Brown University, 1998.

Wolfe, Alan. *Whose Keeper? Social Science and Moral Obligation.* Berkeley, CA: University of California Press, 1989.

Zlotkowski, Edward (ed.) *Successful Service-Learning Programs: New Models of Excellence in Higher Education.* Boston, MA: Anker Publishing Company, 1998.

Zlotkowski, E., (ed.) *Service Learning in the Disciplines,* [an 18 volume series of monographs], American Association of Higher Education, 1997-2000.

ARTICLES

Anderson, J.R. "Acquisition of Cognitive Skill." *Psychological Review,* 1982, No. 89: 369-406.

Beckman, M. "Learning in Action: Courses That Complement Community Service." *College Teaching,* 1997, No. 45(2): 72-76.Checkoway, B. "Combining Service and Learning on Campus and in the Community." *Phi Delta Kappan,* 1996, 77(1): 600-606.

Bringle, Robert G. and Hatcher, Julie A. "Implementing Service Learning in Higher Education," *Journal of Higher Education,* 1996, No. 67 (2): 221-239.

Chickering, A., and Gamson, Z. "Seven Principles of Good Practice in Undergraduate Education." *AAHE Bulletin,* March-April 1987.

Cohen, J., and Kinsey, D. "Doing Good and Scholarship: A Service Learning Study." *Journalism Educator,* 1994, No. 48(4): 4-14.

Coleman, James S. "Differences Between Experiential and Classroom Learning." In *Experiential Learning: Rationale, Characteristics, and Assessment,* edited by Morris T. Keaton. San Francisco, CA: Jossey-Bass, 1977.

Coles, R. "Putting Head and Heart on the Line." *Chronicle of Higher Education,* Oct. 26, 1994, p. A64.

Coles, R. "Community Service Work." *Liberal Education,* September/October 1988, No. 74(4): 11-13.

Cone, R., and Harris, S. "Service-Learning Practice: A Theoretical Framework." *Michigan Journal of Community Service Learning,* Fall, 1996, No. 3: 31-43.

Conrad, D. and Hedin, D. "School-Based Community Service: What We Know From Research and Theory." *Phi Delta Kappan,* 1991, No. 72: 743–749.

Cooper, D. and Julier, L. "Writing the Ties that Bind: Service-Learning in the Writing Classroom." *Michigan Journal of Community Service-Learning,* Fall, 1995, No. 2: 72–85.

Corwin, Patricia. "Using the Community as a Classroom for Large Introductory Sociology Classes." *Teaching Sociology,* July, 1996, No. 24: 310–315.

Cotugna, N. and Vickery, C.E. "Nurturing Social Responsibility: Nutrition Students Volunteer in Hunger Projects." *Journal of the American Dietetic Association,* 1992, No. 92(3): 297–299.

Ellsworth, Elizabeth. "Why Doesn't this Feel Empowering?: Working Through the Repressive Myths of Critical Pedagogy." In Lynda Stone, (ed.) *The Feminist Reader,* 1994, pp. 300–327.

Exley, Robert. "Service-Learning and Curricular Integration." *Service Learning Resource Guide:* A publication of the American Association of Community Colleges, No 1 (1): 1–4.

Equity and Excellence in Education, 1993, No. 26(2). [Entire issue is devoted to Service-Learning]

Furco, A., Bolotte, D., Chung, O., Keaton, T., Muller, P., and Nuttall, S. "Service Learning Faculty Development at Community Colleges." Mesa, AZ: Campus Compact National Center for Community Colleges, 1998.

Gilbert, Melissa Kesler, Holdt, Carol and Christophersen, K. "Letting Feminist Knowledge Serve the City." In Maralee Mayberry and Ellen Rose (eds) *Meeting the Challenge: Innovative Feminist Pedagogies in Action.* New York: Routledge, 1999: 320–340.

Giles, D.E, Jr. and Eyler, J. "The Theoretical Roots of Service-Learning in John Dewey: Towards a Theory of Service-Learning." *Michigan Journal of Community Service-Learning,* 1994, No. 1: 77-85.

Goldblatt, E. "Van Rides in the Dark: Literacy as Involvement in a College Literacy Practicum." *The Journal for Peace and Justice Studies* 1994, No. 6(1): 77–94.

Hayes, E., and Cuban, S. "Border Pedagogy: A Critical Framework for Service-Learning." *Michigan Journal of Community Service Learning,* Fall, 1997, No. 4: 72–80.

Hesser, G. "Outcomes Attributed to Service-Learning and Evidence of Change in Faculty Attitudes about Experiential Education." *Michigan Journal of Community Service Learning,* Fall, 1995, No. 2: 33–42.

Hondaagneu-Sotelo, P. and Raskoff, S. "Community Service-Learning: Promises and Problems." *Teaching Sociology,* 1994, No. 22: 248–254.

Herzberg, B. "Community Service and Critical Teaching." *College Composition and Communication,* 1994, No. 45(3): 307–319.

Hockensmith, S.F. "The Syllabus as a Teaching Tool." *The Educational Forum,* 1998, No. 52(4): 339-51.

Howard, Jeffrey. "A Counternormative Pedagogy." In *Academic Service-Learning: A Pedagogy of Action and Reflection,* San Francisco, CA: Jossey-Bass, 1998.

Illich, Ivan. "To Hell with Good Intentions." Address to the Conference on Inter-American Student Project, Cuernevaca, Mexico, April, 1968.

Kahne, J. and Westheimer, J. "In the Service of What?" *Phi Delta Kappan,* 1996.

Kendrick, J.R. "Outcomes of Service-Learning in an Introduction to Sociology Course." *Michigan Journal of Community Service Learning,* Fall, 1996, No. 3: 72–81.

Langseth, M. and Troppe, M. "So What? Does Service Learning Really Foster Social Change?" *Expanding Boundaries, S*pring, 1997, No. 2: 37–42.

Liu, Goodwin. "Knowledge, Foundations, and Discourse: Philosophical Support for Service-Learning." *Michigan Journal for Community Service Learning,* 1995, No. 2: 5–18.

Markus, G. Howard J., and King D. "Integrating Community Service with Classroom Instruction Enhances Learning: Results From an Experiment." *Educational Evaluation and Policy Analysis,* 1993, 15:410-419.

Matejka, K. and Kurke, L. "Designing a Great Syllabus." *College Teaching,* 42(3):115–117.

McKnight, J. "Why Servanthood is Bad." *The Other Side,* January/February, 1989.

McKnight, J. "Professionalizing Service and Disabling Help." In Illich I. et al, *Disabling Professions,* New York: Marion Boyers Publishers, 1977, pp. 69–91.

McVicker Clinchy, Blythe. "On Critical Thinking and Connected Knowing." *Liberal Educator,* 1989, No 75: 14–19.

Morton, Keith. "Potential and Practice for Combining Civic Education and Community Service." In Kupiec, T. (ed.) *Rethinking Tradition: Integrating Service with Academic Study on College Campuses.* Providence, RI: Campus Compact, Brown University, 1993.

Ostrow, J. "Self-Consciousness and Social Position: On College Students Changing Their Minds About the Homeless." *Qualitative Sociology,* 1995, No. 18(3): 357–375.

Palmer, Parker J. "Community, Conflict, and Ways of Knowing: Ways to Deepen our Educational Agenda." *Change,* 1987, No. 5: 20–25.

Parker-Gwin, R. and Mabry, J.B. "Service Learning as Pedagogy and Civic Education: Comparing Outcomes for Three Models." *Teaching Sociology,* 1998, No. 26: 276–291.

Proudman, W. "Experiential Education as Emotionally Engaged Learning." In *The Theory of Experiential Education*. Warren, Karen, Mitchell, Sakofs, Jasper, S. Hunt Jr.(eds.) Dubuque, IA: Kendall-Hunt, 1995, pp. 240–241.

Serow, R.C., Ciechalski, J., and Daye, C. "Students as Volunteers: Personal Competencies, Social Diversity, and Participation in Community Service." *Urban Education,* 1990, No. 25(1): 157–168.

Serow, R. "Students and Volunteerism: Looking Into the Motives of Community Service Participants." *American Educational Research Journal,* 1991, No. 28:543-556.

Shumer, R. & Belbas, B. "What We Know About Service-Learning." *Education and Urban Society,* 1996, No. 28(2): 208–223.

Sigmon, R. "Service-Learning: Three Principles." *Synergist,* 1979, pp. 9-11.

Stanton, T. "Service Learning: Groping Towards a Definition." *Experiential Education,* 1987, No. 12(1): 2–4.

Stanton, T. "The Experience of Faculty Participants in an Instructional Development Seminar on Service Learning." *Michigan Journal of Community Service Learning,* Fall 1994, No. 1: 7–20.

Teaching Sociology, October 1998, 26(4). (Entire issue is devoted to experiential education.)

Weiler, Kathleen. "Freire and a Feminist Pedagogy of Difference." *Harvard Educational Review,* November 1991, No. 61(4): 449–474.

Westhoff, Laura. "The Popularization of Knowledge: John Dewey on Experts and American Democracy." *History of Education Quarterly,* Spring, 1995: 2747.

Zlotkowski, E. "Pedagogy and Engagement." In Bringle, et al *Universities as Citizens.* Needham Heights, MA, Allyn and Bacon, 1999, pp. 96–120.

Zlotkowski, E. "Linking Service-Learning and the Academy: A New Voice at the Table?" *Change,* 1996, No. 28(1): 20–27.